The MERCHANTS
of VENUS

ALSO BY PAUL GRESCOE

The Money Rustlers: Self-Made Millionaires of the New West (1985, with David Cruise)

Jimmy: An Autobiography (1987, with Jimmy Pattison)

Flesh Wound (1991)

Songs from the Wild (1992, with Karl Spreitz)

Blood Vessel (1993)

Vancouver: Visions of a City (1993, with Karl Spreitz)

Alaska: The Cruise-Lover's Guide (1994, with Audrey Grescoe)

Fragments of Paradise: British Columbia's Wild and Wondrous Islands (1995, with Audrey Grescoe)

101 Uses for This Book (1996)

The MERCHANTS of VENUS

INSIDE HARLEQUIN
and the EMPIRE OF ROMANCE

Paul Grescoe

RAINCOAST BOOKS
Vancouver

First published in 1996 by

Raincoast Book Distribution Ltd.
8680 Cambie Street
Vancouver, B.C.
V6P 6M9
(604) 323-7100

1 3 5 7 9 10 8 6 4 2

CANADIAN CATALOGUING IN PUBLICATION DATA

Grescoe, Paul, 1939-
The merchants of Venus

ISBN 1-55192-010-7

1. Harlequin Enterprises – History. 2. Love stories – Publishing –
History. 3. Publishers and publishing – Ontario
– Toronto – History. I. Title.
Z483.H37G73 1996   070.5'09713'54109   C96-910202-X

Designed by Dean Allen
Project Editor: Michael Carroll
Copy Editor: Dallas Harrison

PRINTED AND BOUND IN CANADA

To Audrey, my romance of 34 years

Contents

*(*All chapter titles have been adapted from the names
of Harlequin/Silhouette books.)*

Acknowledgments

First and foremost, my immense gratitude to the indefatigable and generous-spirited Allan Gould, whose splendid research for a proposed history of the Larry Heisey years at Harlequin provided such a fund of basic data for my book. Of course, the interpretation of this research is my own. Thanks, too, to the equally large-hearted Larry Heisey, Harlequin's former chairman, who released Allan Gould's work for my use and who was so instrumental in making key contacts for me, with no strings attached. Kildare Dobbs's abbreviated, unpublished corporate history of two decades ago also proved useful, for which I thank him. Editor emeritus Fred Kerner, whose high editorial standards still inspire some Harlequin staff, was a helpful guide through the company's thickets. I am also indebted to numerous employees, past and present, for their insights, on and off the record. The chapter on the psychology and sociology of the romance novel owes much to the academic research compiled by Rachelle Kanefsky at Raincoast Books (although she may not agree with my conclusions) and to writer and student Evelyn Vaughan – only one of innumerable romance authors who so willingly shared their thoughts with me.

Various friends merit my thanks. In Toronto dear Loral Dean and David Cobb, who entertained me and helped arrange accommodation with Sandra Martin and Roger Hall, who trusted me with their home for such a long time; and my kind old pal Alan Walker, whose apartment briefly became my home. In New York the always stimulating Pat and Ronnie Romano, who shared their apartment and their love and knowledge of the city. And major thank-yous to my son, Taras Grescoe, for his predictably fine research in France and his wife, Gwénaëlle Callec, for her informed translations; and to my nephew, Dr. Greg Large, and his wife, Myrna, for their thorough tracking down and dispatch of old Harlequins.

The Merchants of Venus owes its existence to Michael Carroll of Raincoast, who leaped on my casual suggestion that I wanted to write it, and who as a former Harlequin editor not only gave me much guidance but also proved to be a sensitive collaborator in the book's creation.

And they all lived happily ever after. . . .
  – Classic fairy-tale ending

I

Sweet Surrender

THE WORLD OF HARLEQUIN

It was Friday night, and the 900 women in the Crystal Ballroom of the Radisson Plaza Hotel in Fort Worth were ready to party. They had freshened up after a day of workshops at the 13th annual Booklovers' Convention sponsored by the fan magazine *Romantic Times.* Many had taken their cue from the Texan setting and were in their western best of white lace dresses and high-top boots, or bright plaid shirts with sheriffs' stars above Levi's and Lizwear jeans. Women from across the United States and some down from Canada – twenty-something singles, retired widows, but most of them middle-aged and married – they were consumers of the estimated 175 million copies of romantic fiction published in North America each year. There would be another night to get gussied up in Scottish costumes to celebrate this year's theme of Brigadoon. They would have other days to talk to the 250-plus authors and 150 book-sellers in attendance, and to take the writing workshops so they, too, might become part of a publishing category that generates roughly $750 million a year on this continent alone. That Friday night, they were there to see the covers of their beloved romances come to life. Real-life male hunks were competing to pose for photographs that would inspire the commercial artists to paint the provocative images that help to sell the 140 new paperback novels that surface in the United States and Canada each month. The 26 contestants strutted onstage to the skirl of bagpipes, flashing their expansive chests and muscular arms. The audience howled its approval. A disembodied voice needlessly urged, "Please welcome the men of Brigadoon." After freezing in place for long moments, they swaggered off with regal waves of the hand to yelps and the occasional screech.

We few, lesser, mortal men shrank into insignificance.

The Mr. Romance Cover Model Pageant was a tangible acting out, a visual parody, of a form of popular literature that has enormous global appeal yet remains much mocked and misunderstood by literary critics and librarians, male chauvinists and feminists alike. The critics seize on what they describe as an unvarying, traditional formula: girl meets boy, girl and boy resist each other's allure, boy finally meets girl's expectations, and by the final page they either wed or bed – all told from the heroine's point of view. In fact, there is only one constant that defines the modern romance novel: the inevitable happy ending. It is a form that, while resonating with the classic themes of myth and legend, had its contemporary incarnation in England, whose female authors fine-tuned the formula, and its most prolific flowering in North America, whose writers transformed the genre. Their audience is enormous, although a widely touted figure suggesting that romance might represent more than 48 percent of all mass-market paperbacks in the United States has since been disowned by the Book Industry Study Group in New York. Whatever the numbers (and there are no other industry breakdowns available to the public), romantic fiction *is* the major genre of all paperback categories. Its current success is really the story of a Canadian company that controls up to 80 percent of the series-romance market as the largest paperback publisher in the world. The company was created by a heroic gentleman adventurer-turned-publisher and his editorially astute wife. They built on the concepts of a British family firm that was the first in the world to treat books like brand-name commodities. Aggressive American-trained, marketing-driven male executives further refined these revolutionary ideas and virtually reinvented

The men of Brigadoon. Male hunks strut their stuff at the third annual Mr. Romance Cover Model Pageant in Fort Worth, Texas. ROMANTIC TIMES

book publishing domestically and throughout the world by peddling romance novels like boxes of soap flakes in the very places where women shop.

While it has many competitors among conventional publishers, Harlequin Enterprises of Toronto wields a white-gloved iron fist to dominate the market in supermarkets and drugstores as well as bookstores, and in lucrative direct-mail book clubs that exclusively feature its Harlequin and Silhouette lines. Through joint ventures and its own independent operations, it sells 176.5 million books a year in 23 languages in more than 100 international markets, including the former East Bloc nations of Europe – a total of three billion books in less than half a century. All this business translates into revenues of nearly half a billion dollars a year. Harlequin has achieved that most desirable of positions in the marketplace – like Coke or Xerox – by having its brand name become synonymous with the generic product. The company made many of its early employees millionaires when it sold out to the Canadian communications giant Torstar. In the two decades since, it has consistently propped up one of North America's largest newspapers, the often ailing *Toronto Star*. And in the first quarter of 1995, running out of traditional markets, Harlequin flexed its muscles even more dramatically and launched coproduction partnerships in a land of 1.2 billion people, China.

That was the same season *Romantic Times* was having its four-day convention in Fort Worth. Harlequin's preoccupation with China might have been one reason why neither its president and chief executive officer, Brian Hickey, nor any of his senior executives was in attendance that evening. The more plausible one was that, alone among publishing houses in the field, the company is so powerful a presence that it need not fear the wrath of the 54-year-old woman who took center stage in the Crystal Ballroom. She was short, with a shock of tightly curled red hair and clad in a vaguely Oriental scarlet-and-gold jacket. Her almost pretty face looked a little puffy because of a thyroid condition that had added 30 pounds to her frame. For much of the audience, Kathryn Falk, the founder of *Romantic Times,* might be a living model, nearly a caricature, of the classic romance heroine. Lady Barrow, she liked to call herself, since she had bought a title in 1994 – the Lordship of Barrow – along with 2,677 acres of freehold land near Newmarket, England. She had dated a European movie star and an Indian maharaja, and now she lived in a Victorian carriage house in Brooklyn with Kenneth Rubin, who had a large jewelry business and was one of America's major collectors of antique coin-operated machines, which furnished their home. In the textbook she compiled and edited for hopeful writers, *How to Write a Romance and Get It Published,* Falk's dedication is to "Kenneth, who took me off to his castle in Brooklyn, where I have lived happily ever after. . . ." She was more a scrappy entrepreneur than a gentle fairy-tale princess; she had been known to assault publicly one of her female rivals for the affection of female readers. Publishers, if they didn't dread her for the clout she had with her 135,000 addicted readers, tended to step lightly around the subject of Falk and her monthly magazine. "It's first and foremost a fanzine," one publisher told me. "It's an ego trip for the writers. It should be a trade journal. So there's a real void in this industry. I'd appreciate if you didn't quote me."

On the ballroom stage, where lights revealed a Scottish highlands bridge set against a backdrop of trees and an impossibly blue sky, Kathryn Falk was saying, "Tonight we've come to celebrate men. That's why we read romance nov-

Kathryn Falk with Fabio, who made a guest appearance at a previous Mr. Romance Cover Model Pageant. ROMANTIC TIMES

els." She knew her readers. They had helped to make media stars out of two cover models, Avon Books' blond Fabio, and Viking Penguin's Topaz Man, the dark and comely Steve Sandalis. Both wore their hair long, the way highwaymen and pirates presumably did in olden days and hockey players and construction workers do now. Those celebrity models and most of the hopefuls in the pageant exemplified the popular image of the romance hero, as perpetuated by nonreaders: the biggest, strongest, most handsome man in the heroine's world, not necessarily the smartest or most scintillating in conversation. (One anomaly was a cute, human-sized contestant with a funny, self-mocking patter who would break a hooker's heart; I took comfort when a thirtyish woman beside me murmured approvingly, "If I took *him* home, he'd still be interesting 30 years later.") Certainly the larger-than-life models could be the physical realization of many romance readers' fantasies: the stuff of some feminine mythology, born of a primal reality that the toughest, boldest, and even most ruthless male might make the best progenitor, the most effective provider and protector, in a world where women were supposedly the weaker sex.

Contemporary writers and editors of these novels would protest, with some justification, that this is an outdated image. The new Harlequin hero might still be physically strong and (at least in the beginning) emotionally silent, but the heroine is no longer the frail, humble, virginal woman of old, no longer the naive young governess to the motherless children of the brooding lord of the manor, nor the compliant, uncomplicated nurse to the worldly wise doctor. Nor is she quite as willing a victim of the quasi-rapes that some publishers were pressuring romance authors to write a decade or two ago (the more disdainful publishers still refer to the typical romance reader as Gladys Stringbag). The most enlightened of today's heroines insist on healthier, more egalitarian relationships. No longer are they content to find their sexual fulfillment in a passionate embrace on the final page. Competing equally with men in careers of consequence – small-business owners, college professors, the odd marine archaeologist and female police sergeant – they act overtly on their need to make love with the men of their dreams before being bound in wedlock. Even readers of *Playboy* have heard the news, if in an outrageously skewed manner: in a recent column, Cynthia Heimel informed them that the modern romance novel, which she calls "women's romance pornography," is "teeming with the hottest sex that can be described using incredibly clichéd euphemisms." Increasingly, romantic fiction is for women who move their hips when they read – "they're masturbation books!" Heimel exclaims, admitting that their attention to sexual detail aroused even her. A recent example is *The Stud*, a title in the gamier Harlequin Temptation series, which offers graphic sex scenes that have the heroine describing how the hero fills her as he thrusts into the tightness of her vagina. (Not all the taboos have fallen, however: Virginia Henley, a Canadian writer whose bestselling romances for other publishers have earned her a winter home in Florida, says, "If I put that c-u-n-t word in, they'll always take it out.")

The other half of the fantasy being played out on the Texan stage that Friday night was that these powerful men, for all their strength and potential for savagery, would be ultimately tamed by the women who loved them. The sheer force of the heroines' femininity would gentle them, transform them from inarticulate beasts into sensitive, supportive men who could express their deepest emotions and their desperate need for romance. Some of the contestants were more articulate than others. Young Jason Sparks of St. Charles, Missouri, began his onstage speech with "My ultimate romantic fantasy is I'd have to be by myself. . . ." He hesitated, to whoops of laughter from the women. "With . . . with . . . a very romantic lady," he finished quickly. Sean O'Brien of Karnes City, Texas, in a tux with a cowboy hat and string tie, received a more respectful hearing when he told the audience that "Women are our gift from God. Those same emotions are there in men . . . but we need your help."

Among the judges of this third Mr. Romance Cover Model Pageant was Judith McNaught, whom Kathryn Falk introduced as a *New York Times* best-selling author (*Perfect, Something Wonderful*). Heather Graham, another judge and an equally successful romance author, has described McNaught as "one of the smartest business women in our field." She was a controller for a large trucking company in 1978 when she wrote her first book, *Whitney, My Love,* in four and a half weeks. It took her more than five years and many rewrites to get it published. The book was categorized as a historical romance, in particular a Regency, which is a novel set in England of the early 1800s during the reign of George III, when mannered society and romantic literature flourished. "The rejections came," the elegantly turned-out, coolly professional McNaught recalls, "because they said a Regency romance was always short, it was fluffy, it was a comedy of manners, it was never sensual, it certainly was not emotionally intense." When Pocket Books finally released it as a paperback at twice its original length, the sensual, emotionally intense *Whitney, My Love* became a best-seller, a new romance classic. Meanwhile, McNaught had written and published two Harlequins, one of them after an initially unhappy experience with an editor whom she still bad-mouths publicly. The novels were what the industry calls series or category romances. Part of a continuing series, under imprints such as Harlequin Temptation or Silhouette Intimate Moments, these are briefer paperback novels of 50,000 to 75,000 words, generally with contemporary settings. They are the traditional, more formulaic Harlequins that churn through the book racks and in-house book clubs every month.

Whether historical or contemporary, romance novels nowadays are too diverse in theme and tone to fit neatly under a single rubric. All historicals have been lumped under the pejorative label "bodice-rippers," so named because of the provocatively posed scenes on their covers. But as well as having diverse locales – England, France, the Caribbean, early America – they fragment into many specific types, such as westerns and Native Americans (or cowboys and Indians); those with pirate, medieval, and Viking heroes; fantasies featuring Druids, genies, and legendary places such as Camelot and Atlantis; supernaturals with ghosts and vampires; and gothics with suspenseful stories, moody heroes, and moldering mansions and castles. Contemporary novels have their own distinctions: humor, like the seminal collection of satirical short stories, *Naked Came the Ladies*; mystery and suspense; fantasies with mermaids and Loch Ness monsters; supernaturals with angels, New Age, and reincarnation themes; and (a popular new category) time travel. Other categories are futuristic and science fiction; New Reality novels that deal with unsettling subjects such as sexual abuse and alcoholism; multicultural stories with black and Latino characters; and overtly gay and erotic novels, many with sadomasochistic overtones. Some series are even written from the male point of view.

Much romantic fiction is mediocre or relentlessly predictable, just as other genres, such as crime novels and techno-thrillers, often are. I know: as the author of a couple of detective novels, I have followed the mystery field, and I realize how much dreck is out there. Harlequin had its own failed experiment with its minor-league and badly marketed line of original paperback mysteries, Raven House, which it tried to package and sell like romance novels. It had similarly wretched experiences with science fiction and teenage imprints, but has revived a series for young adults and continues to market a moderately successful male-adventure imprint called Gold Eagle. Now, it is true that romantic fiction can still suffer from the coy use of euphemism, where "penis" becomes "manroot" (though that is changing); the dependence on cliché, in which pulses race and hearts pound in chests; and the preposterous devices that keep a couple apart until the final clinch. As in this scene from Catherine George's recent Harlequin Romance, *Summer of the Storm,* in which Alec and Cassie, having already made passionate love, fail to consummate another encounter:

> "Enough of that, Cassie Fletcher," he said, breathing hard, "or I'll do something you'll regret."
> Cassie's change of heart was written so plainly on her flushed face that Alec clenched his teeth and shook his head.

"No, Cassie, I've said I'll wait, so I'll wait. It may kill me," he added menacingly, "but never let it be said that Alec Neville went back on his word!"

Gold Eagle, however, offers its own stereotypes, especially in long-running series such as The Executioner (whose legacy includes an embarrassing court case that Harlequin would like to forget). The stories revolve around violence and military hardware and have their predictable happy endings with the good guys always obliterating the bad. Yet because they are written *by* men *for* men, these novels seldom endure the scorn routinely heaped on Harlequin romances.

Not only are many Harlequins and competitive novels competently written, sometimes with spare, plot-propelling prose, most also tell well-paced stories. The kinds of stories they recount have been the subjects of scores of academic theses and several books by serious critics (at least a couple of whom went on to write a Harlequin). In the past, feminists in particular have been highly critical of the dominantly male slant of romantic fiction. Now a revisionist school that is aware of the more realistic themes, the new breed of heroines, and the fact that the men they usually win in the end become more caring has decided that these novels can be empowering for women. Perhaps this empowerment isn't even important: they are, after all, escapist literature, neither more nor less than Stephen King horror stories and Tom Clancy technothrillers can be for men. Readers don't come to them looking for metaphysics or mega-problems. And their upbeat conclusions have an equivalent in the much less reviled mystery novel, where the investigator generally solves the crime and brings order to a chaotic world.

The best romance novels become bestsellers. Today Judith McNaught writes mainstream fiction: much longer, more complex, less conventionally plotted books that have broken out of the category ghetto as single titles with staying power rather than one-month wonders as part of a series. Her books have appeared first in hardcover, found their way quickly onto the *New York Times* bestseller list, and earned her multimillion-dollar contracts. None was published by Harlequin, which, until recent months, when it started its Mira line, had made the strategic mistake of refusing to create a publishing program of hardcover single titles. At the convention's Book Fair, the day after the cover-model pageant, McNaught had an everlasting line of fans, the longest of any author's, as if she were handing out directions to Ponce de Leon's

Fountain of Youth instead of simply autographing her books.

Judith McNaught and Heather Graham, her sister judge at the pageant, are high-profile members of the Romance Writers of America, not all of whom have been as happy with Kathryn Falk. The feisty, nonprofit RWA has more than 7,600 members, but only about 1,500 are published authors; the rest are wannabes. A 1994 issue of the Published Authors Network newsletter, *PANdora's Box*, had an open letter to Falk from several writers who criticized her for, among other things, the pageants, which they felt cheapened the image of their industry. The editor decided to print the letter anonymously: "I think every single member of PAN understands exactly what would happen to any author who dared to sign her name to a letter of commentary such as the one we're discussing. To suggest otherwise is to ignore reality." (Nor are all RWA writers great fans of Harlequin Enterprises. *PANdora's Box* has chronicled their unhappiness with the company's unbending contract terms, its cheesily low royalties for novels sold through its cash-cow book club, and until recently its unbecoming pressure on authors to use pseudonyms, which Harlequin would then own.)

Up on the Fort Worth stage, the formidable Kathryn Falk was introducing another judge in her inimitable way: "Bill Black is the newest male in our harem. . . . He is the president of Leisure Publishing." Black, a trim man with a trademark mustache, would want a younger Burt Reynolds to play him in the movie of his life. I had met him earlier in the day in a lobby at the convention hotel. His eyes closed, he appeared to be dozing, or perhaps he was contemplating how the head of a company that was a niche player in the romance market had been roped in to judge a bunch of men baring their chests and chatting about making love.

Black was then president of Dorchester Publishing, which offers a small line of romances and westerns under the names Leisure Books and Love Spell, as well as marketing historical romances through its own book club. The Backe Group, a media holding company, had bought 25-year-old Dorchester in 1994 and made Black president. He had previously run the children's books program at Scholastic and for a dozen years had been a consultant for Simon & Schuster, Cowles Business Media, and other publishing clients. He seemed well placed to sum up his industry, beginning with Harlequin.

"Harlequin has always been the 400-pound gorilla in the marketplace,"

Black told me after I had interrupted his reverie. "In many ways, they founded this industry. If I were the head of Harlequin, and I knew my core business was in good shape, I would do exactly what they're doing. They're ruthless. . . . If they want shelf space to launch a new series in retail, they'll get it."

In a long soliloquy, Black went on to outline the strengths and weaknesses of Harlequin's competitors on the American publishing scene. Running through the major houses in rough alphabetical order, he sprinkled his commentary with the jargon of *full list* (a publishing program that covers a broad range of fiction and nonfiction), *backlist* (a publisher's previous offerings, still in print), and *midlist* (books that sell moderately well, neither bestsellers nor bombs).

"Avon Books is a house that has always been committed to romance publishing, although their program does tend to rely very heavily on a few major authors. But then if I published Kathleen Woodiwiss, Rosemary Rogers, and Johanna Lindsey, so would mine. They have a full-list mass-market publishing program, and they don't need to have a full-line romance publishing program at the same time."

The Berkley Publishing Group, part of G. P. Putnam's Sons, releases several romance novels every month, actively soliciting and developing new writers. Bantam Doubleday Dell, like Avon, tends to focus on writers such as Iris Johansen, who can be wildly successful, but it also owns Dell, which continues its Candlelight Romance series – "another old battlewagon, squeaky clean sort of stuff," Black said. As for HarperCollins, while its strength is commercial nonfiction, it does well with romance: "Their strategy was to buy their way into the marketplace. They've got more cash than God."

I reminded Black that HarperCollins had just made a seven-figure hard/soft deal for three books from superstar Janet Dailey, who had long ago turned her back on Harlequin to write for its onetime bitter rival, Simon & Schuster. Dailey had most recently been with Little, Brown, a house that Black discounted as a serious romance publisher. "Not a player," he said. "They're a hardcover house, and whatever they do in romance fell out of bed."

NAL/Dutton releases monthly contemporary and Regency romances under the Signet and Onyx imprints, but its sister company, Viking Penguin, has the more intriguing position in the marketplace with its Topaz imprint. "They went out into the field and built customer demand at the local romance-buyer level. They went after the clubs and the newsletters and the associations and all that kind of stuff. They did a terrific job, as opposed to what Avon did with Fabio. Exactly the other way around. Avon did it from the top down – you know, find yourself an alleged star and create product and try to ram it through the marketplace. For Topaz, Steve Sandalis was an add-on. They needed a guy. They happened to pick Steve. They could have picked anybody."

Random House's Fawcett and Ballantine lines, he pointed out, are really two separate businesses. Well before the boom years, Fawcett was involved in romantic fiction with authors such as Georgette Heyer and Victoria Holt. It may have the best romance backlist in the business as well as being the predominant Regency publisher. Ballantine, meanwhile, has ended its program of publishing midlist romance authors in favor of those who might become *New York Times* bestsellers.

Black observed that Simon & Schuster's Pocket Books arm has the best distribution in the business. However, its own romance publishing is sporadic, driven by name authors: "They make so much money distributing Harlequin and Silhouette that they have no interest whatsoever in creating an ongoing genre of romance authors."

Warner Books, he noted, is another house that tends to publish only superstar authors, such as Robert James Waller of *The Bridges of Madison County*, which stayed on the *Publishers Weekly* hardcover bestseller chart for 141 weeks and became a Clint Eastwood film. "Warner as a mass-market house has a very small list and as a romance publisher an even smaller one. But when they publish them, I'm sure they do very, very well."

Black ended his alphabetic monologue with Zebra Books, an imprint of Kensington Publishing, owned by Walter Zacharius. "From the authors' and the agents' perspective, Zebra is, if not the most important player in the game, right up there with anybody else. They consistently publish new authors. They will on the other hand pay a lot of money for major bestselling authors. They're constantly adding new lines and new line extensions. They're not as important as Harlequin. . . . The model in this business if you're a writer is Janet Dailey and others who started writing for Harlequin and then broke off and built their own following and became hugely successful.

"From a reader's perspective, no publisher other than Harlequin is identifiable. I mean, a reader doesn't give a flying fa-too whether Avon publishes a book or we publish it or Zebra publishes it. From a distributor's perspective –

the people who buy the titles and then put them on the shelves – Zebra is on the one hand a major player and on the other an endless source of confusion, angst, and difficulty because they're always creating new stuff and terminating old stuff. Distributors don't like that a lot. But they are obviously a major, major player in this business."

At the cover-model pageant in the Radisson Plaza, Kathryn Falk was calling Zebra Books' Walter Zacharius a father figure as she introduced him to the audience. The balding, 71-year-old publisher, his tall form tuxedoed, hesitantly stepped onstage. His privately held company was a cosponsor of the event with *Romantic Times*. Zacharius and Falk, once enemies, had made their peace. He now professed to admire her entrepreneurial chutzpah, and she gave him a platform to express his sometimes unpopular views to romance writers and readers.

Zebra Books, the last privately owned paperback publisher of any size in North America, represented one of Harlequin's failures. In 1992 the giant tried to buy its sassy pip-squeak competitor, presumably because of Zebra's strong position in the historical-romance market and its imaginatively marketed contemporary lines. It was a textbook clash of cultures: Harlequin's buttoned-down, M.B.A.-educated corporate executives – CEO David Galloway and president Brian Hickey – versus the shambling, streetwise Walter Zacharius. After Harlequin signed a letter of intent, the deal crumbled. Depending on whose story you believe, it was either because Hickey offered a much lower price after his accountants had investigated all of Zebra's numbers or because a frustrated Zacharius walked when Harlequin wouldn't give him time to get over the recent death of his longtime partner, Roberta Grossman. "I will say one thing about them," Zacharius would tell me later. "They're some of the smartest business people I've ever met. Because they know how to take what they have and make the most out of it. Publishers they ain't. They admit it."

During the previous decade, Harlequin had another failure that belied its reputation for corporate smarts. Torstar acquired majority control of it in 1976, and three years later – in an act of arrogance that this untypically Canadian company sometimes displays – Harlequin decided to stop distributing its products through the relentlessly efficient Pocket Books arm of Simon & Schuster. Henceforth, it would deal directly with American wholesale newsstand and bookstore distributors. Simon & Schuster, under volatile president Richard Snyder, then began publishing its own romance line,

Silhouette, head to head with its former business partner. For four years, the two houses bled as they battled for readership. Finally in 1984, Harlequin bought Silhouette and reverted to the Pocket Books distribution channels that it had so haughtily deserted. David Galloway, then Harlequin's president, now Torstar's C E O, confesses that the needless war cost his company tens of millions of dollars.

It was a strategic mistake born of the sheer hubris that a self-important, monopolistic corporation can demonstrate. Until the mid-1970s, Harlequin had been a light-footed, responsive, independent company, run by a marketing genius named W. Lawrence Heisey. Larry, as anyone who knew him longer than a day liked to call him, was a gregarious, charismatic man; even today, retired at 66, with a bounty of silvered hair haloing his warm, handsome face, he looks (as one of my observant Jewish colleagues says) like a gentile Ben-Gurion. Heisey had an M.B.A. from Harvard Business School, as did Galloway, and had been a marketing specialist with Procter & Gamble Inc. in Canada, as Galloway had been with General Foods. In 1981, five years after gaining majority control of Harlequin, Torstar swallowed it up as a wholly owned subsidiary. Heisey then invited the parent company's David Galloway to become executive vice president and, soon after, president. But the bitter truth was, the decision to abandon the Pocket Books distribution system had already happened under Heisey's leadership, and it was up to Galloway to attempt to rectify it – which he did, after tremendous corporate bloodshed.

Until that time, Larry Heisey had made only a few major missteps. By the beginning of the 1980s, he had fashioned Harlequin into the world's leading romance publisher, whose revenues of almost one-quarter of a billion dollars were contributing nearly half of Torstar's consolidated earnings per share. And he had done it by positioning books in the marketplace as products that could be delivered to targeted consumers the way Procter & Gamble distributed cooking oil and shampoo – with the same marketing verve and in the same supermarkets and drugstores that women frequented. Like packaged goods, the books were standardized at 192 pages apiece to save on printing costs and to fit six at a time in a pocket on the display rack. Moving beyond bookstores and positioning the books so prominently in such busy retail centers helped Harlequin to keep its returns on sales down to 25 to 30 percent compared with the industry average of 40 to 50 percent in the United States.

Heisey, however, had not invented the commodity style of publishing. Media observers of the time, and ever since, have credited him with this extraordinary concept of selling books by their brand names rather than by their authors. North American as this heretical approach to bookselling sounds, it was the creation of a couple of Englishmen. Gerald Mills and Charles Boon founded the London publishing house of Mills & Boon in 1908, and, between the two world wars, they made the fortuitous decision to specialize in romantic fiction. It was they who conceived some of the best ideas that Harlequin would adopt decades later, among them the marketing of books as generic brands. Boon's sons, Alan and John, would further develop the family firm into Britain's most successful publishing house and a logical target for a strategically shrewd acquisition by Harlequin in 1972. The Boon brothers continued to oversee the house, proud of their carefully groomed reputation as gentlemen publishers who coddled their female authors and paid them handsomely at a time when other houses held back. Meanwhile, behind the scenes, they would allow a financial imbroglio to erupt, one that contradicted their well-preserved public image and mightily embarrassed their overseas owners.

In hindsight the conjoining of Harlequin and Mills & Boon – which the Boons still prefer to call a genteel merger rather than the lopsided buyout it was – seemed inevitable. Harlequin had the marketing savvy, M & B had the product.

Not surprisingly the first North Americans to appreciate fully the worth of the English firm's special commodity were a couple of women. Harlequin and its competitors have been controlled and run largely by men – the Boons, Heisey, Galloway, Hickey – but the industry's creative heart has been the writers and editors they employ, only a handful of whom are male. This dichotomy, so richly reflected in romance literature, was true from the beginning. Harlequin was the contrivance of a man, the dashing Richard Bonnycastle, who launched it in 1949 in the cold Canadian heartland of Winnipeg, Manitoba. At first romance novels were only a small part of Harlequin's publishing program. Then Bonnycastle's secretary, Ruth Palmour, and his wife, Mary, recognized the classless appeal of romance novels. It was Mary who made certain that they did not transgress her rigorous standards of good taste. And, after the founding father died, it was the Bonnycastles' business-savvy son, Richard, who had the foresight to realize what business Harlequin was really in – packaged consumer goods rather than traditional books. Dick Bonnycastle Jr.

transformed his parents' private little company into a big public enterprise, expanded it into the United States, moved it to Toronto, hired shrewd managers such as Larry Heisey, and eventually sold out to Torstar. Now, as Harlequin's star was no longer in the ascendant over North America, the parent company welcomed the fact that the romance publisher was orbiting in new and exotic places such as China.

That March evening in Fort Worth, Texas, a collective sigh arose spontaneously from the audience with the arrival onstage of host James Bartling, one of the three Nebraskan hog-farming brothers who had entranced last year's convention in Nashville in their roles as romance cover models. Jim Bartling, he of the hawk nose, jutting jaw, and long blond ponytail, toyed with the women by quoting an old but legitimate psychological survey: "You know that readers of romance novels make love 74 percent more often?" And when the glamorous hostess at his side, a local T V celebrity, reported that the average romance reader spends $1,200 a year on books, he replied, "I might have spent that much on hair conditioning." If Mary Bonnycastle were alive today, and a guest at the *Romantic Times* Booklovers' Convention, I doubt whether she would recognize what her beloved heroes and heroines and her own sweet Harlequins have become.

We get hundreds of letters from women telling us how wonderful
it is to read a pleasant, well written book without being subjected
to psychological and sexual problems. I had always said that
women wanted that kind of book.
— Mary Bonnycastle, 1969

2

Born Out of Love
THE BONNYCASTLES

The love story of Dick and Mary Bonnycastle was the stuff of a Harlequin historical romance.

When the wire arrived that morning, Mary felt a pang of cold dread. The day had dawned sunny and bright, with all the warmth of a Manitoba Indian Summer. But as she sat in the comfort of the parlor in her parents' home in Winnipeg, she knew her Richard was Up There, aboard a supply ship doing battle with the unforgiving Arctic ice. For the past five months, she had only his photographs as a reminder of those lanky, sun-blond good looks, that chiseled chin, and the energy and curiosity that could never be captured by a Kodak.

He descended from an aristocratic Canadian family. The eldest of a judge's six children, he was named for a gallant ancestor. Sir Richard Bonnycastle had been a captain in England's Royal Engineers, and he had been knighted for his services in helping to fortify the new Province of Canada against American invasion after the Rebellion of 1837. Her Richard had the same sense of adventure. He had attended Wadham College in Oxford and played center on the world-champion Oxford hockey team.

But after reading law, he soon grew weary of practicing it with a distinguished, stuffy legal firm in Winnipeg. When the local British consul mentioned an opening for an accountant with the legendary Hudson's Bay Company, Richard eagerly applied for it. Soon he was in the Far North, traveling down roiling rivers in a canoe and running 30 miles a day behind dogsleds to oversee the fur-trading company's dealings with Indian and Eskimo trappers.

Six years later, on one of his winter layovers in Winnipeg, he had asked for her hand. In local society, Mary Northwood guessed, she would be considered a catch. An architect's daughter, she knew that some people considered her beautiful, with her wide smile and elegant features. She had accepted his proposal unhesitatingly, and they were to be wed in October, in five weeks' time. Now, as she opened the telegram, a small shiver ran through her. MY DEAR MARY, it read. TRAPPED IN ICE OFF CAPE BELCHER. . . .

Like the plots in the books that Richard Bonnycastle would come to publish and that Mary would edit, their story would have the happiest of endings. But the debut of their married life was more fraught with harrowing adventure and portents of tragedy than those romance novels could ever promise their readers. Bonnycastle was 28, a fledgling lawyer who had accepted a junior accounting position in 1925 with the Hudson's Bay Company; within three years, he was the manager – the chief fur trader – of its Western Arctic district. King Charles II and a group of English nobles and merchants had created the Company of Adventurers of England Trading into Hudson Bay in 1670 as an incorporated joint-stock merchandising venture (in which all shares are fully and publicly transferable), and it remains the oldest such enterprise in the English-speaking world. It once owned 40 percent of what would become the Dominion of Canada; two and a half centuries later, the business operations of the tradition-choked company were foundering in the Far North. Many of its managers there were either inept or knavish, while free-trading competitors were buying furs from the Native people and selling them southern goods at more attractive prices. The Canadian government was investigating the company's relations with the Natives.

Dick Bonnycastle, in caribou parka and Eskimo moccasins and snowshoes, traveled by boat, bush plane, and dogsled through Canada's Northwest Territories as he tried to restore a semblance of order to the Hudson's Bay posts. He was forever in fear that he would be fired. The diary that he kept faithfully records the everyday problems, as in this entry on January 15, 1929: "I had to foot it pretty nearly all the way to Hay River. The going was either glare ice or snowdrifts. . . . We had a cold trip. The thermometer hasn't risen above 40°F below since we left Providence. My feet are sore, blisters under the soles and skin off the knuckles of my toes. The blood came through my socks. . . . However, *c'est la guerre.*" Everywhere he met benightedness and poverty. "April 15, 1931: I started out for Tuktoyaktuk with seven dogs and an empty toboggan. . . . The people here have very little food. . . . All they had, as far as I could see, was a little flour and an old white whale head which nearly made me sick to look at. Thirty of us slept in one room, all over the floor, beds, and everything, men, women, and children. This life isn't all it's cracked up to be!"

Life turned much worse in mid-September of that year, when an old Hudson's Bay Company supply ship tried to outrun the winter ice in the Arctic Ocean. Bonnycastle was homeward bound, via Vancouver, aboard the steamship *Baychimo*. Three years earlier, he had taken a stomach-turning trip on the ship that had caused him to write: "I swore all day I would never again come into this horrible country. I really hope I don't come back, although I am feeling a little better now." Now he was on the vessel again, hoping to arrive in Winnipeg a couple of weeks before his long-planned wedding to Mary. Within a week, the steamer was off Point Barrow, on a northern verge of Alaska, trying to batter through pans of congealing ice. By the time the *Baychimo* approached Cape Belcher, menacing floes 12 to 15 feet high were closing in around her. "It seems to me we haven't a ghost of a chance," Bonnycastle recorded, worried that the ship would be iced in for the winter. At the end of September, he wired his fiancée from the ship, warning her that he would not be home before October 21 at the earliest. "I *do* so want to be married on October 31," he wrote in his diary just a month before the already postponed wedding date. "I am afraid the wire will cause some consternation. I can't say anything else. It is wretched."

The captain, whom he considered incompetent and a coward, ordered his crew to scavenge ship's materials and begin building a shack on shore in which they could winter if necessary. "The captain is a terrible man, bull-headed, overbearing, and knows it all," the diarist noted. Meanwhile, Bonnycastle was negotiating with Alaskan air-transport companies by wireless radio to attempt a dangerous landing on a frozen lagoon and to carry the passengers out. As a

Hudson's Bay manager, he had been a firsthand witness to the revolution the airplane was wreaking in the Arctic. Two years earlier, he had taken his maiden flight; only that summer, he had flown with bush pilot Bill Spence in a Fairchild seaplane, from Coppermine to Victoria Island (well north of the Arctic Circle), in a 600-mile round trip, the farthest commercial flight north ever made to that time. Here he was, only weeks later, arranging an air-rescue mission. Finally in mid-October, two Stinson-Detroiter monoplanes touched down on a runway of ice near the ship, and eight people clambered in them, Bonnycastle included. One-third of their 320-mile trip to Kotzebue, Alaska, took them through a mountain range with no possible landing spot. They arrived just before darkness with only 20 minutes of fuel left. "It was pretty darned risky," Bonnycastle confided in his diary. Newspapers across Canada headlined the drama: SAVED BY AIRPLANE IN NORTH TWO MEN RES-CUED FROM ARCTIC NOW ARE ON WAY HOME. Not until October 23 was he aboard a ship in Nome, Alaska, heading to Vancouver. A relieved but prudent Mary had delayed their wedding again, to November 27.

It was a match made, if not exactly in heaven, at least in its honeyed, moneyed suburbs. Both were well-born, properly educated, attractive young people. Mary Frances was the eldest of four daughters of a prominent local architect, George Northwood. Winnipeg, the Manitoba capital, was then a yeasty mix of upwardly mobile European immigrants (like my family) and landed gentry at least a couple of generations away from their British roots. As the midcontinental hub of the transcontinental railroads and the center of the grain trade, the city was the supplier of the bountiful Canadian breadbasket, a much smaller counterpart of Chicago. The Northwoods grew up in Winnipeg, except for a brief time when their father was in the service during the First World War and they lived in California. Mary attended the private Rupert's Land School for girls and spent the requisite year in Europe, being finished at an exclusive school in Versailles. Her parents and teachers bred a woman who believed in traditional values that embraced service to the community, but not at the expense of the family. "A mother misses so much," she pointed out, "if she's not at home to meet her children and hear their enthusiastic accounts of

The fur trader and the lady. Richard and Mary Bonnycastle (extreme left) *finally got married on November 27, 1929.* JUDITH BONNYCASTLE BURGESS

their day's events." The family had suffered financially in the 1929 crash but always insisted on maintaining appearances. On separate occasions, Mary's mother, crippled with arthritis, traveled to Florida for a winter holiday and to the Empress Hotel in Victoria, on the West Coast, for a proper English-style Christmas; for both trips, she just hailed a taxi in Winnipeg, in the middle of the continent.

Mary met her husband-to-be on a local golf course; they both liked the game, and would one day enjoy gardening together. Theirs would be an uncommonly tranquil marriage ("I never heard them quarrel," their youngest child, Judith, told me recently. "There was a great loyalty, one to the other"). They shared a patrician handsomeness, with long, highbrowed faces, though Mary was at least a head shorter than Richard's six foot three. If Richard Henry Gardyne Bonnycastle had the dash of a romantic hero – in fact, he could be a role model for the Harlequin male – he inherited it from both sides of his family. His mother's father had fought against the Métis (mixed-blood) army of Louis Riel in what is now Manitoba; 15 years after being captured, sentenced to death, and winning a last-minute reprieve, Major Charles A. Boulton successfully led his Boulton's Scouts against Riel during the Northwest

Rebellion of 1885. After his heroics in the Northwest Rebellion, he became a Canadian senator and a newspaper publisher in rural Manitoba. And, of course, there was Dick Bonnycastle's knighted great-great-grandfather, whose name he bore: the commanding royal engineer in Canada West in the 1830s, and the author of five books about this new land. (One of them included a criticism of the United States, which would not dissuade his book-publishing descendant: "In England the cautious, the slow, and the sure plan prevails; in America the go-ahead, reckless, dollar making principle prevails.")

Dick Bonnycastle was born three years into the century in the village of Binscarth in south-central Manitoba. His father, who had come west from Ontario in the early 1890s, was among the farming community's local elite. Angus Bonnycastle was as popular in public as he was with his family, whom he entertained as a one-man band playing the fiddle, harmonica, and drums. A teacher-turned-lawyer, he eventually became a provincial magistrate, county court judge, and Conservative member of the provincial legislature. All this was the doing of his wife, Ellen, according to family legend. "He had no great ambition . . . ," his architect son-in-law, Anthony Adamson, recalls in his privately published memoir, *Wasps in the Attic*. "He was however not married by Ellen for that sort of thing so he went along reasonably well with her high aims for him and her children." Ellen, a published poet and short story writer, was the editor of her father Charles Boulton's *Russell Chronicle and Free Trade Advertiser* for several years. Most of her fiction was genteelly romantic in nature, like the novels her son would publish someday, although a surviving story called "After Many Days," featuring a minister hero, has an un-Harlequin unhappy ending.

At various times, the Bonnycastle family lived in Binscarth, Russell, Dauphin, and the only city of any size in the province, Winnipeg. Angus and Ellen insisted that their six children know the customs of the Old World as well as the New; the boys might hunt for rabbits, but they also got dressed for afternoon tea (even if the Spode pot was cracked). Staunchly Church of England, the Bonnycastles sent their eldest – nine-year-old Dick – to the Anglican St. John's College in Winnipeg, and later to the church-supported Trinity College in Toronto. His sports were golf and tennis in summer (he was a tournament tennis player in Western Canada), hockey in winter. In his late teens, Bonnycastle went to England to study, to Wadham College in Oxford, where he played on the same world-beating Oxford hockey team as a future Canadian prime minister, Lester Pearson, and a future governor general, Roland Michener. His future seemed foreordained: he was preparing to be a lawyer, like his father. But like his father, he found it difficult to blinker his life: as well as touring with the team around Europe to earn a place in the Hockey Hall of Fame, he laced his studies with college larks such as riding a motorcycle while formally attired in white tie and tailcoat. Visiting London, he met the American movie and stage actor Clifton Webb and, through him, the British theater star Gladys Cooper (later Dame Gladys); they asked the charming young Canadian to accompany them to Gstaad, Switzerland. Nearly three-quarters of a century later, his daughter Judith quotes him as noting in his diary on three successive days "Definitely can't go. Must study" and then 10 days later writing "In Gstaad." Dick Bonnycastle considered his English experience to be the most formative and useful of his life: "No matter where I have gone since, I have met someone I knew there."

After becoming a member of the Honourable Society of Lincoln's Inn in London and passing his bar examination, he came home to practice law with the Establishment Winnipeg firm of Aikens, Macauley. He lasted a year. Bored with his chosen profession, he leapt at a chance to work for the Hudson's Bay Company, with its promise of excitement and travel. Starting as a junior accountant at a salary of $1,200 a year, this well-bred, educated, and diplomatic Canadian represented a significant break in tradition for a hidebound, England-based commercial enterprise: in the past, it had always hired either tough Britishers used to isolation or the Canadian Métis offspring of immigrant Scots who had taken Native wives.

Bonnycastle stayed with the company throughout the Depression and the Second World War. Within a year of his eventful voyage on the *Baychimo* in 1931 (the deserted ship disappeared in a storm that winter and was spotted at sea for the next five years), he had proved himself by decreasing the western Arctic debt dramatically. Five years later, he was secretary to the company's Canadian Committee, the liaison officer with London headquarters, and personnel manager for its fur trade. That year, 1937, he took his final trip to the Arctic, a journey of several weeks that made the cover of Henry Luce's new *Life* magazine. Margaret Bourke-White, whose extraordinary black-and-white photograph of Fort Peck Dam had graced the magazine's first cover just a year before, photographed Bonnycastle shepherding Canada's governor general along the Mackenzie River in a sternwheel steamer. Lord Tweedsmuir was known to thriller readers as John Buchan, the author of *The 39 Steps,* the classic man-on-the-run novel. His Hudson's Bay host enjoyed his kind of book (decades later, he became a James Bond fan) and works of adventurous nonfiction, such as Vilhjalmur Stefansson's recent *Hunters of the Great North.* In his second career, Bonnycastle would publish British contemporaries of Buchan such as Victor Canning *(Panther's Moon)* and Edgar Wallace *(The Four Just Men).*

Although Buchan was nearly three decades older than Bonnycastle, the two hit it off like a couple of English remittance men come together in the colonies. "He was a good scout," the younger man said, offering his highest accolade for a fellow adventurer. And the two men befriended the assertive, obsessive photographer in trousers and tartan shirt – Maggie – who had brought along 10 chrysalises of the mourning cloak butterfly that she was chronicling on camera. Eventually there would be a family story among the Bonnycastle daughters that the 31-year-old Bourke-White (who later married Erskine Caldwell, the author of *Tobacco Road*) had fallen in love with one of the men she met on that trip – "and we think it had to be Dad," Judith, the youngest, told me. Perhaps, but the photographer herself would later note that "from the start there was a kind of affectionate friendship between His Excellency and myself." The agile governor general, at 62 only three years away from death, was an outdoors man, a mountain climber. When he came upon Bear Rock at the riverside fur-trading post of Fort Norman, there was nothing for it but to ascend the 1,300 feet of its sheerest face. Bonnycastle, who had climbed to the peak before, took the less perilous wooded slope. Packing thermoses of tea and a flask of whisky, he reached the top by the easier route, worried about the fate of his vice-regal guest on the precipitous mountainside. In fact, he found him stuck 10 feet below a rocky overhang of eroding shale. "Give me a hand," Buchan said. Bonnycastle used a broken tree branch to pull him up. Years later, his rescuer, writing about the climb in *The Canadian Alpine Journal,* modestly avoided mentioning the governor general's predicament, but he did allow that "He had made the ascent with great difficulty, and was very pleased with the result, saying it was one of the nastiest climbs he had ever made and would make the blood of experienced

Dick Bonnycastle on his final trip to the Arctic in 1937, during which he accompa-
nied Canada's governor general, Lord Tweedsmuir, better known as John Buchan.

MARGARET BOURKE-WHITE

Alpiners curdle." (Buchan's wife, Susan, reading about the climb in the newspapers, wired his secretary accompanying him: "This tomfoolery must
stop.")

That kind of high adventure wouldn't recur in the years that followed, as
Dick Bonnycastle, a family man in his late thirties, sat out World War II with
the company's Canadian Committee at home in Winnipeg. He and Mary had
a son, another Richard, and then two daughters, Honor and Judith, whom he
would entertain with tales of his years in the Arctic. "Dad would tell us about
having to cut off a man's arm that had become gangrenous," Judy says. "These
were our bedtime stories. We never got Cinderella. He used to take us tobog-
ganing behind the car – totally naughty – and we'd go mushing up the river."
By war's end, stuck in an office, working in a suit and tie instead of a parka,
he was as restless after two decades with the old firm as he had been after a
year in law. Peacetime prospects beckoned; it was a period of optimism and
opportunity for an ambitious man. "I wanted to go somewhere and get into

something I could run myself," he said later. "I knew I'd never be able to run the Hudson's Bay Company."

In truth, his son told me, Dick's architect father-in-law – whose impatience had begun with the much delayed wedding – had been pressing him to do the right thing by Mary and the family and take a position that would promise a more secure future. The well-connected Northwood talked to an old friend, Doug Weld; they had been prisoners together in a German camp during World War I. Douglas S. Weld was involved in a family printing firm, Bryant Press of Toronto, which had a branch plant in Winnipeg. Advocate Printers, founded at the turn of the century, had been struggling financially and needed an entrepreneurial, visionary helmsman. Dick Bonnycastle enthusiastically accepted the position of managing director. Mary recalled, "It was a terrific decision, after twenty years in the Hudson's Bay Company, to go into something new. But I was all for his doing what he wanted to do."

Another woman in his life was not so content. In his role as secretary to the Canadian Committee, Dick had a $125-a-month personal secretary named Ruth Palmour. An insurance salesman's daughter, a trim woman in her early twenties with pleasing blue eyes and blond features, she was a graduate of Winnipeg's Success Business College. "Mr. Bonnycastle," she says, formal even 40 years later, "always liked something new." She was disappointed to see him leave the company, although he sometimes worked his staff as long and hard as he did himself. "But he was charming, and knew how to communicate with people. He made you feel that you wanted to do your best for him." And after a tough day, the boss would sometimes take the employees out for dinner. So a month after he left for Advocate Printers, when Mr. Bonnycastle asked her to join him there, Ruth Palmour was pleased to accept, though a bit apprehensive: "I'm not the adventurous type. But it seemed like something different, and the other place was staid and proper."

She left the wide corridors and carpeted offices of the Canadian Committee for the wood-partitioned and cement-floor confines of a general printing plant. Advocate's hot-lead Linotype machines on the first floor of a six-story building and its flatbed presses in the basement produced stationery, accounting forms, annual reports, advertising material – and, for a publisher in eastern Canada, a line of 25-cent paperback reprints called Collins White Circle

Pocket Novels. Ruth Palmour's boss was intrigued with the success of these paperbacks. By 1949 Dick Bonnycastle, applying the coolheadedness and diplomacy he had honed in the North, was turning Advocate around and began looking for a fresh adventure. He had no experience in publishing, but he did have the right presses and the excess capacity to print this increasingly popular hybrid form of the book.

Paperbound books date back in North America to colonial times; in 1777 John Bell published a 190-volume series of British poets. The idea of reprinting original books in cheaper form, a forerunner of the contemporary paperback industry, surfaced in Germany in 1837 with a series of softcover books from the Tauchnitz publishing house. Tauchnitz Editions featured British and American authors in English for European readers who wanted to practice their language skills. A decade earlier, a group of Bostonians had idealistically but unprofitably published cheap paperback books as the American Library of Useful Knowledge. In 1839 two New York journalists started a popular newspaper-like supplement called *Brother Jonathan* that carried the complete texts of pirated British novels and became America's original mass-market paperbound books. Because the supplements could be mailed at low newspaper rates, other publishers leapt into the market, dropping prices so much – to six cents – that when the post office raised the mail rates within a few years, the industry died. Meanwhile, dime novels with western themes and other popular fiction flourished as paperbacks during the 19th century, at one point representing a third of all books published in a single year. No longer confined to bookshops, they also appeared on newsstands and in dry-goods stores. Prominent among them were pirated works by British and French writers, until the Copyright Act of 1891 stopped the practice. In 1917 a former New York bond salesman named Horace Liveright and a Greenwich Village bookstore owner began publishing the instantly successful Modern Library of classic literature in modestly formatted, low-cost hardbacks for widespread distribution.

The ultimate concept – inexpensive softcover reprints of both popular and serious books for a mass market – came together during the Depression. In 1935 England, grammar-school dropout Allen Lane of The Bodley Head, a faltering hardcover house, created the Penguin Books line of sixpence literary paperbacks, which sold splendidly in unconventional locations such as Woolworth stores. Within four years, Penguin had launched an American distribution office run by Ian Ballantine, a 22-year-old American graduate of the London School of Economics, and Betty, his British bride. The couple arrived in New York only a few weeks after publisher Robert Fair de Graff, a Dutch American high school dropout, and the principals of Simon & Schuster had distributed 10,000 copies of each of 10 titles of the new line of 25-cent Pocket Books. "Complete and Unabridged" reprints in a portable 4¼-by-6 ½-inch format (soon to be 4¼ by 7 inches), the paperbacks bore the logo of Gertrude the kangaroo on their plastic-laminated covers. They were as diverse in tone and content as James Hilton's fantasy *Lost Horizon* (the first Pocket Book), Agatha Christie's *The Murder of Roger Ackroyd*, and Samuel Butler's literary *The Way of All Flesh*. Placed in department stores and drugstores as well as with news dealers and booksellers, they all sold as quickly as candy floss at a carnival. As World War II ended, Pocket Books was selling more than 40 million copies a year, a seductive enough figure to prompt liberal newspaper publisher and department store tycoon Marshall Field III to buy the company and its parent, Simon & Schuster.

This paperback phenomenon was propelled by the advent of large, high-speed, rubber-plate rotary presses. By 1949 bookshops and even drugstores were selling these pennies-per-unit products from a growing list of publishers: Avon Books, Dell Publishing Company, Popular Library, N A L (New American Library of World Literature, which published under the Signet fiction and the Meteor nonfiction imprints), Pyramid Books, and Bantam Books. Ian Ballantine – whom Penguin had fired after the war – launched Bantam for New York publisher Grosset & Dunlap. One of its backers was the Curtis Circulating Company, the potent distribution arm of the company that published heavyweight periodicals such as the *Saturday Evening Post* and *Ladies' Home Journal*. "Just saying Curtis was our distributor was enough for people to believe in us," said Ballantine (who went on to publish paperback originals under his Ballantine Books imprint before selling out to Random House in 1974 and rejoining Bantam; he died in 1995).

Dick Bonnycastle knew that Curtis Circulating's strong sales force had a hammerlock on independent distributors throughout North America. Through his printing of White Circle paperbacks, he had met the sales manager in Curtis's Canadian office in Toronto, known there as Curtis Distributing. Jack

Palmer had discussed with him the idea of creating a publishing company specializing in mass-market reprints. Palmer would handle the selection of titles, the marketing, and the distribution across Canada, Bonnycastle the printing.

At the beginning, there was no thought of being a major player in the industry. In the words of his daughter, Judy Bonnycastle Burgess, "When empty presses came along, Father thought it would be fun to publish the 'new' paperbacks." Ruth Palmour agrees: "Harlequin was a filler for a nice, steady business." Bonnycastle was certainly not interested in making his fortune from publishing. "He couldn't understand people who just worked for money," recalls his son, now a wealthy businessman, who looks back on the origin of the company with a little awe and a lot of hyperbole: "This may be the only company in history that required no money to start – because they had to pay the printing bill in 60 days, but Curtis paid them in 30 days." The partners in this apparently blessed enterprise were Doug Weld of Bryant Press and Jack Palmer, with 25 percent each, and Advocate with 50 percent; Dick Bonnycastle was not a shareholder.

His hobbylike approach to publishing pervaded the birth and first year of Harlequin Books. No one now alive remembers where the corporate name came from (most likely from Palmer), but Bonnycastle's daughter does recall the joyous family meeting in which her parents discussed the choice of logo. The harlequin figure – in a ruff-collared jacket and tights of many colored patches, and often wearing a mask – originated as a stock character in the commedia dell'arte theater of 16th-century Italy. The harlequin in these improvised comedies and romances was the dumb but shrewd servant, an athletic type whose somersaulting and stilt-walking prompted his Italian name, Arlecchino, or "always airborne." This slapstick theater helped to inspire French comic opera and English pantomime productions, as well as artists such as Picasso. "I can remember sitting around the table," Judy says. "Dad had done a squiggle of this little guy in the diamond, and we chose the logo." Her father's sketch evolved to the design that remains to this day: a black-and-white harlequin playing a lutelike instrument while sitting cross-legged within a diamond shape. Harlequin employees now refer to him as Joey.

Deciding on the logo was the easy part; the problem was choosing which books to reprint. The first title, released in May 1949, was *The Manatee*, by a now forgotten American author, Nancy Bruff:

Jabez Folger stepped off his whaler on a hazy July morning in 1830 and, detaching himself from the enmity of his crew, walked away.

He strode through the raucous activity of the Nantucket docks bearing the dark streamers his thoughts had woven during the long, unlucky voyage. These were almost visible as if he had stumbled into an ancient, smoky spider's web and carried it away clinging to his head and brow.

In the darkness of its tone and content, the novel was hardly a prototype for the fluffier Harlequin romances that would soon follow. Set in the whaling town of Nantucket, Massachusetts, it tells of the violent Jabez, who feels more for his ship than for his pious, gentle Quaker wife, whose love he has "deliberately and viciously . . . murdered." Yet there *is* a happy ending, and there *are* characters named Luke and Saffron. And, more to the point, I see strong portents of the publisher's eventual direction in the way the book was designed and promoted. The jacket copy – in describing *The Manatee* as "a classic tragedy of gods and devils played out against a setting of sea, sky and fabulous island" – manages to include the word *love* four times. The front cover shows a cartoonlike painting of a woman in a long gown at the top of a staircase, looking down on a handsome man in a sailor's cap. "Strange loves of a seaman," says the descriptive text above the title. Next to this cover line, in the upper left-hand corner, perches the harlequin logo and the number *1* – from the first, the company had the bright idea of following up an innovation of Mercury Publications earlier in the decade to number the books, which made them collectible. And prominently displayed at the bottom of the cover is the phrase that would one day become a brand: *A Harlequin Book*.

The two dozen other Harlequins published that first year and retailed at 25 cents apiece (the almost universal price point at the time) were a stew of crime novels (*Blondes Don't Cry*), westerns (*Painted Post Outlaws,* by the aptly named Tom Gunn), and a few titles that at least had the ring of the romances to come *(Honeymoon Mountain, Virgin with Butterflies)*. One book even combined a medically oriented plot with a vaguely feminist title: *His Wife the Doctor*. And there was *Gina,* a novel by George Albert Glay, who would have another book, *Beggars Might Ride,* on the list three years later and who would become a senior editor with Harlequin more than two decades later. From Toronto Jack Palmer chose the books and arranged to buy the reprint rights, and then he sent his selections, along with cover art and copyright information, to

The very first Harlequin book, released in May 1949 – perhaps a portent of things to come. HARLEQUIN ENTERPRISES

31

Winnipeg for printing. He was ever enthusiastic: "We'll do well with this one!" he promised. Or: "This will go great guns!"

At first Palmer's choices seemed mildly successful. The Bonnycastle kids would hear their father exclaim at home about the number of readers who were buying Harlequins in little places such as Plum Coulee, Manitoba. In the first year, it looked as if they made a profit, even after wholesalers has taken their 36 percent share of the retail price and brokers a further six percent. On paper, anyway, earnings in 1949 appeared to be about $150,000, and that was the figure on which the company paid taxes.

"Things looked rosy, and then the returns came in," Ruth Palmour recalls. "We started seeing the true facts of the business. It could have folded then; we were *behind*." Bonnycastle's son is blunter: "They were broke." Unfortunately the books had been distributed on consignment, which meant that retailers had not paid anything for them in advance and could return any unsold copies. Which they did, to Harlequin's surprise. Until that time, returns had virtually been unheard of in the paperback publishing industry. In fact, they were usually called "exchanges," because the publisher would send a new title to the wholesale distributor instead of following the consignment system of refunding the cost of an unsold book. During the war, with paper shortages and a demand for reading material, recalls Pocket Books executive Bud Egbert in *Two-Bit Culture: The Paperbacking of America,* "every book that was printed was sold. If anybody made a return, you called them up and asked what was wrong. . . . By 1949, that was over." When all the accounts were in and the returns on sales of 818,000 books topped 17 percent, the principals of Harlequin faced a disquieting fact: they had lost $80,000. The blood continued to flow in 1950, when returns on 1.6 million books reached 26 percent. And with the federal tax laws then in effect, Harlequin wasn't allowed to carry any loss back to the previous year. Simply put, the company couldn't recover the money it had paid in taxes on nonexistent profits.

Part of the problem was simply that Bonnycastle's attention was diverted. He was managing the printing house. He was a partner in, and sometime chairman of, a sheet-metal company called Selkirk Metal Products, which made a fast-selling line of self-cleaning, insulated metal chimneys. A consortium of a half-dozen Winnipeg businessmen and professionals had put together the company with only $600 apiece; within a few years, after taking out healthy dividends, they would sell out for $3.6 million ($200,000 of it Bonnycastle's). A dealmaker named Daniel Sprague led the group: "He was the financial wizard of these things. My father was a good manager," Bonnycastle's son says, while admitting that his father mismanaged Harlequin in the beginning. In 1952 the consortium bought Advocate and another printer, Stovel Press, to create Stovel-Advocate Press. The business moved from downtown Winnipeg to the polyglot north end (where I grew up, aware of the printing house's reputation as a respected local institution). Bonnycastle became president and general manager of the new company.

Amid all this, the middle-aged Jack Palmer died in Toronto of a heart attack. It was left to Bonnycastle to sort out the financial mess Harlequin was in. Fortunately there was another prominent player in the business who shared his problem, the head of Curtis Distributing's parent company in the United States. When he flew in to see Bonnycastle, he had one brisk piece of advice: keep publishing, however modestly. If Harlequin shuts down, the retailers will want to return all your books right away. Then Curtis will have to swallow the losses. And if there isn't any new product in the pipeline, the booksellers will consider you out of business, and Curtis can't argue against any returns. So keep publishing – even one title a month. And we'll tell the retailers we are not going to accept any returns because this is an ongoing publisher.

The self-serving advice saved the business. Having the heft of Curtis behind Harlequin, actively pushing its product, also helped: throughout North America, the distributor had the reputation of playing hardball with local wholesalers and retailers, threatening to withdraw its popular *Saturday Evening Post* and *Ladies' Home Journal* if they failed to carry the books Curtis wanted them to sell. Encouraged, Dick Bonnycastle continued publishing, at almost the same frequency as before. But now he had another problem: Jack Palmer had been responsible for selecting all the titles. Who was going to manage their publishing list?

Harlequin had been reprinting the works of some well-known names, Americans such as Midwestern novelist Wallace Stegner and science fiction writer A. E. Van Vogt, and Britons such as mystery writers Agatha Christie and John Creasey (within a couple of years, even W. Somerset Maugham's *Catalina* would appear as an anomaly on the list). Among the British authors was popular crime writer James Hadley Chase (René Raymond), whose first coarse, brutal book, *No Orchids for Miss Blandish,* had scandalized and/or excited readers in 1939. According to one critic, the dead or wounded included "Guys rubbed out: 22, guys slugged bad: 16, guys given a workover: 5, dames laid: 5." George Orwell, author of *1984,* the literary classic whose lurid paperback cover in 1950 had read "Forbidden Love . . . Fear . . . Betrayal," noted that Chase's book, supposedly dealing in violent sex, was really about power. British crime-writing critic Julian Symons commented that in Chase's novels, "love, where it occurs, is often used as a means of obtaining dominance over another individual." My point in mentioning all this is that Harlequin, which would make its reputation in soft-core romance, was originally publishing some hard-core violence – in its second year, Chase's *No Orchids,* and the next year, his crudely titled *Twelve Chinks and a Woman,* which the Toronto police department pulled off the shelves, much to Bonnycastle's embarrassment. This was the year, though, that the boom in sensationally presented paperbacks began to ebb in North America, as the U.S. House of Representatives created a Select Committee on Current Pornographic Materials to ferret out prurient content in books, magazines, and comics.

Balancing Chase's initial Harlequin appearance in 1951 was *Beyond the Blue Mountains.* It was the first of many historical and gothic romance novels on the company's list by England's Eleanor Hibbert, a reclusive woman who became a worldwide bestselling author in hardcover under the pseudonyms Jean Plaidy, Victoria Holt, and Philippa Carr, among many others.

Another writer, who would soon move on to much more serious themes, made his debut that year as an author, not just a Harlequin author. The first two novels of this Belfast-born Irishman, transplanted to Montreal, were as up-front as their titles: *Wreath for a Redhead* and *The Executioners.* They were originals, first published by Harlequin. The cover of *Wreath* portrays a "titian temptress" in deep décolletage who is about to be strangled by a scarf held by a pair of gloved hands. *"Montreal Means Murder!"* the cover line hollers, and the story is a thriller about a sailor who goes searching for a missing redhead and finds himself the target of the police and an illegal combine "whose tentacles stretched across Canada." *The Executioners* is about "A Fast-Talking Canadian Adventurer vs. Imported, Ruthless Killers," and the opening paragraphs signal the writer's embryonic style:

This is the story as you'll never get it in the newspapers or the police files – though the files are thick enough by now to fill six books, bigger than this, and they all add up to the same question. What happened to the old man?

The cops have been over the ground with fine tweezers and about six countries have put men on the case. But there is no lead, after London. And the only man who might tell us, won't ever say. His boys aren't talking either, not that they could say much. In their set-up, they were stooges who carried out orders. That's all.

He is one of my favorite writers, one whom Graham Greene called "my favorite living novelist." The author of *The Luck of Ginger Coffey, Lies of Silence,* and *Black Robe* (one of five of his books that became films), he has twice won the Canadian Governor General's Literary Award for Fiction as well as a special award from the U.S. Institute of Arts and Letters. And Brian Moore has long since renounced those two crude but compelling potboilers. For instance, in a 1986 documentary by Canada's National Film Board, *The Lonely Passion of Brian Moore,* he says, "I was halfway through my first novel. I was writing *Judith Hearne.*" Of course, *The Lonely Passion of Judith Hearne* – which, despite its title, is *not* a romance novel by any definition – appeared in 1956, five years after he apprenticed with Harlequin.

The company's list in the first five years, averaging about 60 books annually, made only a few more perfunctory bows to Canadian content with the odd domestic fiction (*Royce of the Royal Mounted*) and nonfiction (*The Black Donnellys,* a tale of an Ontario family's blood feud). There were a handful of other nonfiction titles, including *Rasputin and Crimes that Shook the World,* and how-to books on cooking, knitting, and *Health, Sex, and Birth Control,* which went into seven printings. But of all the bestsellers, Ruth Palmour remembers, "these nice little romances stuck here and there seemed to be the popular ones."

Almost from the beginning, she had noticed that the more romantic-sounding the book, the better it sold. In the company's second year, *Gambling on Love* and *Portrait of Love* virtually sold out compared with titles such as *Murder over Broadway* and *Speak of the Devil,* which had returns of well over 50 percent. Jean Plaidy's well-received historical romances began appearing regularly after 1951 (*Beyond the Blue Mountains* had only 48 copies returned on sales of 30,000). Two years later, Harlequin published the seminal volumes in a subgenre that would soon be inextricably linked with its name: medical romances. The first two that telegraphed their subject in their titles were by the American Lucy Agnes Hancock: *General Duty Nurse* (Harlequin No. 235) and *Community Nurse* (No. 264). In 1955 almost a third of the 25 titles were Hancock's nurse-and-doctor romances, which sold for 35 cents each.

By now Ruth Palmour was intimately involved in Harlequin as de facto manager. It was she who had been dealing with Palmer by letter and phone, getting the books printed and delivered to the wholesale distributors. Never to marry, she was the archetypical employee who was wed to her work, if not to her employer. "How could she not have been madly in love with him?" wonders her boss's younger daughter, Judy, who would one day collaborate with her. "Ruth was extraordinary, the quintessential organizer of the century. She was like stepping into a cool lake, wonderfully calm. It wouldn't have happened if it weren't for Ruth."

After Palmer died, his 25 percent stockholdings went to Bonnycastle, who now had his first piece of the company. And as the business faced ruin and its future seemed bleak, Doug Weld of Bryant Press returned his seemingly worthless stock to the new shareholder, whose son recalls a Sunday morning in 1954. His worried father commented after breakfast, "I've got this 25 percent of Harlequin stock, and I just don't know what to do with it."

"I'll buy it, Dad! I'll give you $160 for it." Richard Junior, a 20-year-old university student with a financial bent, was ready to empty his savings account.

"No, it wouldn't be a suitable investment for you," his father said. "It's a bit speculative." After pondering for a while, he said, "I know what I'll do: I'll give it to Ruth."

Ruth Palmour's memory is that she actually received the shares several years later when Bonnycastle remarked, "Ruth, I think we'll give you 25 percent. It might be worth something sometime."

Probably a *bit*, she thought at the time. "I didn't twig to what it could be," she says now. "It was a generous thing to do, and I appreciated it."

In the early 1950s, Dick Bonnycastle realized that he not only had a strong woman running things in the Harlequin office, he also had an equally capable woman he could call on at home. The Bonnycastles were more complex characters than the caricatures who appear at the beginning of this chapter suggest.

Mary Bonnycastle in her twenties. One of Winnipeg's most prominent socialites, she was also Harlequin's first editor.
JUDY BONNYCASTLE BURGESS

Dick was a reasonably successful businessman who was not ultimately intrigued by business. He became a respected, almost revered politician, a supermayor, while loathing the practices of politics. He was a man known to his friends and colleagues for a wit as dry as a prairie dust storm, to his daughters as a father who imported fun into their lives – yet a sister-in-law, Mary, married to his younger brother Larry, recalls that while "he could be perfectly charming and as funny as could be, we didn't see it often. There was always a sadness about him." His life, like his father's, appeared to be a quest for newness, for another adventure, and Harlequin was just one interesting stop along the way. Its success was never an obsession with him; it was, in the end, happenstance. If he hadn't had the inspired – frustrated? desperate? – idea of turning to his wife at this time, listening to her advice, the company may never have been more than a modest little publisher in the business of reprinting other people's books.

Mary seemed the soul of upper-middle-class Winnipeg society, which in one sense she was. At Greywood, their elm-shaded home on South Drive whose well-tended grounds slanted to the banks of the Red River, she had created an oasis for the family. There she gardened, did needlepoint and knitting, and one day would take up oil painting, sipping iced tea with female friends in the summer as they painted on the lawn. But like her husband, who followed his father in embracing public service, she moved out of the castle to engage herself in the larger community. Some of her involvement was expected, ordinary, such as being president of the Anglican Parish Guild and the Ladies' Section of the St. Charles Country Club. More ambitious was her work as a volunteer and an executive member of the guilds of the general and children's hospitals and her serving on the board of the Victorian Order of Nurses, on the finance committee of the provincial Girl Guides, and on the women's committees of the symphony, the art gallery, and the Royal Winnipeg Ballet. Yet she insisted on being available to her children, young Richard, Honor, and Judy: "Too many parents today are too much preoccupied with activities outside the home."

So when Dick had asked Mary in the past to help out and read proofs of Harlequin books before they were published, to make sure there were no typographical or grammatical errors, she was interested: this was useful work she could do at home. She was always reading, anyway – biography, history, the classics, especially Charles Dickens and Jane Austen. The reality of reading books as a business was something else. The ones that Jack Palmer had picked were, with some exceptions, not her glass of iced tea. Books by that Chase man, for instance. She had even threatened to stop proofing such trash, and when her husband mentioned that Harlequin was losing money, she asked, perhaps rhetorically, "Do you know why?"

"The only books we're selling well are the nurse romances."

"You see! What women want is a nice story with a happy ending."

Now, with Palmer dead, Dick came to Mary once more and asked her to act as an at-home editor, reading and recommending titles the company could reprint.

"I'll have nothing to do with those sex books. . . . And I don't know anything about the business part."

"I'll look after that."

It was settled. Ruth would correspond with publishers across the continent and ask them to submit books for possible reprinting, which she would then feed to her boss's wife for approval and perhaps some editing. Mary read while knitting, relaxing in the sunroom, even propped up in bed, and, over the next few years, she remarked on how popular the nurse-and-doctor romances were. She went to the local branch of the public library and looked

One of the earliest Harlequin nurse-and-doctor romances – soon to become the company's bread and butter.

HARLEQUIN ENTERPRISES

through a number of books that all shared the imprint of an English firm. They were medical romances, they were decent, and, of their kind, they were quite enjoyable.

Ruth was also visiting the library, a branch near the office. "I'd go in and look over the shelves. They had a lovely corner with four or five shelves, the romance section." She started reading books from the same London publishing house that Mary had identified. *Oh, boy,* she thought, *this is a real gold mine.* When she learned that a new employee at Stovel-Advocate came from England, she asked her: "Do you know anything about these?"

The young woman, a publican's daughter, was surprised: "Oh, you don't know about Mills & Boon? They're just wonderful!"

Ruth sent a sampling of the books to Bonnycastle, with the suggestion: "Let's do these."

This convergence of interest in an overseas publisher that few people in North America had heard of was enough to convince Bonnycastle. The two women he was depending on were already convinced. He directed Ruth to write a letter, one that would eventually change the face of publishing on this continent and around the world:

8th May, 1957

<u>Air Mail</u>
Mills & Boon, Limited,
50 Grafton Way,
Fitzroy Square,
LONDON W. I, England.

Dear Sirs:

We are looking for light romances dealing with doctors and nurses for publication in our Harlequin line of paper-covered pocket-type books, and
wonder if the Canadian reprint rights for any of your books of this type
might be available to us.

Our royalty rates are 1.4¢ per copy sold in a 35¢ edition, with an advance
against royalty of $200. payable on publication which would be within a
year of completion of agreement. Our initial printings of nurse and doctor
titles are presently 25,000 copies.

If you are interested in submitting books to us, we would be glad to
receive copies of some of your doctor and nurse titles. Mary Burchell's
"Hospital Corridors" might be particularly suited to Canadian readers if, as
I understand, it has a Montreal setting.

We shall look forward to hearing from you.

Yours very truly,
HARLEQUIN BOOKS LIMITED,
(Miss) Ruth Palmour,
Secretary.

John has suggested that our books are better than Valium.
  – Alan Boon
They could be prescribed by National Health.
  – John Boon

The Splendid Legacy 3
MILLS & BOON

In 1903, the year Richard Bonnycastle was born, a visionary Michigan inventor founded the Ford Motor Company in Detroit to build the world's first inexpensive automobile. It took Henry Ford five years before he developed the $850.50 Model T, described as a vehicle of all bone and muscle and no fat. That year, 1908, Ford hired an efficiency expert to devise a production process that became the first automotive assembly line, an innovative system to mass-produce a better and cheaper – and standardized – product. "Me," he said, signaling a major theme of the century ahead, "I like specialists."

The same year, across the Atlantic, two Englishmen founded a company that would someday become the assembly line of the publishing industry, mass-producing the Model T of books. They would come to specialize in a cheaper if not necessarily a better product than their competitors, one that would share the uniform characteristics, the homogeneity, of Ford's black-only flivver: a series of predictably gentle romance novels with instantly identifiable brown bindings and the good-as-gold guarantee of a happy ending.

Gerald Mills had been the educational manager and Charles Boon – C.B. – the sales manager of Methuen and Co., a London publishing house launched in 1889. Methuen published Rudyard Kipling, Joseph Conrad, and Queen Victoria's favorite author, Marie Corelli, whose florid *The Sorrows of Satan* was England's first acknowledged bestseller. The firm was showing exceptional growth in the first decade of the new century, propelled by its Sixpenny Library of current and classical authors. The middle-class Mills was a public school and Cambridge graduate, gentle in manner; the working-class Boon had left school at 12 and earned a reputation as a corporate despot. What they had in common was the belief that though their 10 years of combined efforts had helped to fuel Methuen's expansion, their employers were failing to reward them amply. With £1,000 – Mills had private money, Boon scraped together his share – they started their own house to publish fiction and non-fiction of general and educational interest; as a trade journal remarked, the partners of Mills & Boon "propose to throw their publishing net widely."

Significantly their first book was a romance. Released in 1909, *Arrows from the Dark* was by the young Sophie Cole, who would write 60 Mills & Boon novels, into the 1940s. The subject matter was significant only in hindsight, for at first the publishers had no thought of focusing on light romantic fiction (though Boon gratefully gave Cole 50 shares of the company, which he later bought back). During the century's second decade, they did publish a series of high-society novels with aristocratic characters; the covers bore the logo of a Cupid, which was to resurface in the 1940s in a box announcing "A Mills & Boon Love Story." Laura, Lady Troubridge, a relative of Virginia Woolf, wrote seven of these upper-crust stories on the theme of love and trust. And while another of the company's early novels was a love story called *The Prince and Betty* by humorist P. G. Wodehouse, most of its books veered wildly from that specialty. Among them were educational titles such as *Nerves and the Nervous*; the first two (and unsuccessful) novels of Hugh Walpole, who then jumped to another house and was later knighted for his prolific work; and the autobiographical adventure yarns of an immensely popular American, Jack London, whose *Cruise of the Snark* and *John Barleycorn: or, Alcoholic Memoirs* replenished M & B's cash flow. They even released a pro-suffragette play, *Votes for Women*. Their first year, the partners grossed an encouraging £16,500 and awarded themselves a £52 raise, to £312 a year; the office boys got £5, 4 d to reach £26. "It was obviously an up-and-running firm with a spirited editorial direction," Boon's son John says.

But with the First World War, the firm lost all its senior staff to the military or the government; C.B. was in the navy, and Mills was in bad health. "Its financial resources were small, and it didn't have much of a backlist," John Boon says. "Basically, during that difficult time, it lacked direction, and moreover – which was probably worse for a publisher – it lost its contacts with authors and with the book trade. The business was actually run by my Aunt Margaret, a charming woman but not known for her business acumen." C.B. returned to a house that was crumbling, in danger of collapse. The bottom had fallen out of the market for M & B's series of one-shilling cloth editions, a precursor to its six-penny paperbacks, and, at the time of Jack London's death in 1916, the firm still had 250,000 unsold copies of his *Valley of the Moon* ("the particular brilliance of Aunt Margaret," her nephew notes wryly). By then the company had begun releasing novels with exotic settings and its first medical romance, Louise Gerard's *Days of Probation*. Yet over the first two years of the 1920s, sales fell by nearly half. Workers' strikes were crippling the economy, culminating in the General Strike of 1924. At times the sinking firm borrowed money from Mills's wealthy brother to stay above water.

During this decade, the eventual direction of the firm was foreshadowed by a series of lighter-than-air novels inspired by Charles Boon's attendance at frothy shows at London's Haymarket Theatre and by the publishing of a romance by Georgette Heyer. Writing at the time under the pseudonym Stella Martin, Heyer was a British author who would become renowned for her Regency romances, which enjoyed a North American revival in the 1960s. The M & B list included other imminently prominent names in romantic fiction, such as Elizabeth Carfrae, whose risqué *Payment in Full* deals with adultery. A 1924 advertisement heralded the future marketing strategy: "It is not necessary for Fiction readers to make a choice from a new Mills & Boon Fiction list. They can rest assured that each novel has been carefully chosen, and is worth reading."

In 1928 the ailing Mills died ("I don't want to knock the memory of Mills," says John Boon, "but he did take life pretty easily"). He had had the bulk of shares in the company, and, under the terms of his will, they had to be bought out. Charles Boon was without funds; the firm faced the prospect of selling to a rival. Fortunately a former office boy at Methuen, J. W. Henley, had access to cash, thanks to his father, and, in taking over about a third of Mills's shares, he became joint managing director of M & B, a partner with C.B. – "as far as he ever had a partner, for he was always an autocrat," son John says. Henley quickly made his mark in production: finding that the printing bills were high, he and C.B. took one of their main printers to lunch and asked him to reduce prices, which he did without a murmur. One year into the new decade, sales were up 12.5 percent, while profits increased by an astonishing 300 percent.

With fresh equity and rising yields, M & B was poised during the Great Depression to capitalize on the burgeoning popularity of the commercial tupenny libraries. Among them were the Boots Booklovers Libraries, which the British pharmacy chain had begun as a loss-leader in 1899. By the 1930s, lower-middle and working-class readers could rent a hardcover book, which sold for seven shillings and sixpence, for twopence or more a week from these pay-as-you-read libraries. They surfaced in almost every village, run by tobacconists, news agents, and other shopkeepers throughout England, including the exclusive Harrod's department store in London. Their success even forced the bookselling chain W. H. Smith to meet the tupenny rate and drop its demand for a half-crown deposit for its lending-library books. Mills & Boon moved with dispatch into this new market for escapist literature, soon recognizing that the women in their readership welcomed any romance novel on the list. For a quarter of a century, the firm would specialize, publishing only in this genre and distributing almost exclusively through the libraries rather than bookstores and newsstands.

"Although most publishers had hard times, our business was up and up because we were selling to the libraries," recalls John Boon. "My father had a rough career, but he knew a winner when he saw it, so he went entirely into the romantic fiction field. We didn't corner the market as we still had a lot of competition [such as Hodder and Stoughton and Collins], but we were the market leaders." His brother Alan joined the firm in 1931, 17 years old and fresh from public school. He says the partners didn't really appreciate what they were then establishing: "A line all in brown bindings, a most unattractive color. And the ladies used to ask in the shops for the books with the brown bindings" – or "the books in brown." The hardbound bindings had the Mills & Boon logo perched in the upper right-hand corner and the name of the author and the title in black embossing within a black border. The front covers had artless three-color line drawings, which became fancier four-color ones by the end of the decade. So similar were the fat volumes in appearance (not to mention in subject matter) that the more resolute readers would even put their own mark on the backs of the books to indicate whether they had already read them.

In effect, without fully realizing the implications at the time, M & B had created a brand: a recognizable product that it could sell repeatedly as a mass-produced commodity – as a series of books, not single titles, all of them released under a dependable publisher's imprint. This ability, together with an efficient distribution network through the libraries, meant that the firm had no reason to spend much if any money on advertising. Instead, it promoted its romantic fiction at the back of each novel, with up to 16 pages of titles, often preceded by a full-page promotion that advised readers: "Really the only way to choose is to limit your reading to those publishers whose lists are carefully selected, and whose fiction imprint is a sure guarantee of good reading." This was the rebirth of what would become, along with Penguin, the best-known name in British publishing and the only one that readers would buy for its own name rather than an individual author's. Mills & Boon also pioneered the use of a mail-order catalog, launched before World War I, to market its monthly new releases. Readers who got on the mailing list for the catalog would often approach lending libraries in advance and create demand for the firm's forthcoming books. This was the start of the Reader Services, or book clubs, that both M & B and Harlequin would effectively exploit in the decades ahead. Later chroniclers of the romance industry would wrongly attribute both the brand name and the book club notions to Harlequin in North America (which admittedly did build on the ideas by adding marketing campaigns to promote its full line of books as a brand name).

Despite the Depression, Mills & Boon became so attractive that a much larger publishing house, Hutchinson and Co., offered to buy it, but M & B was so confidently successful that it could reject the offer.

Many of those romances in the 1930s differed from the more formulaic ones that followed. As Alan Boon points out, "the authors would have subsidiary plots and descriptions of scenery which now our authors don't have time for; they just have to get the guy and the girl together and go through 192 pages."

John adds, "In a curious way, they were more permissive then and dealt with things that we wouldn't deal with today. There was much more divorce." More everything, it seemed: Louise Gerard's 1934 novel, *Strange Paths,* has a hero who trots around in women's clothing for much of the book.

By now it was possible to detect trends, decade by decade. Jay Dixon, who worked for Mills & Boon in the 1980s, left to research a history of the firm – attempting to read every one of its books at the British Museum, which has the only complete collection. "Right from the start," she said, partway through her labor of love, "they were portraying social problems. In one of the first novels, *Wardour Street Idyll,* published in 1910, a woman falls in love with a married man whose wife is a drug addict. By the 1910s you get attempted rape, by the twenties full rape and adultery. In the early thirties, the hero suddenly becomes younger than the heroine. She is the one with the power in the relationship, emotionally and financially."

Yet some of the abiding idiosyncrasies of the genre existed from M & B's earliest days. A tendency to purplish prose, for instance: in Sophie Cole's 1913 book, *Penelope's Doors,* the hero brushes against the heroine's shoulder, and she feels "a little thrill of an electric shock run down her arm into her finger tips." By 1932, in her first novel, *Beggars May Sing,* Sara Seale had introduced the young orphan as heroine, who would become a popular figure. Seale was one of many authors who submitted first novels because of a promise printed in each of these early library-edition books that Mills & Boon would read every manuscript it received. Today the firm and its parent, Harlequin, may be the only major publishing houses still maintaining this policy.

"So we sailed through the thirties," says John Boon, as if he had been there. In fact, he did not join the firm until 1938 – and then only for a year. "I loathed it, I must say. I found it absolutely gruesome. I was put on editorial. I did all sorts of things. In a way the outbreak of war was something I didn't regret." Brother Alan, three years older, was there throughout the decade, at first as an invoice clerk. In his freshman year with the business, he became so intrigued with romantic fiction that he wrote his own romance ("It was pretty awful," he admits). Eventually "I worked for the old man on the editorial [reading manuscripts]. There I picked up any knowledge I have of romances. But the old man didn't delegate very much. . . . He wanted to keep the power to himself."

As children, the younger of three brothers, Alan and John had been fast friends, sharing a bedroom and later playing rugby together (with the Wasps First Fifteen), almost like fraternal twins despite their age difference. Even in appearance they were alike, especially in their plumper, balding years when Harlequin president Larry Heisey saw them as "Tweedledum and Dee – they looked like they were clearly brothers and bore substantial physical resemblance to each other. Alan is more large and shambling, and John is a little tighter." Alan, wanting to be involved in publishing, as an editor if not a writer, decided against university to work for the family firm. John went to Cambridge, where he graduated well with a Double First in history from Trinity Hall, his specialty the romantic era of Charles II. Considering a career in journalism, he idled away his post-university year at Mills & Boon, until World War II catapulted him into the infantry with the South Wales Border Regiment, with whom he landed on D-Day. Alan served as a petty officer with the Royal Navy, fighting at Narvik and Crete.

The year the war began, the firm had more than 450 titles in print by over 50 writers and was selling in Europe, Australia, and New Zealand. Some of its more fecund writers had to adopt pen names to get around a ban that many libraries, Boots Booklovers among them, placed on accepting more than two books a year from the same author. The business continued to flourish in the war years; despite paper rationing, M & B managed to print at least 4,000 copies of each new hardcover (John Boon seems to recall as many as 10,000 for some titles) and sold them as fast as if they were paperbacks. It successfully argued with the Ministry of Supply for its allocation of paper on the basis that it was enhancing the morale of the women working on the home front. Their spirits might have lifted mightily with this scene from Sylvia Sark's *Once to Every Woman* (1940), in which Jon carries his new bride, Gail, to a couch and there transports her even farther: "She felt Jon loosen her dress, slip it from her shoulders, felt his lips on her throat and breast. My husband, my lover, her heart said, but her lips were silent. In this sweet, wild moment neither of them had need of speech. Their love flowered swiftly, more passionate, more searching than it had ever been before."

Some M & B titles of the era reflected the fact of the war: Barbara Stanton's *WAAF into Wife*, for example, in which the Auxiliary Air Force heroine is smitten with a Polish Freedom Fighter, and Fay Chandos's *Away from Each Other*, featuring a left-behind wife led astray by a captain billeted in her home ("We

Side by side – Alan (left) *and John Boon, scions of British romance.* HARLEQUIN ENTERPRISES

haven't time for prolonged discussions in ethics and conventions," the wily seducer says. "Haven't you heard that there's a war on, darling?" To give the heroine her due, even while succumbing she recognizes that line as one her father had used on her mother in a previous war). But most of the romances – whose covers now routinely had the Cupid with a placard proclaiming "A Mills & Boon Love Story" – pretended things were peacetime normal or placed the characters in relatively untroubled settings such as Scotland. Romance is escapism, after all. And publishers felt at first that hostilities wouldn't last that long and that books with wartime backdrops would become too dated to reprint. After the war, however, reality reared its less pretty head in novels that dealt with issues such as shortages of housing for families and jobs for women. Jane Arbor's protagonist in *Ladder of Understanding* (1949) hungers for mean- ingful employment: "Was her undoubted talent for her own chosen career to be buried henceforward beneath a welter of ministering-angel work?"

Like that M & B heroine, John Boon wanted his own independent career. But he came home from the war to a wife, Felicity, their children, and the need for an immediate job; reluctantly he rejoined the family business. Charles Boon had died in 1943, his powerful presence waning in his final years. "My father was an extremely difficult man, and working for him was not the most enjoyable of experiences," John told the *Sunday Times* years later. "I'm sure I would never have stayed if my father had lived." John was to confront other family problems. Alan, now a husband and a father, had returned to a comfortable niche in editorial and he was a pleasure to work with. But their eldest brother, Carol, was involved in production with the firm, and his character, like that of the remaining partner, Henley, was archconservative. "It was Dickensian," John says. "They always bought secondhand typewriters, and an office boy came around with big bottles and filled the ink wells. Several of the staff sat on high banker benches – stools! The accountant wrote up the books twice a year, so we didn't know literally what the profit of the company had been until April and sometimes June of the subsequent year. There was a curious psychological dead hand on that side of the business. Not only that side. You see, we'd had such a bad time with educational books and general books, and we'd done so well with fiction. And my father's imprint – he was a very strong character – was so heavy on the firm that no one would change anything about the business. I'd just come out of the army, after all, and my God, you had to fight Henley and Co."

John Boon was well suited to the task. He had an outgoing manner and political instincts that would one day lead him to the presidencies of the British and the International Publishers' Associations and earn him the honor of a Commander of the British Empire. Alan has described him as "a very strong character, not easily deflected, and he says what he thinks. He never stands any nonsense. In the firm, he has had a slightly higher profile than me, as he's the one who goes round the office and talks to everyone every day." John would take over the tasks of sales, finance, and general organization – and, in his early years, combat duties against managing director Henley and brother Carol.

That was far from the only battle to be waged: the younger Boons were facing a shift in reading habits. With the war over, people had more money to buy books, and public libraries began sprouting; inevitably the commercial libraries that M&B depended on were disappearing. "We were playwrights without a theater," Alan Boon says now. And as the 1950s arrived, television became another threat.

By this time a more rigid editorial formula was falling into place, based on Alan's so-called "laws" and outside pressures. Alan applied two major criteria to his editing of romances. One was "nature's law," the rule of the Alpha Man, who was "strong, brave, mentally and physically tough, intelligent, tall, and dark." Boon has long argued that "all women gravitate towards this type of man, and wimpish heroes are not successful." Nor, he has pointed out, despite evidence to the contrary in many of today's Harlequins, are very aggressive heroines successful. His other yardstick was Lubbock's Law, named for English literary critic Percy Lubbock, which translates roughly into the obvious notion that romance novelists should write from the heroine's viewpoint (although not in the first person) so that readers will identify with the main character.

The external influences on the content of romance novels came from the editors of British women's magazines, such as *Woman's Weekly* and the *People's Friend,* who bought authors' manuscripts to run as serials before they appeared as novels. They insisted on some moral uplift, which meant that overt drinking and sex were taboo – no more sherries before dinner or men dressing up like women. And the serial technique demanded that chapters end with cliffhangers, which sped up the pace of a plot. The most legendary of these moralistic magazine editors was Winnifred (Biddy) Johnson, whose nickname gave new meaning to the phrase "old biddy"; as Alan Boon admits, "Miss Johnson undoubtedly had a big influence." An editor of *Woman's Weekly* and *Woman and Home,* she occasionally stretched her strictures to allow a plot device known as MINO, or "Marriage in Name Only," in which a bachelor and a single woman could be thrown together to live intimately in the same setting – a trumped-up situation that heightened a story's sexual tension in a morally correct manner. Because she and other editors paid as much as £500 for serial rights (of which M&B took 10 percent), they had a strong hand in how the stories were written, especially in an era, as in the 1930s, when Mills & Boon paid a first-time author such as Ida Cook an advance of only £30 (for *Wife to Christopher* in 1935). Cook, whose pseudonym was Mary Burchell, recalled her first meeting with Charles Boon, when she was anxious to sign the contract he handed her.

"No, no, no," Boon had said, softening his hard edge for the young writer. "You must take it home and read it. Then show it to your father. If he approves, and you agree, sign it then, not before."

In spite of that paltry advance, Cook went on to write more than 130 popular books for the firm before her death in 1987. She was a pioneer in the more down-to-earth romance: that first novel turned on the heroine's tricking a man into marriage, bearing a stillborn infant, adopting her sister's love child, yet still managing a happy ending. And though in later novels she might let her protagonist have an illegitimate child, she maintained a code of rectitude that was insisted upon by the high-minded editors of Scottish magazines who serialized her work. This balancing act of morality and reality made Mary Burchell novels bestsellers in the 1950s and beyond.

And it was a Mary Burchell novel, *Hospital Corridors,* that Ruth Palmour suggested Harlequin was interested in when she wrote her door-opening letter to Mills & Boon in 1957, requesting paperback reprint rights to "light romances dealing with doctors and nurses." (Harlequin legend – and Larry Heisey – have it that Ruth asked M & B for full North American reprint rights, a distinction that might have become important when Harlequin later moved into the U.S. market with a vengeance. In fact, while she only requested Canadian rights, Harlequin would then assume it also had the American ones, and so would Mills & Boon.)

This letter from an unknown woman in someplace in Canada called Winnipeg – or Winny-peg, as the Boons pronounced it – came at a propitious time for them. The younger brothers were still battling to bring the firm into this century against the inertia of managing director Henley and brother Carol. John says, "I can remember saying to Carol in the late fifties: 'You don't really care if this business grows and succeeds or not.' And he said: 'No, I don't.' It was rather depressing." Finally John and Alan would win their war by forcing out the two unambitious executives – "chucked" them, in John's words; "booted" them, says Alan – and by hiring some business-management consultants to update their accounting process so they could determine how much money M & B was making in the same year the firm made it.

But at the moment Ruth Palmour's letter arrived, they were grappling with another problem: the dramatic decline of the commercial lending libraries. Without this network of outlets in place, they desperately needed an alternative distribution system for their romantic fiction. They had no sales force to speak of – well, there were two fellows over 70, one who had been with the firm virtually from the beginning, and the other an uncle to the Boon boys. Not until now had M & B ever really needed salespeople. At one point, casting about for options, it tried to increase its sales through the mail. That scheme went nowhere. In 1955 it had reintroduced a general list of books, including crafts titles such as the immediately successful *Discovering Embroidery,* and had later acquired the Allman educational textbook line. But how, in this new climate, could it sell hardcover romances? Perhaps in paperback?

John Boon was told by a friend, an experienced sales director with Collins: "You must go into paperbacks." *We can't,* Boon thought. *We just haven't got the distribution nor the sales force nor the finance – we cannot gamble on the large printing orders and advertising budgets that paperbound books demand.* Instead, knowing that many small villages had no bookstores, the firm began to use news agents to sell the romances in their usual clothbound editions.

When the Harlequin letter came across their desk, the Boons saw only the opportunity to earn a small bonus for themselves and their authors from paperback reprints of their romances in Canada. Five days later, they composed a brief reply:

13th May 1957

Dear Miss Palmour,

Thank you very much for your letter. We note your interest in the Canadian reprint rights of doctor and nurse titles. As you request, we have today forwarded you a copy of Mary Burchell's HOSPITAL CORRIDORS, and, as you suggest, in the next day or so we will also be forwarding you some other titles we have published which have hospital/doctor etc. backgrounds.

Yours sincerely,
MILLS & BOON LTD.
Alan W. Boon
Director

The two firms were now in bed together, although it would be nearly a decade and a half before they formalized their union. In 1957 Harlequin published its first Mills & Boon romance, Anne Vinton's *The Hospital in Buwambo* (Harlequin No. 407), followed in 1958 by Mary Burchell's novel and several others by M & B authors. Many of them were medical romances, a staple of the English firm since *Days of Probation* had appeared in 1917. In the 1950s they became a subgenre, although not until 1977 did they have their own series, called Doctor Nurse Romance. As later M & B editors would point out, "they are usually more rooted in reality, a 'feet-on-the-ground fantasy,' if you like. . . . Whilst deaths do occur in the stories, the ending is always upbeat, leaving the reader feeling happy." The books occasionally contained surprising medical detail, as in Alex Stuart's *Master of Surgery*, published in 1958 by both firms. A female junior house surgeon explains her own ankle injury: "It was a Pott's fracture-dislocation, involving rupture of the internal lateral ligament, and the fibula was also fractured obliquely five centimetres above its lower end. The foot was everted and displaced backwards, with the internal malleolus projecting through the skin." The immediate success of these books overseas led the Boons in an entirely new direction that would transform their business within two years, as they became convinced that paperbacks could work for them, as well.

First they had to forge a relationship with this strange little company in the heart of Canada. John Boon visited Richard Bonnycastle's Harlequin in Winnipeg some years later to find "a *very* small organization which consisted of him and Ruth and one other person. I thought he was ashamed of it. The printing was carried out in an extremely effective plant run by an immigrant who refreshed himself at regular intervals by drinking from a bottle of Jack Daniels." In 1960 the partners in Stovel-Advocate sold the printing house, but the deal did not include the company's 50 percent shareholdings in the Harlequin operation – which the Bonnycastles now acquired in Mary's name for $20,000. The other shares were already owned equally by Dick and Ruth Palmour.

From 1955 on, Harlequin published one romance title almost every month, nearly all of them with nurse-and-doctor themes, usually with print runs of 20,000 to 25,000. By the time it approached Mills & Boon, the firm was often releasing two medicals a month and experimenting with regular romances. Even those written by Americans, and set in exotic locations, followed the romance recipe developed in England. While Peggy Dern's *Nurse in the Tropics* takes place in a hot, lush Haiti, it has a coolly discreet ending in which nurse Martie finally confesses to plantation owner Hugh on the second-last page:

*A Mills and Boon
romance of the late 1980s.*

HARLEQUIN ENTERPRISES

"You darling idiot. If you don't know I've been madly in love with you for ages, then you're the only one in the world that doesn't." And then she takes his face in her hands, stands on tiptoe, and kisses him. "After that, there was no need for words." Some medicals had a North American setting: *Three Doctors* by Elizabeth Seifert has one of the American doctors typically fall for a virginal schoolteacher and, on the penultimate page, propose to her with a kiss, but he is untypically well read – "He knew his Lewis and Dreiser, his Anderson and Cather." (This 1956 novel had some of Harlequin's earliest marketing: four pages at the end offering five backlist books for a dollar, with a mail-order coupon.)

The production and editorial team of Ruth Palmour and Mary Bonnycastle, gifted amateurs though they were in publishing, were well primed for the M & B books. Ruth had them set in type by Linotype machines and, later, had molds supplied from England made into rubber plates ready for printing. She was already working with cover artists whom Jack Palmer had found in Toronto and with a Winnipeg commercial artist, Bernard Smith, whose wooden illustrations came to exemplify the distinctive Harlequin look. Years later, when the books still had flatly drawn couples posed stiffly against a cardboard backdrop, often with the heroine squarely in the foreground, *Publishers Weekly* commented, "These covers are an art director's nightmare," and quoted a cheerful Larry Heisey saying, "Foreign reprinters and repackagers reject our covers all over the world, sometimes with horror. . . . You don't change a winning tennis game." In fact, from the late 1950s on, Ruth Palmour had rejected the more professional covers that Mills & Boon used on their original hardbacks: "We didn't feel theirs were right." But like M & B's, Harlequin covers of the period reflected the movies, with heroines and sometimes even heroes resembling actual film stars; *Strange Countess* in 1959 has a Ronald Reagan look-alike.

Ruth read the books first, eventually speeding up to one a day, before sending boxes of them home with her boss, who returned them with his wife's comments. (Dick Bonnycastle never read a single one, his son says.) Mary was no pushover. Her shorthand remarks ranged from "OK" through "Will do" to a flat "No," sometimes with her rationale for rejection. Of Pauline Ash's *Nurse for the Season*, she wrote: "Unpleasantly unkind to plain nurses. After all most of our readers are not beauties!" Of Sheila Ridley's *Star of Love*: "Poorly written – jumps around too much. Wrong approach to African natives – very poor and dependent on charity – not good in modern times." Occasionally she became practical, when Ruth pressed her for more product. For example, her critique of Rose Burghley's *A Moment in Paris*: "Not up to much – the poorest one of this lot but no worse than some we have printed." Mary did some editing, deleting 25 pages at a time for space reasons or whole paragraphs that offended her. "I cut out all the swearing," she reminisced years later to writer Kildare Dobbs. "I applied the standards people seemed to like. If the villain of the story was a French-Canadian, for example, that was obviously something that had to be changed. Of course, I turned down any books that were not well enough written in the way of good English." She did retain the Britishisms, finding them charming, such as a doctor being called "Mister" and a nurse "Sister." But for Gladys Fullbrook's *Nurse Prue in Ceylon,* she advised Ruth: "Delete some of the superfluous 'darlings' in first few chapters." And assessing Hilda Nickson's *For Love of a Surgeon,* she admitted, "Didn't care much for this – nothing much wrong with it so if you need it, okay – see what you think – I thought a bit too gloomy and far-fetched but maybe we need a slight variation!" Ruth needed it; it was published.

The wholesale rejection and pecking away at books that Alan Boon had edited would come to irritate the British brothers who published the originals. Especially when they were thinking that their novels should become slightly more daring. "Our books were pretty prim," Alan recalls. "We felt they had to be more realistic, which really means a bit more sexy. Mrs. Bonnycastle felt they shouldn't bring a blush to the cheek."

Another Mary Bonnycastle, married to Dick's brother Larry, recalls the day Dick was summoned to the Winnipeg office of the Anglican Archbishop of Rupertsland. As she tells the story, the archbishop held aloft a slightly steamy Harlequin and said, "One of my parishioners has brought me this book. I will not have it!"

"I'm very sorry, sir," Dick responded. "It won't happen again. That one must have gotten by."

After that his wife made certain nothing more than the odd "damn" slipped by.

By the mid-1960s, their daughter Judy was helping Mary with the reading burden. "I would suspect she had enough – I mean, you read hundreds a year." After graduating in English literature from the University of Toronto and working in the Far East, Judy had been a freelance fact checker for *Maclean's* magazine, had edited a small sports magazine called *The Curler,* and had written for the early *Toronto Life,* owned by her publisher brother-in-law, Michael de Pencier. Although fancying a career in publishing since age 10, she had never read Harlequins as a girl; reading them now was "kind of a duty, sort of pass-on-the-mantle." She had no illusions about the books: "This was not literature." Judy, in her mid-twenties and living in Toronto, brought a different sensibility to the task, as some of her typed comments to Ruth Palmour indicated. "*Not* suitable for publication," she wrote of Madame Daniel Gray's *Portrait of Lawrence.* "This book is ridiculous. Really." Judy was much younger and much less tolerant of writers than the Boons, rejecting about a quarter of the British titles. "Alan Boon was a total darling," she says, "but he had more trouble telling an author it was a dud." As for the Boons, John says, "It drove Alan mad, to dismiss a novel with three words!" (A decade later, some authors not only complained that M & B didn't edit its books, they also suspected that Alan Boon himself read no more than the first and last pages of a manuscript before sending it off to the printers.) Boon, meanwhile, was becoming much more tolerant of the sexual scenes being introduced by his writers. In 1967 Nan Asquith's *The Garden of Persephone* became the first Mills & Boon title to allow the hero and heroine to consummate their relationship in full view of the reader – to *do* it, orgasmically, if in flowery prose.

Across the Atlantic, the books that escaped the Bonnycastle women's net received a warm reception with readers. At the time, Maurice Mousseau was a warehouseman in Winnipeg for a periodical distributor, the Canadian News Company. He delivered skids of new Harlequin releases to the book departments of major department stores in the downtown core, the T. Eaton Co., and the Hudson's Bay Company, Dick Bonnycastle's former employer. "I'd come in first thing in the morning and lay out 100 copies of each title on the table, immaculately straight," Mousseau says, "and by the time I went for coffee at 10:15, they'd be demolished. Then I'd put out another 100 of each. I'd be back twice a week to Eaton's and the Bay to check every title in the store and replenish them." Medical themes were then outselling general romances; the overall sell-through of Harlequins in the Manitoba and northwestern Ontario region was 85 percent, an impressive figure for any publisher in that era when returns started to soar.

Some of the firm's success in Canadian retail outlets was due to the aggressive Lloyd Van Alstyne of Curtis Distributing, the Toronto-based branch of the Philadelphia company that had helped to save Harlequin in its early years. Curtis was distributing the books, along with those of competitors and a full range of magazines, to local wholesalers. "Van Alstyne was the terror of the industry," says Jack Shapiro, who owned a wholesale news company in Saskatchewan. "He represented the biggest publisher in North America. What made local distributors handle Harlequins was the enormous pressure he brought to bear. There was always the threat to lose Curtis" – that is, its popular magazines, such as *Ladies' Home Journal* and *Jack and Jill*. And Curtis in turn was motivated by the growing popularity of Harlequins; "we wielded a good stick over their heads," Ruth Palmour says. So popular were these naive-looking romances, Shapiro notes, that in Saskatchewan – a province with the odd reputation of having the highest per capita readership of *True Story*, the American confessions magazine – "within five to six years, *True Story* almost disappeared, and Harlequin satisfied the desire for romantic reading more than it ever did."

In 1963 Dick Bonnycastle, recognizing that the same desire might be satisfied across the border, organized a sales force of three strategically located agents in the western and Midwestern states. All were retired Curtis representatives who approached their friends in the business to place this new line specializing in paperback romances. With a cover price of 40 cents and then 45, matching the current Canadian figures, the books performed well enough in the United States over the next four years that Simon & Schuster's high-powered Pocket Books division agreed to distribute them in all states but the 16 where Harlequin had launched its American offensive with its own salesmen.

The impetus for the move southward had come from the founder's son, Richard, who, after a series of personal financial ventures, was becoming more interested in the family business. It was he who had convinced his father to hire an executive vice president, Jim McCartney, a former industrial engineer who was working in Winnipeg with the management consulting firm of Clarkson, Gordon (and who ran the first federal election campaign of local Liberal Lloyd Axworthy, now Canada's foreign affairs minister). "I saw Harlequin as a great opportunity," the young Bonnycastle says, "but it needed somebody to march it off to war." Meanwhile, worried about Simon & Schuster producing its own competing line of romances, he went to New York himself with a few sample books and was shunted off to a vice president. "Would you like to distribute these books?" he asked the executive, who browsed through them and said, "We couldn't do covers this bad."

"I knew right away that they wouldn't do these books," Bonnycastle Jr. told me recently. "The real secret of Harlequin was the egotism of the New York publishers. The key thing they wanted to do is have more bestsellers than the other guys. They didn't do any research."

Larry Heisey, who would become president of Harlequin, mentions that the senior Bonnycastle went to New York later and met with Leon Shimkin, the squat, dynamic president of Pocket Books. And Shimkin agreed to distribute the books to direct retail accounts that were not served by periodical wholesalers, including bookstores, supermarkets, and dime-store chains such as Woolworth, where Pocket Books had pioneered paperback distribution. He later had s & s publish Harlequin titles under a sub-rights license, paying the Canadian company a straight royalty on sales. Sy Turk worked for Shimkin at the time, having started as a junior accountant and ending up as president of s & s. In his gravelly voice, he explains the understanding the two companies had about the American version of the books: "We were the publisher, and Harlequin was the 'author.' We published the books, we printed them, they provided the covers, and we took the risk of inventory." Larry Heisey told me that "Leon always said he didn't understand the way we put the covers together or anything about it – and he said Simon & Schuster shouldn't change a thing. He merely added a 5 to the front of the number of each book so you could tell who had actually published it, and where the returns should go, in case there was ever any confusion. That was the only difference in the books."

After his visit with Shimkin, Bonnycastle Senior wrote a follow-up letter to the U.S. wholesalers. He pointed out that "Harlequin romances continue to be the leading paperback line in terms of copies sold in Canada," and he added, perhaps with too much Canadian modesty, "we suggest there is no particular reason why Harlequin romances should not eventually be one of the top selling lines in the United States. . . ."

That was June 1968, when Dick Bonnycastle was otherwise occupied. The whole family was preparing for the summer wedding of Judy, who was marrying television producer Kenneth Burgess. After the ceremony in Barbados, there were 40 guests for the outdoor reception. About 120 black villagers stood watching on a hillside. Dick, in a typical gesture, waved them all down to the party, where they danced to a steel band and dined with the gussied-up Canadian visitors. The cook who prepared the dinner was so put out at no longer being the only local at the reception that she refused to speak to the family for days afterward.

Bonnycastle was immersed in the public life he preferred to his businesses and in a renewed passion for flying. Prodded by his son, he had toyed with the idea of buying Mills & Boon to ensure the source of supply but had never got around to it. He'd also had offers to go east, primarily from a financial powerhouse among the Canadian Establishment, J. A. (Bud) McDougald, whose Argus Corporation of Toronto was a specialized investment and holding company. "But he wasn't interested," his son says. "He was interested in the West, the outdoors, Ducks Unlimited. That's why he never went into

Richard and Mary Bonnycastle in later years. JUDY BONNYCASTLE BURGESS

business big-time. He was into public service, he was Metro chairman, and Harlequin was sort of a nice little thing whose balance sheet he looked at once a month and saw what was going on."

He had all those other matters on his mind, primarily his role as the first supermayor – officially the chairman – of the Metropolitan Council of Greater Winnipeg. Known for his overseeing of the Manitoba Business Advisory Council and the Winnipeg Chamber of Commerce, Bonnycastle was appointed to the $12,000-a-year post by the premier of the province in 1960. For six years he held together an unruly band of 19 mayors and reeves representing an area of more than half a million people. I was a young newspaper reporter in Winnipeg then and noted the general approval of the diplomatic way he was handling his role. He became a central figure in the city's life; an article about the Art Gallery Ball pictured him and Mary "swirling gracefully" and smiling in their costumes. Perhaps the most flattering tribute Bonnycastle received upon retiring was the editorial comment that he had never been a political animal; as the *Winnipeg Free Press* said, "he rarely lost his temper, rarely retaliated, even in the face of the most villainously unfair attacks. . . . He was given a very difficult job to do. He has done it very well." A year later, in 1967, he was named the first chancellor of the new University of Winnipeg.

Dick Bonnycastle had been the national president of Ducks Unlimited, the habitat-conservation group, which reflected his love of duck hunting in Manitoba's Turtle Mountains and Delta Marsh with his black Labrador retriever, Joe. He visited the northern lakes in his own Cessna single-engine 180 floatplane, bought for $3,000. In 1963, still seeking adventure as he entered his sixth decade, he had learned to fly, graduating at the top of his class. "He felt he was getting old," his daughter Judy told me, "and there was something he was missing out, something he hadn't done." Bonnycastle was increasingly aware of time's passage: he had developed a heart condition and was having his blood pressure checked regularly. In August 1968, he flew into the northern Manitoba town of The Pas to retrace old routes and find old friends along the Mackenzie River, which he had traveled decades before by boat and dog team.

A month later, he was flying his Cessna over Lake Winnipegosis, in west-central Manitoba, with a former official of the provincial government's natural resources department. Bonnycastle made a decent landing on the lake at the junction of Waterhen and Long Island bays. After taxiing to a stop and undoing his seat belt, he slumped in his seat and died of heart failure.

Five hundred mourners filled St. Paul's Anglican Church in Winnipeg to pay their respects to the 65-year-old public servant and businessman. Of all the obituaries that appeared in praise of him, none mentioned Harlequin Books, the quietly successful private publishing company that he had cofounded and that would soon go public and begin to flourish internationally.

4

Prince for Sale

THE   BOOK   AS   SOAP

Over his four-decade business career, Richard Bonnycastle Jr. seems to have
had all the attention span of a puppy. Always sniffing out fresh possibilities,
leaping into each new situation, cocking his leg and imprinting a project just
long enough to make it his. Then plunging off to investigate something novel
and exciting. He has had, however, two enduring passions. Neither of them
has been his father's enterprise, Harlequin Books. Like his dad, early on he fell
helplessly in love with the West – which for him would mean that most
American of all provinces, Alberta – and, in place of his father's planes, he fan-
cied racehorses. While Bonnycastle Senior was being supermayor and running
Harlequin with the index finger of his left hand (pointing out what had to be
done, but not doing it), his son was displaying the symptoms of a kind of
attention deficit disorder. "I found that as businesses get big," he told me
recently, "I lose interest in them."

    He was christened Richard Arthur Northwood Bonnycastle. The family
called him Rich, fittingly, given the personal wealth he would accumulate
(over $100 million by his mid-forties). Schoolmates called him Bones, short
for Bonnycastle and an apt nickname for the big-boned tackle on the St. Vital

Bulldogs football team. He had attended private boys' schools, Winnipeg's Ravenscourt and then Trinity College School, Canada's oldest, in Port Hope, near Toronto. He came home to the University of Manitoba and to amateur football; at six foot four and 250 pounds, he was a good enough tackle to consider a professional career in Canada. (A man who worked for him years later describes his "Cagney-like body language, a face chiseled out of concrete, and vitality bursting out of him.") After graduating in commerce, he spent a year trying to sell group insurance with Great-West Life Assurance, a prominent North American firm based in Winnipeg (which he still calls "Great Waste of Life"). But a high-profile local hockey player beat him to most of the major companies in town, and Bonnycastle sold only one piece of group insurance in his year as a salesman. He did, however, make contact with a local clothier, Ralph Drewitt, and together they created a small athletic-clothing and sporting goods venture, Bonwitt Manufacturing. Bonnycastle invested $2,500, an inheritance from his godfather. "Well," his less entrepreneurial father said dismissively, "you might as well lose it in that as something else."

Bonnycastle Junior recalls: "That's where I really learned about business, because we made every mistake that's ever been made. For example, ordering enough baseball cloth to make uniforms for every team in Canada for the next 20 years. Literally. I mean, I learned about receivables. I had to jump in my car and go to Kenora [across the border in northwestern Ontario] because that was the nearest account receivable, and my car broke down and I had to thumb my way. Almost froze to death on the highway in minus something in this light coat and pulled a log across the road to stop the next car. I got down there, and I found the guy in a beer parlor, made him give me a check for $300, and, at one o'clock in the morning, I was thumbing, got a bus back to Winnipeg, and finally put the check in the bank to make a payable." All in all, it was a trip that lacked the romance of his father's mushing through the Arctic's frozen wastes behind a dog team. Another time, in a deal that might have made his respectable father's eyes roll, the partners had to approach a bookie named Davie Johnson in Winnipeg's grittier north end. "I walked in there and said, 'Davie, we need five grand.' He said, 'Okay, it's 10 percent paid monthly,' and pulled five grand off a roll of bills, and that's how we financed the business."

There were other businesses to distract Bonnycastle Junior, including a travel agency with Ralph Drewitt and what he calls a whiskey agency. A fellow student at Trinity College School had been Charles Bronfman, an heir to the Montreal Bronfmans' Seagram Corporation fortune, who now asked Bonnycastle to set up a Winnipeg agency for the company's lines of Adams whiskey and Jordan wines. He earned $40,000 a year merely for arranging banquet permits and occasionally suffering through a morning drink with a bartender. It was the whiskey agency that dashed any hope he had of a pro football career. Both he and a promising player he had hired to work for him were offered Canadian Football League contracts. But if they left at the same time, he would lose the agency – and football for a nonstar was worth a piddling $1,500 a year.

In 1963, after his father had cashed out of his printing company with $200,000, Bones Bonnycastle decided it was time to stop playing around and learn about big business. He sold his shares of Bonwitt and the travel and whiskey agencies for "a little money, not a whole bunch." Approaching Jim Richardson, a fellow Establishment scion helping to run the local financial conglomerate James Richardson & Sons, he suggested himself as the person to launch an underwriting presence in eastern Canada for the family's private investment house. For two years in Toronto, he did just that, trolling western Ontario and some northeastern states for business. What he discovered was that most of the companies he called on were subsidiaries of U.S. parents and were not about to give him any underwriting action ("and that's why Canada really ended up getting sold out and why we're in the problem we're in today").

It was during those years in Toronto that he became more intrigued with his own family's business, successfully urging his father to expand in a United States that was then devoid of any serial romance novels like Harlequins. The three salesmen the company hired, in Dallas, Minneapolis, and Seattle, were ex-Curtis hands who approached their friends in the industry. "And these guys would give them the chance and put the books out, and ooh, they sold! – surprise!" the son told me, still sarcastic after all these years.

Surprisingly the warm reception the romances were receiving in the American marketplace began to concern the young Bonnycastle. Harlequin's sole source of supply remained Mills & Boon, with whom it had only a sort of gentlemen's agreement, renewed every year when Bonnycastle father and son had a nice lunch in London with the Boon brothers at their same special table at the Picadilly end of the Ritz Hotel dining room. "I got a little worried," the son recalls. "Two things. One: we never had an agreement with Mills & Boon – Ruth had written one letter – and two: here we are starting to build a business in the States with all the big publishers watching." Contemptuous as he was of the publishers' blinkered pursuit of bestsellers, Bonnycastle realized they might start paying attention to the Canadian upstart developing the romance market in their backyard and go after Mills & Boon themselves. He pressed his father to acquire M & B – to no avail. But he did take some comfort in the fact that Simon & Schuster's Pocket Books division later agreed to distribute the romance line in the 34 states where Harlequin didn't have its own sales force.

By then Dick Bonnycastle Jr. had left the Toronto he loathed, transferred by Richardson's to Calgary, the burgeoning oil capital of Alberta. "I had too much of my old man's blood. I just couldn't stand looking at those high towers and cement. I'd been ranching where my uncle had a place near Consort, Alberta; I went there every summer until about 1950." He would settle permanently in the province, acquiring three ranches where he raised purebred cattle, becoming a partner in a stud farm, and pursuing his love of thoroughbred racing with well over 100 horses that carry the colors of Harlequin's trademark black-and-white diamond pattern. (In 1978 a Bonnycastle filly, Enstone Spark, won the British classic The 1,000 Guineas as a 35-to-1 shot.) One of his partners has been Robert Sangster, who ran Vernons, the biggest of the British soccer pools; another is George Gardiner, the Toronto investment magnate with whom he bought the 60 racing and breeding horses owned by Conn Smythe, the financier and founder of Toronto's Maple Leaf Gardens. (Gardiner became a director of Harlequin in 1973, invested heavily in the company, and profited perhaps more than anyone when it was sold years later.)

To finance his racing stock, Bonnycastle has had a gusher of cash from oil and venture-capital investments. About to fly from Toronto one day not long after he moved to Calgary, he was sitting beside an attractive young blond woman who was asked to give up her seat for another passenger, a man. Annoyed at his new seatmate, he refused to talk to him until the plane landed, only to learn that he was an oilman from Calgary. The two arranged to meet again, and soon they formed a small company called Ulster Petroleums, which bought land beside the Canadian Arctic's Beaufort Sea. Only days later the enormous Prudhoe Bay petroleum boom began in the area, and Ulster's stock soared twelvefold. Bonnycastle stayed in the oil business. He became what author Peter C. Newman calls – in his chronicle of the Canadian Establishment, *The Acquisitors* – "the most imaginative player in the Oil Patch," with "the knack of backing winners."

But in September 1968, having left Richardson's and with his career in the oil game still embryonic, Dick Bonnycastle had to change horses and deal with the aftermath of his father's death by assuming the presidency of the family's privately held publishing business.

Now he could carry out what he had long been prodding his reluctant dad to do: take Harlequin public. If the company was to stay in the field, if not to take the lead, and if it was ever going to buy Mills & Boon, it needed fresh financing. Going public would not only make it easier to raise money than if the company stayed private but also allow his widowed mother to cash in her holdings. Dick Bonnycastle worked fast to get the company in good enough shape to attract investors. In 1969 he moved the company's headquarters to the Toronto-Dominion Centre in downtown Toronto; his small offices were across the hall from Chicago lawyer George Cohon, who was just launching the Canadian branch of that Harlequin of fast-food restaurants, McDonald's. Jim McCartney, Bonnycastle's executive vice president, moved east, while Ruth Palmour stayed behind in Winnipeg as secretary-treasurer.

Unfortunately, as a company doing only about $300,000 worth of after-tax business in the chancy world of book publishing, Harlequin couldn't attract any underwriters to put it on the stock market. Needing a better financial story to tell, Bonnycastle found a company for sale in the then-attractive field of learning materials. He bought Jack Hood School Supplies of Stratford, Ontario, for $2 million, and to run it hired Martin Reaume, a gentle, bespectacled accountant with Clarkson, Gordon, Canada's oldest and largest firm of chartered accountants and management consultants. The acquisition suddenly gave Bonnycastle a combined operation with $500,000 in earnings and a stake in a hot sector – just interesting enough to make his former employer, Richardson's, take on the public underwriting.

On the surface, Harlequin seemed to have a good story to tell: the best-seller among all paperbacks in Canada, the leader in the underpopulated romance field in the United States – a company suddenly valued at more than $10 million. Its initial 400,000 common shares, pre-priced at $7.50 apiece, went on the market in May and opened at $9.50 to brisk trading. Of the $3 million in shares, Bonnycastle's mother was allocated $617,000 worth, and Ruth Palmour received $315,000 worth. Mary Bonnycastle was named chairwoman, and among the directors was Daniel Sprague, who had put together the Selkirk Metals deal in Winnipeg that the family had profited from many years before.

In 1970 Dick Bonnycastle needed a good financial man to backstop him. At first Jim McCartney recommended a fellow Clarkson, Gordon alumnus named William Willson, a young-looking management consultant in his mid-thirties, but then seemed to waffle on hiring him. Bones Bonnycastle, still a football fan, was at the Grey Cup championship in Montreal with a friend and asked him if he knew a guy named Bill Willson. "He's twice as good as the guy you've got," the friend said, in a slighting reference to McCartney. Bonnycastle flew back to Toronto and hired Willson as a $20,000-a-year vice president of planning and development; a year later Willson also succeeded Ruth Palmour as corporate secretary. The pragmatic Willson's most unorthodox act might have been the wearing of bow ties. "He was no social butterfly," Martin Reaume says. "He was a no-nonsense guy." Bonnycastle calls him "a very straight arrow, as straight as you can get." Even if Willson had argued hard against a decision of his boss, he would loyally carry it out.

The same year, Bonnycastle hired a second vice president. The round-faced, melodiously named Richard Bellringer had left high school in a village near Kingston, Ontario, to seek work in Chicago and had returned the day he received a draft notice. Back home, he spent one decade running southern Ontario branches of the national Kresge's dime-store chain and the next decade developing Coles Book Stores into a franchise operation of three dozen outlets as far west as Winnipeg. Dick Bellringer, in his mid-forties, became VP in charge of sales, at $25,000 a year. He was a homebody, preferring to be with his wife, Alma, than out drinking with the boys. He was considered a rough diamond in the Harlequin setting; Larry Heisey says he tended to mock those with a college education. On one of the North American executives' first visits to England, the Mills & Boon staff took them to see the vast St. Albans abbey in Hertfordshire. "There's a lot of wasted space here," Bellringer said. "We could have a bookstand here and a McDonald's there." Martin Reaume admonished him: "Dick, we're just visiting."

Now Bonnycastle needed a president. In his mind, none of his current executives qualified. Bellringer was in exactly the right position. And Willson, who didn't want the top job, had underlined Bonnycastle's own sense that Jim McCartney was wrong for it. "He had no strategic outlook on where the company should go," Willson reminisces. "And Mills & Boon didn't get along with McCartney, and Bonnycastle wanted to buy Mills & Boon." From the start, Bonnycastle felt that he should be going after someone with a background in consumer products, rather than books – preferably someone from a major American corporation. His Uncle Larry recommended that he approach a firm in Chicago, Heidrich and Struggles, the first major head-hunter in North America.

The new public company desperately needed direction. By the end of 1969, earnings had been $363,677, or 30.5 cents a share. A year later, as the economy dampened and returns climbed in the mass-market paperback industry, profits were down to $238,984, or 17.2 cents a share. Meanwhile, the struggling Jack Hood division had a loss of $127,122. Early in 1970, trying to bolster Hood's earnings, Bonnycastle paid $750,000 for the well-run Nor-Ed Supplies, another learning-materials company, based in northern Ontario. As he recalls it, Nor-Ed's partners wanted Harlequin to warrant that Hood's margins would be more than about 22 to 23 percent. Martin Reaume, who became Harlequin's $14,000-a-year comptroller, had assured Bonnycastle that they were about 28 percent. After the deal was signed, "Reaume came in bawling that he'd made a mistake. He'd added instead of subtracting, and instead of 28 percent it was only 16." Reaume's memory is that when he checked Hood's books, "there was a one-sided journal entry. I had only half of it. It showed the balance sheet was 250 grand more than it was. On the basis of that, Nor-Ed came on board." In the wake of the error, Bonnycastle felt the deal was doomed, but Harlequin's lawyer, Gar Emerson, reassured him that it had been signed in good faith and should stand. However, Bonnycastle did renegotiate better terms for Nor-Ed's partners, and the one who assumed control of the new division, Glenn Johnson, stayed with Harlequin and eventually represented the company in Australia.

But at the time, the school-supplies division was severely depressing

Harlequin's stock, and the only good news for shareholders in the 1970 annual report was the announcement that as of January 1971, Harlequin had a new president: W. Lawrence Heisey.

Larry Heisey was 13 when he came to the dinner table one evening and announced to his widowed mother and two brothers that he knew what he was going to do when he grew up. "What's that, son?" Alice Heisey asked.

He had been up in the bathroom and, on a bottle of her perfume, had seen a listing of the parfumier's branches in major cities around the world. "I'm going to have a company that has offices in Toronto, Montreal, New York, London, Paris, Rome, and Sydney."

"If that's what you want, son, I hope you get it," though that wasn't what she wanted for him.

"Do you know what you're going to manufacture?" asked his older brother, Alan.

"I have no idea," Larry said.

"Hot air," Alan replied. "Hot air."

The family used to retell the story at Larry's expense until the time, not long after he had joined Harlequin, that he could tell it on himself. "I woke up one morning," he said, "and I had it all." Last laughs are delicious.

If it wasn't truly his own company that he built into a global giant, but one in which he was just a significant shareholder, Heisey would run it as if it were. He operated with a broad-stroked entrepreneurial style that he didn't learn in the lecture halls of Harvard Business School. He absorbed it early on growing up in Toronto. His father, Karl, was a mining engineer and mine owner from a family of Swiss-German extraction that had migrated to Canada from Pennsylvania in the early 19th century. He died in the Depression year of 1937, when Larry was seven, leaving Alice an estate too small to be taxed. The largest asset was a hotel with a $95,000 mortgage, which his widow reluctantly but enterprisingly ran for a decade and sold for a profit that she invested wisely in stocks. "There were heavy expectations," Larry remembers. "She loved quoting things like 'Where much is given, much is expected.' And I kept asking what I'd been given – my father died when I was a kid." The brothers grew up, United Church-goers of old Canadian

Larry Heisey (left) *and Richard Bonnycastle Jr. – building an empire of love.* HARLEQUIN ENTERPRISES

stock, in the Dufferin and St. Clair area of Toronto, which immigrants would transform into Little Italy. At their mother's urging, he and his older brother, aged 10 and 12, were selling their neighbors 90 dozen eggs a week from a cousin's farm, charging two cents a dozen below the local A&P ("We should have been pricing them three cents over because they were farm fresh"). Larry knew about marketing even then, using a toy printing set to label the cartons HEISEY BROTHERS EGGS. They split the profits with their patroness.

Fatherless for most of his youth, Larry tried to please the most important person in his world, his mother. "I found it convenient to tell people that I was going to be what my mother thought I should be, because she had wanted to be: a lawyer." This role of pleasing women would be a constant throughout his career, in two of the three companies he worked for and in one of the ventures he launched as an entrepreneur.

As Alice Heisey's stocks prospered, they moved to much tonier Lawrence Park, where he attended high school, proving his big brother's hot-air crack by winning a provincial dramatic-verse speaking award. Culturally attuned, he frequented the Art Gallery of Ontario to drench himself in painting and sculpture, a lifelong infatuation he was later able to indulge with his Harlequin earnings. Like his mother, he took piano lessons, which left him accomplished enough to be a bar pianist if he had wanted. Which he never did: "My mother was entrepreneurial and I was entrepreneurial." Larry took his bachelor of arts at the University of Toronto's Trinity College (where Bonnycastle Senior had gone). He studied both political science and economics to allow himself the option of law or the business career he preferred. For fun he acted in college theatricals, honing the presentation skills that would make him such a beguiling marketing man. Blond, with penetrating blue eyes, he was almost Hollywood handsome – a rugged Brian Dennehy perhaps, rather than a perfect Paul Newman. He stood taller than his five foot ten and had all the ease of a fifth-generation Canadian who knew his place in the world. He worked summers at a brokerage house where he once heard a hot tip – "and I sort of put my entire summer's earnings on this moose pasture that we were flogging. The two stocks were dead within the year. Mother thought it was a real good lesson." He had another source of income, a profitable *Time/Life* magazine subscription service for students that he marketed on letterhead with six different typefaces.

In 1952 he eagerly took up his brother's invitation to visit him at Harvard Business School, where Larry sat at the back of a classroom and watched the school's classic case method in action. The next day, he had a successful interview in which he was accepted for the Cambridge, Massachusetts, finishing school that fall. Then he had to go home and tell his mother.

"But you've always said you were going to be a lawyer."

"Well, I changed my mind," he replied, determined to please himself this time.

Earning his two-year M.B.A., Heisey responded to the challenge of jockeying with his peers to solve real-life business cases. In his first year, he finished in the top eight percentile, but after a working summer he was less determined, anxious to be out in the world, knowing for certain what he wanted to do. He had worked for Procter & Gamble in Toronto, a job he had landed in spite of a lousy first interview. He hadn't realized that Don McCaskill, a fellow he had first met at summer camp and whom he was now casually chatting up at P&G, was in fact the job interviewer – until McCaskill showed

Heisey the door. After McCaskill wrote him a rejection letter, he took his case to an interviewer for the U.S. parent company on the Harvard campus. With his charm and youthful brashness, he asked for three minutes of the man's time, during which he told him how shabbily the Canadian subsidiary was handling job interviews. He not only got a second chance and a summer job – which led to a full-time position – but also had another last laugh: nearly three decades later, the Toronto branch of the American Marketing Association would vote him marketing man of the year, an award named for Donald B. McCaskill.

Larry Heisey learned his trade over 13 years at Procter & Gamble. *The Financial Post* book *The 100 Best Companies to Work for in Canada* describes P&G as "a middle-of-the-road company, with high ethical standards; a company that takes a great deal of time and care in developing its products." The Cincinnati-based parent, colloquially known as "the soap company," whose prime target is women, is in fact a multiproduct corporation offering brands for both genders. P&G's promoters and critics routinely call it one of the world's great marketing machines. Heisey begs to differ: "Everyone celebrates it as a marketing company. But it is a product company. They will not go to market without a product that has advantages over the competition. The management of the company is not available [to outsiders] to discuss anything, so the world perceives them the way the press perceives them – with all those damn commercials, they're a marketing company. But they found the way to win the day is to make a better mousetrap; nobody's ever made anything better than Tide." His initiation was eight months in the British Columbia interior, schlepping products around small-town stores, learning market anomalies such as the popularity of Crisco among British Columbia's religious Doukhobor colonies because the shortening had no animal fat. His first office job in Toronto was assistant brand manager on the Tide account in Canada. At the time, P&G stressed internal competition with a single marketing specialist assigned to each product as brand manager, who acted as a mini-czar with his own fiefdom. Although the company dropped this approach in the 1980s for a team concept with coequals from various departments, Heisey profited from the independence of mind it bred. "I felt very possessive about my products – Tide, Crisco, Fluffo, Ivory Soap, Comet."

His latent entrepreneurialism surfaced at least twice during his career with

P&G – once in publishing. He had observed the success of a Tide promotion that offered a five-color Rand-McNally world map with every box; in place of a coupon for 25 cents off, each map cost the company only about eight cents on a one million press run. Deciding that print products could be profitable – how profitable he would eventually learn at Harlequin – Heisey and two colleagues launched a weekly magazine called *The Canadian Green Book*. It capitalized on the fact that a company such as P&G paid grocery stores to run advertising that promoted its products. The magazine was simply a compilation of such co-op ads, as they were called, to inform the P&Gs and General Foods that their advertising money was actually being spent. When the first issue drew $20,000 worth of subscriptions, or $4,000 less than it would cost to print the magazine for a year, the partners sold it for a modest profit of $1,000 apiece; the magazine survived for a decade.

Another venture was even less lucrative. In the late 1950s, the Canadian government had printed a 50 cent booklet of physical fitness exercises developed for the Royal Canadian Air Force. Called 5BX, the five basic exercises became all the rage, and Heisey and a friend thought what the world needed was a mechanical device to time the exercise sessions. Working through Don McCaskill, they placed an ad in *Reader's Digest* that cost them about $5,000; it sold 38 timers – "It was an absolute wipeout," Heisey says. "I think everyone who's in advertising should have one consumer product that they try to sell through direct mail."

Fortunately he kept his day job at Procter & Gamble, where he eventually became manager of advertising productions, a new position to which the media, market research, copy, and commercial production departments reported. That proved to be his pinnacle at P&G. Early on he had told his superiors that he didn't want to uproot his wife and two children and move around the world with the company – even while realizing this was the only way he could be groomed for the one position he wanted: the Canadian presidency. In 1967, stalemated, he was primed to accept the offer of another job.

It was on a different floor in the same building at Yonge and St. Clair. Standard Broadcasting operated four radio stations in Montreal and Toronto (including CFRB, Canada's largest) and handled advertising sales for many more stations across the country. Heisey became executive vice president of its sales arm, with a good salary and stock options that he took up. They weren't enough to ease the sense he soon had that overseeing a group of self-starting radio salesmen was not his strength. "I came from a different kind of culture than most of these guys," he recalls. "I had a college degree, and there were very few of those around." There were other problems: "One guy who was at a senior level in the firm asked me to prevaricate if I got asked about a certain issue. Well, I don't like to live with untruths." His lack of admiration for many of his colleagues was palpable and colored his performance. Within two years, the chairman fired him.

He was then a single father, raising daughter Janet and son Mark. In 1958 he had married Donna, a physiotherapist on staff at a Toronto hospital. It was no storybook marriage. She began displaying the effects of serious emotional problems, and after eight years they separated. Donna, who had taken the children, presumably suffocated on a combination of prescription drug and drink in 1969. "That was not an easy period in my life. My wife had died, and I had a house to run with two kids." And no job. He did, however, have an inheritance from his mother's estate and golden parachutes from his two previous positions. They emboldened him to start his own business; he thought he would never work for anybody again.

He and a friend acquired two Toronto boutiques named Gambit that sold panty hose. Heisey and retail were not a good fit. "I don't think I made the best choice of partners or industry," he told me. "And it was my own fault. I certainly didn't do due diligence. I didn't talk to people who might know more about the business than the obvious ones." While Gambit would expand by another half-dozen shops, the industry was about to be ripped apart by a technological development. Hosiery had been a specialty item that came in various sizes. Now a new stretch yarn allowed one-size-fits-all panty hose. Suddenly every drugstore and clothing shop could stock all the hosiery they needed in little kiosks. Eventually the partners announced they intended to wind up their business in a month's time; instead, creditors who were owed $20,000 immediately forced them into bankruptcy court. Heisey had learned that he was not a single-minded entrepreneur.

Late in 1970, when a headhunter called him from Chicago, wondering if he might be interested in discussing the presidency of a small, publicly traded company in Toronto, Larry Heisey listened.

Learning the company was Harlequin Enterprises, which published romance novels – yet another product for women – did not dissuade him. He had seen the books on cigar-store newsstands but had never opened one ("I was amazed at row after row of these innocent, unlined faces peering out at me"). In the racks now were titles such as *The Arrogant Duke* by Anne Mather, *Nurse Harriet Goes to Holland* by Betty Neels, and *Girl with a Challenge* by Mary Burchell. The books certainly had a competitive price: 50 cents, half the average price of a paperback. This time Heisey did his due diligence by reading a few, talking to some book retailers about their sales, and then studying Harlequin's promising first annual report, which had reported earnings of $363,000 for 1969. The only drain on the company seemed to be the school-supplies business, not publishing. The company was releasing eight new titles a month, which accounted for more than 14 percent of all the mass-market paperbacks sold in Canada and about three percent in the United States. Obvious room for growth down south.

Heisey saw at once that a Harlequin was a product, like soap or shortening. It had a brand name, even a logo with that little guy in the diamond, and covers that virtually appeared identical, book after book. "They were publishing the same book eight times a month – I mean, the same story, retold another way." Harlequin, he concluded, was nothing more or less than branded literature that could be promoted like any other branded consumer product, like Tide or Crisco.

His first impression of Dick Bonnycastle was of a big man whose mind darted around as if it were on skates: "He doesn't hold in one line, one direction, before he's on to something else." And a man who didn't seem wedded to Harlequin: "It didn't occur to me that he was intimately involved with the business or wanted to be. He was really looking for others to take care of it for him." A well-placed broker friend of Bonnycastle, Christopher Ondaatje, defined his need: "Harlequin needed not so much a publishing person as a marketing superstar. Heisey was highly intelligent and presentable, the perfect person, with his Procter & Gamble training," to expand the product's base. Bonnycastle, impressed, sent him on to meet one of Harlequin's directors, his Uncle Larry – Dick Senior's younger brother – who was vice chairman of the Canadian Corporate Management Company headed by former federal Liberal finance minister Walter Gordon. Larry Bonnycastle asked him why he had got into the hosiery business. Good question, Larry Heisey replied, knowing he was now one step behind in the interview. But he had noted that Harlequin's investors were not doing well, having lost $128,000 on the sale of securities in each of the previous two years. So why, he asked Uncle Larry, would you be a director of a little company that was losing so much of its shareholders' money on portfolio investment? Bonnycastle admitted that he just hadn't been paying enough attention. At that point, Heisey knew he was even, and maybe one step ahead, in the interview.

Dick Bonnycastle also had him meet Bill Willson, who was essentially sizing him up as his potential boss and, despite being miserable with a cold, warmed to this Heisey fellow. "Willson was absolutely, totally dedicated to Dick Bonnycastle," Heisey says. "And he tried to oblige him at the same time as being ruthlessly honest. He was a very smart and diligent, outspoken man." But the candidate met neither Dick Bellringer nor Jim McCartney, who wanted the presidency so badly, Heisey says, that "he could taste it."

What Larry Heisey didn't know was that he was second choice. Bonnycastle had asked the headhunting firm to find him candidates outside the book industry. "I didn't want someone to sell books – we're selling *product*. I had the idea of getting a guy out of a senior U.S. company who'd run a big division. So he came up with two: one ran a $300 million consumer-products division of Borden, and Heisey. I was favoring the guy from Borden. Just because Larry was a little bit . . . *effeminate*" – and here the rough-cut western rancher is passing judgment on the cultured eastern urbanite. "But the other guy turned us down. So I was left with Larry – which was probably a damn good thing, because it turned out he was exactly right."

It was late December 1970, and a dithering Bonnycastle told Heisey to call him on the 31st. When the hopeful candidate called from the ski slopes at Georgian Bay in northern Ontario, Bonnycastle said there was just one more thing he wanted to check. Later that evening, Heisey phoned back and was told to start the next business day. Bonnycastle would tell the staff they had a new president. The salary was $25,000, just reasonable for the time, but Heisey bought shares in Harlequin, which Bonnycastle pledged to buy back at cost plus five percent interest if Heisey left the company within six months.

By this time, Harlequin had moved from downtown Toronto to suburban Don Mills, Canada's first architecturally controlled subdivision, a bland mélange of residential districts and pockets of nonpolluting industries, where the company remains to this day. His first morning, Larry Heisey entered the small reception area to find no one there. The company had only a dozen employees on the publishing side, all of them obviously busy. After ringing a bell twice and waiting, he reminded himself, "You're president," and strolled down a hall until he came to an office. Looking in, he introduced himself to a surprised Richard Bellringer: "I'm your new president." Bellringer hadn't heard the news. "Dick Bonnycastle hadn't got the message through. Dick's forgetful," Heisey explains.

From the start, he took to Bellringer and Willson, and together they took delight in this company that seemed on the ascendant. "None of the three of us came from the publishing world, but we recognized that we had a tiger by the tail," Bellringer would recollect years later. "All we had to do was squeeze that tail and hope by heck it would jump in the right direction." Jim McCartney was another matter. Dismayed at not getting the presidency he thought Bonnycastle had promised him someday, he decided to leave, giving Heisey three months' notice. His new boss tried to convince him to stay. He knew that despite a lack of vision, McCartney had often served the company well – particularly in cleaning up a mess that Dick Bonnycastle had left him the year before. "Dick forgot to deliver a contract to Simon & Schuster in New York that was very important they receive by a certain date," Heisey told me. "It was a contract to end our sub-publishing agreement with them. And Dick had failed to deliver it, in his own forgetful way. So McCartney went down and pounded their ears, and they finally agreed to give up sub-publishing rights if they could do something else with the distribution." Despite Heisey's plea, McCartney did quit to go to New York and become president of Paperback Library, owned by Warner Communications, where he stayed less than a year.

One of his legacies at Harlequin was what became known as McCartney's Bar. It was a Scandinavian-style liquor cabinet disguised as an innocent piece of furniture in the boardroom. Heisey and his lieutenants would wander in after work and brainstorm over drinks, often calling their wives about 7:00 p.m. to say they were going to be a little late and then arriving home no earlier than 8:30. "Lots of great ideas came out of those sessions," he says, including the idea that they wouldn't bother pursuing any project unless it had the potential to add more than 10 percent to their profits. "Is that a five percent idea?" he would ask his colleagues. "A 10 percent idea or a two percent idea?"

Heisey infused Harlequin with a sense of possibility: "Great idea! Go do it!" In the words of William (Josh) Gaspero, who ran the North American book division for him a decade later, "Larry is a big-picture guy with a panache that you normally don't find in corporations. He created an atmosphere to let us flourish." And an ambience of fun: Gaspero recalls fondly the evenings they would close a bar down with Heisey at the piano – the bar always had to have a piano – and the men's-night parties when Heisey and his executive pals would have a black-tie dinner, shoot pool, and play cards.

Dick Bonnycastle's relationship with his management team was one of absentee chairman, with little hands-on interference on the publishing side. Their meetings together would often be boisterous, brimming with yells and curses – "a knock-'em-down, drag-'em-out management style," he says – but only once did he pull rank on the subject of books. He insisted that Harlequin publish a nonfiction book featuring the work of naturalist and artist H. Albert Hochbaum, who had been a friend of Bonnycastle Senior. When he announced to his executives that they were going to do *To Ride the Wind*, they studied the figures and called their boss back in to say: "We shouldn't do this project. We're going to lose $100,000 and not gain much experience to do anything else."

"Boys, we're going to do this book. And if you don't believe me, pull out your shares and we'll have a vote."

"Richard," Heisey said, "we're going to do it."

The next day Bonnycastle called him to say: "Well, you beat me yesterday. I hate giving people orders."

Heisey later told his employer that rather than loudly trumpeting it as a Harlequin title, the prominent imprint would be "A Richard A. N. Bonnycastle Book" – "I'm going to let you have the pleasure of having your name on the book." Published in 1973 in a luxury leather-bound edition that cost $250, the book lost about $100,000.

Three months into the job, Larry Heisey was sitting alone in a hotel room in Chicago one evening when he wrote a prediction of what might happen to Harlequin in the next five years. Among the projections that more than panned out: shareholders, including himself, would make a profit per share equal to what the shares were then selling for – roughly about $3 apiece. Not everyone in the company had his faith. Martin Reaume, for one, raising four children and far from the gambler that Heisey was, sold his shares in 1975 and bought a cottage. Those less optimistic than Heisey might have worried about Harlequin's educational arm depressing profits. That night in the hotel, he predicted that the learning-materials division would grow in its new incarnation as Scholar's Choice, an amalgamation of the failing Jack Hood School Supplies and the more successful Nor-Ed Supplies. He was wrong. Jack Hood had begun losing its markets when the Ontario government decided to consolidate school boards, which then used their concentrated clout to bargain directly with suppliers rather than through an intermediary such as Hood. "Jack Hood fell on instant bad days and gave a kick in the teeth to the price of the stock," Heisey says. "The shares plummeted from $7 to $1.90."

A more satisfying focus of his first year as president, one that would reap him and other stockholders profits beyond their imagining, was the acquisition of Mills & Boon. Heisey had met the Boon brothers soon after joining Harlequin, accompanying them to the Frankfurt Book Fair, where they pushed their nonromance list and made what he considered bad foreign deals for their romances in as many as 20 countries. Alan Boon had been going to Frankfurt since early in the 1960s. "We weren't frightfully busy, but we had the best bar there."

Heisey sums up their approach: "They were prepared to do traditional business. They exported to Australia and New Zealand [about a million books a year], Hong Kong and the Bahamas, and they did sales in Greece and the south of France and all those things that Englishmen did. But they never really had the sense of what could be, I don't think. Alan thought about being into other countries, but he didn't know enough about business to figure it could be done. And he thought you had to stand back and let other publishers do things in their own countries." John Boon, after all, was one of the originators of England's competition-quashing Net Book Agreement, only recently repealed, which insisted that books must be retailed at their full price, with no discounts.

Mills & Boon was ripe for a takeover. The Boons were concerned about estate planning, brother Carol and their sister were interested in cashing out their shares in the business, and M & B had been talking with the old English

The men of Harlequin, circa 1979. Standing left to right: Alan Boon, John Boon, Larry Heisey, Dick Bonnycastle Jr., Dick Bellringer. Staircase left to right: Patrick Nakagawa, Josh Gaspero, Bill Willson, and Vincent Walter. HARLEQUIN ENTERPRISES

firm of Heinemann and at least one U.S. company. As Larry Heisey says now, "anyone who really understood what it was should have given the Earth for it."

John Boon remembers a crucial moment in the late 1960s when Dick and Mary Bonnycastle went to London with their son. During lunch at the Ritz, Bonnycastle Junior sat making notes and offering opinions. "He was very shrewd; I wondered what would come of it." After his father's death, he began planning a takeover, urged on by Chris Ondaatje to sew up his source of supply: "You absolutely must buy the supplier. Then you control your own destiny." His friend didn't need much nudging. When Harlequin was going public, he told the Boons that the underwriters were demanding that he sign Mills & Boon to a five-year agreement to provide romances; the brothers signed. To cement his relationship with the horse-loving brother, Bonnycastle says, "I thought it was politic to get a horse there with Alan." He got more than one, which gave him the excuse to visit often: "Every time we got a rumor of them selling, I'd go whipping over there, ostensibly to look at the horses."

"Dick formed his management team," John Boon says, "and they came over to woo us more hotly." At one point the Boons mentioned that Hutchinson, the venerable English publisher that had tried to buy Mills & Boon during the Depression, was also interested. Bonnycastle suggested a three-way deal and went to London to negotiate it in the Rothschild investment banking house. He remembers about 18 people around the table as the Rothschild's man said, in effect, "I'm here to see how *you*, Mr. Hutchinson, are going to buy *your* company, Mr. Boon, with *your* money, Mr. Bonnycastle." To which Bonnycastle replied: "Well, that wasn't quite the way I had it figured out." The meeting adjourned without further ado.

Other companies had expressed their interest in Mills & Boon. "We were not in a good negotiating position," John Boon admits. "We were very profitable, but 60 percent of that was from subsidiary rights in North America and elsewhere, not from sales. We almost clinched a deal with Heinemann, and I wrote a long letter to Dick in 1971, explaining our position. He feared his great plan would collapse."

Although the market was bad, Bonnycastle had his friend Christopher Ondaatje raise the financing. Ondaatje, the Ceylon-born, British-educated son of a Dutch tea estate manager, was a published author (and the brother of poet and novelist Michael, who was to win Britain's Booker Prize). More than that, he was a fellow publisher. Bonnycastle had sold him the family's Greywood Press of Winnipeg, still publishing the remnants of Harlequin's slim list of steady-selling nonfiction. Ondaatje also owned a small house called Pagurian Press, which he had started with $3,000 and whose cash flow would help to finance an investment company with eventual assets of more than $500 million. With his high-cheekboned elegance and London School of Economics education, Chris Ondaatje – then a partner in the Bay Street institutional brokerage house Loewen, Ondaatje, McCutcheon & Company – was an ideal salesman for Harlequin. He recalls not having to do more than five minutes' worth of research on why the deal would be a good one for investors. "Romance is escapism, and escapism is a drug. Romance had always sold. It's a gold mine." The financing vehicle was a $4 million sliding-scale debenture

– "it was my invention" – in which interest rates slid up and down; for example, "if you bought a six percent debenture and the rates went to 11 percent, you got 11 percent. It did very, very well. I made my first $2 million out of Harlequin. I bought my house at 45 Howland Avenue [in Toronto] with the proceeds. I planted a harlequin maple there, and it's flourishing."

While Dick Bonnycastle choreographed the actual deal making, he had Larry Heisey out in the marketplace helping to raise $1 million from venture capitalists. As Ondaatje points out, Heisey would also profit enough to buy a big house and more. Harlequin's bank had insisted that the company approach potential investors with an attractive enough vehicle before it would lend the company any money. Heisey was sent out to talk to them about the stock issue. Unfortunately Bonnycastle had neglected to give him all the details. At one meeting, Heisey asked a would-be investor: "What *is* it we're offering?"

"It's a convertible debenture yielding nine percent – convertible at $4 a share." "My goodness," Heisey replied, "that's a very good deal – as a matter of fact, it's almost too good."

He wasted no time in teaming up with a friend to buy one of the 10 $100,000 units himself. "It was a wonderful investment," he says. "And I didn't know what it was until I was telling this chap why it was a good business and he told me what the deal was. That's typical Dick. He can be very forgetful." (Another time Heisey told me: "We were a very small group of people, and Dick often played things very close to the vest.")

Bonnycastle, meanwhile, had his vice president Bill Willson negotiating the fine details of the Mills & Boon buyout. Willson, John Boon says, "was a hard bargainer, not a skillful negotiator; he offered us a derisory amount. I got very angry and lost my temper: 'It's a bloody waste of time!' They were ball-aching, nit-picking negotiations. We had one telex from Willson that was 30 feet long; we laid it out in the corridor." At one point "Bill Willson said if we didn't do the deal, they'd compete and take our authors. It was the wrong tone to adopt in negotiations such as these. It really turned us right off. But Bill did what Dick told him. I told Dick and Larry: 'Bill is impossible.' "

"John," Heisey responded, "I know it's a tough time, but just think about it this way: when we get this deal done, he'll be working for you."

They came to terms. John Boon would oversee the business operations in

London, while Alan would oversee all the editorial for both Mills & Boon and Harlequin. To finance the acquisition in early 1972, Harlequin borrowed $1.5 million from the bank and issued $1 million worth of nine percent, 10-year debentures convertible into common shares at $4 a share. The final purchase price was $3,069,381 (about half for assets, half for corporate goodwill), plus five-year warrants entitling the holders to acquire 100,000 Harlequin shares at $4.50 a share. About a year later John Boon told Larry Heisey that he and his brother believed they might well make more money from the warrants than they had from the cash sale. "Believe it, John," Heisey said. "Believe it." Not long ago, a former colleague of theirs at Harlequin told me: "You know they lost all the money they got from the first payment because they didn't figure on taxes. They didn't set themselves up in a Swiss corporation. They lost it all on the basis of the 95 percent tax or whatever it is in the U.K." However, when Harlequin sold to Torstar and continued expanding, they did make millions.

At the time of the takeover – which the Boons have always preferred to call a merger – the brothers had mixed emotions about selling the family publishing house. "John was not thrilled with the Canadians taking over," says Paul Scherer, who managed Mills & Boon's United Kingdom, Australian, and New Zealand markets in later years. Production director Arthur McKay says, "The Canadians treated it like cans of beans, and it hurt us a bit." Dick Bellringer went over to clean house, and within a week he had made major changes such as firing the entire sales department.

Nor was Dick Bonnycastle as happy as he should have been the day the deal was signed in London. The hard-eyed businessman who had inherited his own family business had already told Larry Heisey not to fall in love with the company: "You have to be ready to sell and trade." On the cab ride back to their hotel, Heisey suggested that he would be visiting Mills & Boon immediately to get a few things straightened away.

"Oh, shut up," Bonnycastle told him. "Get on the fucking plane and fly back to Canada and let them think about the new way of doing things for about six months. I'm sad for them today, giving up their company."

Harlequin celebrates its 25th anniversary this year, and
though it's hardly possible that earnings will triple again,
silver does seem to shine in the offing.
    – Publishers Weekly, 1973

5

The Bonds of Matrimony

TORSTAR BUYS IN

The wedding was in the gracious home in Lawrence Park that was once his mother's. Larry Heisey was in his Harlequin office at three o'clock when someone told him, "Go, you're getting married." That late-July day in Toronto was steamy, still nearly 90 in the evening. Larry and his bride had waited for the Unitarian minister, who was late. They phoned his home and got his wife, who said he had left, and then the minister arrived with his girl-friend, who stayed for the party. *Unitarianism has its charms,* Heisey thought. The ceremony was in a tent on the lawn, and the 20 friends and family in attendance burst into applause at the end. With dinner the rain came, miring the backyard in mud, and the house had just one air conditioner to moderate the humidity.

A few years later, Ann Heisey was still rhapsodizing about their courtship and marriage: "You know, this would make a good Harlequin Romance." For its *Maybe This Time* series, perhaps. Heisey and Ann Barclay, the daughter of Norval and Llewellyn Smith, had met the year his wife died, and Ann's hus-band had left her and her daughter. She and a girlfriend, another abandoned wife, were staying the week at his brother's cottage. Larry was taking his two children home after the weekend when these two attractive women arrived, burdened with groceries and a dozen bottles of beer. Ann, a compact woman with slender legs and a full figure, had a typical Harlequin-heroine reaction to the man she was about to fall in love with: she resented him. It wasn't only that he was drinking some of the beer they were trying to ration over the week, but also because he was male – and she and her friend were currently down on men. Heisey, however, decided to stay on, and by week's end Ann had melted sufficiently to start dating this kind and easygoing man back in Toronto.

They were married four years later, in 1973 (one year short of Harlequin's silver anniversary, despite what *Publishers Weekly* thought). By then Larry Heisey had conducted Harlequin to an increasing crescendo of success. The annual report for that year would set the tone for the bountiful years to follow. The company – easily the world leader in romantic fiction, its products appearing in 80 countries on every continent – sold more than 35 million books, 10 million more than in the year he had joined. Returns remained at the 20 percent level, contrasting nicely with the industry paperback average of more than double that. North American revenues of $12.9 million leaped by nearly two-thirds and pre-tax profits of $5.4 million by more than three-quarters from the year before. While British and overseas revenues of £1.45 million rose by only 14 percent, pre-tax profits of £364,000 climbed by one-third. The combined net revenues of $20.3 million from all activities increased the company's per-share earnings by 69 percent to $1.57. (Among current shareholders was Western Broadcasting of Vancouver, which had more than 30 percent of the company.) The figures, and the results over the next two years, were to make Harlequin an enticing enough catch to attract its own manly, deep-pocketed suitor.

What the self-described old soap salesman had brought to the often antediluvian world of publishing were all his marketing smarts from Procter & Gamble. "He was a very dynamic marketing guy," says Sy Turk, who was then president of Simon & Schuster. He remembers attending a joint sales conference at which Harlequin editors and executives were promoting the new batch of books and Heisey referring to them in terms of their series numbers instead of their titles. "Just the numbers," Turk says. "He did not discuss anything about the contents. That was brilliant. He was dealing with *product*." In 1973 Heisey introduced the technique of sampling, common in his former indus-

try, at an unprecedented level in the hidebound book business. Ordinary publishers, because of the variety of books they offered, could use it nowhere near
as effectively as the distributor of a branded line. At Harlequin sampling was
born of necessity: the company was still not feeling flush enough to do any
major product advertising. As Heisey says, "Of the classical promotional
devices in the consumer-goods business, the best of them is sampling." And
he recalls a quotation from Socrates that applies: "If you have a great quantity
of sweet nectar for sale, it may be prudent to give each person his first glass for
no charge. If your wares are hemlock, be paid before any lips are wet."

Heisey's wares were as sweet and seductive as honey. Paperbacks were
cheap to print at the time. Harlequin got the rights from a popular British
author, Violet Winspear, to publish her *Dark Star* in a run of two million
copies, which cost little more than five cents apiece to print. (Years before, the
Cockney factory worker had submitted her first, handwritten manuscript to
Mills & Boon in a shoe box; now she was in England's 83 percent tax bracket.)
Although this Harlequin Sampler carried a price tag of 15 cents, the company
gave retailers 100 to 200 copies at a time to pass on to their customers as a special promotion, particularly during National Harlequin Month in the United
States. Accompanying material reminded dealers that Harlequin had the lowest returns in the business and that customers bought an average of four copies
at a time. "It sampled an awful lot of people with the nectar," Heisey says. "We
did some testing and proved that it built business."

Another technique, which other publishers had never attempted on a
nationwide scale, proved equally successful: advertising on television. In 1974,
Harlequin's 25th anniversary year, the company test-marketed commercials in
Calgary and 10 American cities, including Chicago, Dallas, and Oklahoma
City. Over six months, book sales in those markets jumped by an average of 79
percent compared with a 27 percent increase elsewhere on the continent. The
following year, the company spent $650,000 in the last quarter for 30-second
network commercials on weekday soap opera and game shows in the United
States. (A $250,000 follow-up campaign across Canada led an Eaton's depart-
ment store in Winnipeg to move its housewares department to accommodate
an expanded Harlequin display and a Simpsons in Toronto to restock its entire
Harlequin inventory – 2,500 books – three times in eight days.) In one of the
three commercials, a pretty young mother says, "Nap time for the twins, an

W. Lawrence Heisey: the old soap salesman who helped to revolutionize book publishing.

HARLEQUIN ENTERPRISES

now it's *my* time to curl up and disappear with a good book. Do you know what I read? Harlequin Romances. . . . They're well written, exciting – a good love story always is – and the characters go to foreign places and see things I dream of seeing. They're my disappearing act." Others featured a little older mother with a career, and a serene middle-aged woman who told the camera: "I know what it's like to be in love. And these help me to remember. . . ."

Harlequin has since claimed to be the first publisher to advertise during prime-time TV and in prime time for continuous months. Appearing on *Kojak* and *Laugh-In* helped the company's profile with wholesalers and retailers as well as readers. Commercials were not without their problems. Dick Bellringer pulled one off the air because the actress's nipples could be seen through her blouse. And another that surfaced on the bizarrely funny *Mary Hartman, Mary Hartman* series instead of on the benign *Happy Days* drew a ᵉnt of letters from unhappy Harlequin fans. The TV advertising worked: ⸍ 72 million books sold, 30 million more than two years earlier.

ᵒmmercials were produced by Compton Advertising of New York,
ᵛ't been Heisey's first choice of an agency. He had originally
ᶠriend. "Bellringer and I went off to Chicago and talked to Paul
ᵂonderful little agency, Tatham Laird, that used to do Mr.
⸍ Gamble. We had been old friends. Paul would come up

north, and we'd go fishing. But he never really understood what I was talking about. He couldn't believe that anyone would be publishing books that looked like this. And he made it really quite clear – even though we told him what kind of money we had and what our gross had been – that he wasn't interested." Fortunately Milton Gossage at Compton had done his homework, and he welcomed them as clients.

As well as television, Harlequin went into print with a vengeance – within a few years, it wouldn't blink at spending $1.7 million on full-color, full-page ads in 18 national women's magazines – and into many other things as well. Such as Kotex boxes: Violet Winspear's *The Honey Is Bitter* was packaged in 100,000 boxes of feminine napkins in Canada. "The Harlequin reader profile closely parallels that of our brand," the Kotex brand manager explained. By this time, Harlequin had a North American marketing director, Dave Sanderson. Not yet 30, a psychology grad from the University of Western Ontario, quick of wit and temper, he had been a brand manager in the Toronto office of Carnation Foods. Organizing the Kotex promotion for Harlequin, he sat in on a meeting of serious-minded Kimberly-Clark executives as they discussed a sudden upsurge in sales of the product. As he listened to them wonder aloud what might have accounted for the increased use of their sanitary pads, Sanderson asked, "Did you ever consider they were perhaps used as mattresses for gerbils?" There was a long silence; no one smiled; he explained he was kidding. "Since that day," he says, "I've stopped being a smart-ass."

Harlequins also became a premium in Canada with Ajax cleanser and a Bio-Ad presoak laundry detergent, while Colgate-Palmolive offered two different romances as a free mail-in with the purchase of its products. But when 60 McDonald's restaurants across the country gave away the romance novels on Mother's Day, the chairwoman of the Status of Women Society in the small Ontario town of Cambridge asked women to boycott the chain – "and then we could see if McDonald's would distribute the leftover novels to men on Father's Day." In a less controversial campaign in the United States, Avon handed out nearly 1.5 million Harlequins with its cosmetic products.

When Dave Sanderson was hired, Larry Heisey told him: "You know the supermarkets. We sell the books like soap or soup. Don't think about publishing. Go make it happen." *If that isn't a dream job*, Sanderson thought, *what is?* His major marketing coup in the mid-1970s was getting Harlequin into supermarket chains – most of which until then had stocked only publications such as *TV Guide* and *Good Housekeeping*. "I came from a business that knew how to sell in supermarkets," he recalls. The sales pitch to the Loblaw's chain in Toronto was a 10-store market test to turn one and a half square feet of space into $1,100 a month in sales. Periodical distributors, who had been trying for years to crack the supermarket field with paperbacks, would install the racks and restock the product once or twice a week. The only concession the distributors had to make was to carry Harlequins in the same trucks they used for the women's magazines also destined for the supermarkets. The test worked, and with further promotions Harlequin pioneered paperback sales in supermarkets across the continent. The display stands evolved from wine racks to plastic spinners it called Booktiques. Supermarket managers liked romance books simply because they sold by brand identification rather than by author or title. As *Advertising Age* has observed, "they turn over quickly and often generate higher profit per sq. ft. than auto supplies and housewares." Sanderson says, "Once this started to take off, the growth of Harlequin became exponential."

At that time, the marketing director was traveling endlessly, crisscrossing North America, and he didn't appreciate that an off-site Harlequin meeting had been called on a weekend in Nashville. Among the dozen attendees was Lou Krupat, who had been hired from Northern Telecom in a senior financial role. In Sanderson's eyes, he was a bureaucrat among entrepreneurs, a nickel-squeezer. Late Saturday morning, Sanderson gave his marketing report – and at one point, Krupat said, "That's not right."

"Lou, I know what I'm talking about."

They continued to argue the point – as Sanderson recalls, "it turned into a pissing contest between Lou and Dave." It turned ugly, he says, when Krupat said, "That's a lie."

Sanderson swung at him, missing his nose by an inch. Then he stomped out and flew home to Toronto, telling his wife they had better start saving their money and buy generic brands from now on. At work late on Monday, he had a phone call from a secretary, saying, "Mr. Bellringer wants to see you." And this wasn't a "Mister" kind of company.

"You've got a volatile temper," Bellringer told him. "You can't take swings at people."

"Why didn't *you* stop him?"

"Can you still work with him?"

"I can work with the good, the bad, and the ugly," Sanderson said.

"You *must* control your temper," Bellringer advised him.

By the mid-1970s, Harlequin was printing 450,000 copies of each title (with the difference between the fastest and the slowest selling averaging about two percent). Such enormous runs convinced Heisey to head south for cheaper printing prices on the two-thirds of its North American books that sold in the United States. Harlequin would save one cent per book, or about $500,000 a year. And when Canada imposed a large increase in foreign postage rates, the company also transferred the American mailings of its reader-fulfillment service across the border. Moving these operations from Canada meant a loss of about 100 jobs to the United States.

The Harlequin Reader Service had begun quietly in 1970 as a way of ful-filling requests for backlist paperback titles. The next year, the division, based in the Shakespeare Festival town of Stratford, Ontario, started republishing books in hardcover under the Golden Harlequin Romance imprint. By 1974 it was releasing Mills & Boon titles in softcover specifically to market to direct-mail customers – and discovering that it had created a lucrative book club. As comptroller Martin Reaume says, looking back, the idea behind this service to readers was a no-brainer: "Just simply mail them out the new titles each month and keep doing so until either they didn't pay for a couple of months or they died." Very soon mail order became an incredible cash cow, providing as much corporate profit as regular book distribution. The statistics were staggering: of the 14 monthly titles then being offered, well over half the club members took all of them; eventually many faithful subscribers were buy-ing two dozen a month. "One of the tensions," Reaume says, "was trying to keep [the fact of] the staggering growth of the Reader Service from the whole-salers and retailers who might diminish their efforts and shelf space accord-ingly. But sales increased in those markets as well." In recent years, a similar tension has risen among Harlequin writers, who receive only two percent in book club royalties compared with a standard six percent for retail sales. They argue that this direct-mail business is highly profitable, a fact that their editors valiantly try to downplay – although Larry Heisey says that "it's probably the largest segment of profitability to the company." And his successor, David Galloway, told Harvard Business School alumni that with double the margins made from retail sales, "the real magic of Harlequin is its book club."

The same is true in Britain for Mills & Boon, which, at the North Americans' urging, improved its direct-mail operation, even though such aggressive marketing was considered the unsavory end of the publishing industry. In 1973 turnover was £42,800 with fewer than 1,000 subscribers, four years later £353,200 from a membership of 5,000, and by the mid-1980s more than £3 million from at least 50,000 members spending about 85 pence per book. M&B's Reader Service reached the point where, John Boon says, "in the end, it contributed 50 to 60 percent of the profit."

Sam Whitfield, a slim, outspoken Englishman who had been second in command at the Columbia Record Club in Canada, came to the Harlequin Reader Service in 1971 when it was a quarter-million-dollar business. The Harlequin he was a part of "was not warm and cuddly. It was an aggressive, high-tension atmosphere." At the time, Simon & Schuster's Pocket Books division had built up its own mail-order business with ads at the backs of Harlequins offering readers a catalog of previously published books. It had a list of about 6,000 people to whom it sold eight titles apiece each month. With the sub-publishing agreement ending, Larry Heisey met with S&S and, after some hard bargaining, arranged to buy the list for $100,000, or a mere $16.66 per name (a reader who stayed with the Harlequin club for a year could spend almost three times that amount). S&S president Sy Turk says, "That was a tough negotiation. When our agreement was over, Harlequin took back everything, including the mail order. They were arrogant. They said they owned everything." Meanwhile, Dick Bellringer had organized an unsophisticated survey by placing 200,000 questionnaires in Harlequins sold through retail outlets, offering readers free books if they responded. An astonishing 53,000 did, from across North America, and from that response Harlequin created its own mailing list for the Reader Service.

In 1973, to further promote the club, it started the monthly *Harlequin Newsletter Magazine,* which eventually sold (badly) on newsstands but was designed as a bonus for subscribers who bought a certain number of books a month. A 72-page product, mostly on newsprint and as unsophisticated as its name, it included author profiles, travel, fashion, puzzles, poetry, a reprint of a complete romance novel, and sometimes short stories by Harlequin authors. Most of all, it promoted the Reader Service in several full-page ads. The magazine remained a subscriber incentive for five years.

Whitfield had the reputation of being a lone wolf, planning promotions without informing the rest of the Harlequin managers, but he was effective. Three months after he joined the company, the book club's membership had more than tripled to 25,000; by decade's end, he says, there were 400,000 subscribers – and bad debts from delinquent members never rose above four percent.

Among the product being marketed by direct mail and sold in retail stores was a new line known as Harlequin Presents. Or what the people within the company called "Heisey's Heavy Breathers." Harlequin was being reluctantly propelled into an unaccustomed literary boldness by events beyond its walls. In 1971, just after Heisey got into the business, an editor at Avon Books in New York took home an unsolicited work that was languishing in the publisher's socalled slush pile. Nancy Coffey, a former teacher who used to edit children's books, read the thick manuscript nonstop over the weekend and, she recalls, "I became convinced it had an enormous sales potential." It was *The Flame and the Flower* by Kathleen Woodiwiss, a 32-year-old housewife in Princeton, Minnesota. A native of Louisiana, a born-again Christian, she had been a model in Japan, where her air force husband had been stationed. Her book, which had sold 1.7 million copies by the mid-1970s, proved seminal – if that is not too coy a word – in the history of romance publishing. Set in the England of 1799, the 430-page original paperback was the first in a new genre of heavily promoted erotic historical romances – Woodiwiss's heroine marries the man who has raped and assaulted her. The genre has since been described, in phrases mightily resented by authors, as rape sagas or bodice rippers. As Alice K. Turner observed in *New York Magazine* back then, "the erogenous zone directly referred to with frequency and prominence (so to speak) is the full, rounded breast, which is so often unlaced, unstayed, uncorseted, and nakedly exposed that these heroines should be in collective danger of consumption."

Harlequin by now was feeling the lukewarm breath of competition.

Bantam Books, one of the best-run paperback publishers in North America, had nudged into its market in the early 1970s with a series called Red Rose Romances, which struggled along until 1977. There were others: Curtis's Valentine Romances, New American Library's Rainbow Romances, Fawcett's Hamilton House Romances (which lasted about half a year), and Dell's Candlelight Romances, the only line to survive the decade. Harlequin took a while to move into historical romances and never did fully embrace the field. It did, however, respond to the increasing permissiveness in romantic fiction – as well as to pressure from the Boon brothers to introduce more sophisticated books in North America – by launching the series called Harlequin Presents. Somewhat steamier and more expensive (75 cents to the Romances' 60), the paperbacks had distinctive covers that, then as now, portrayed a close-up of a couple within a circle set against a predominantly white backdrop. For the first time, the author's name became much bigger than the title.

Presents made its debut in May 1973. At first the three titles being issued each month all featured the more passionate prose of a trio of popular British authors: Winspear, Anne Hampson, and Anne Mather. Alan Boon says, "Mather probably led us – in fact, she'll claim she did – into more sexy situations where the hero and heroine could have sex together." The popular Winspear brought similar passion to her prose. "I put all these cruel manly words into these men's mouths," she once explained, "and then work so as he makes a grab for the girl. And then she's half fainting, you know what I mean, with a burning desire, which she doesn't even understand herself. And then he's bruising her mouth with his urgent, demanding kisses, and he's got this strange steely light in his eyes. And I get it so as the girl says to herself, 'What does it mean, what does it mean?' Good God, I tell you, honestly, sometimes I get so worked up myself writing the stuff that I don't know what to do."

There had long been tension within the company between London and Toronto, and in matters of publishing – as opposed to marketing – Dick Bonnycastle tended to side with Mills & Boon: "I was constantly protecting the Boon brothers from the depredations of the Toronto people who all imagined they were publishers. They weren't – they were distributors. The Boons were in the book trade." Toronto had earlier managed to convince London that it should be in the business of paperbacks, and in 1974 the first with the famous M & B red rose covers appeared, Jean Macleod's *The Black Cameron*.

For their part, the Boons had been telling head office that Harlequin was not using their best books. Mary Bonnycastle didn't approve of the work of Mather or Winspear, among others. Alan Boon says, "I wrote to Judy and her mother to reconsider, and they did." John Boon, still touchy decades after the fact, says, "We reached a situation owing to Mary's attitude where we were unable to publish three of our best authors. We feared they'd go somewhere else." The Boons scoff at the idea that Dick Bellringer created the Harlequin Presents line. John says, waspishly, "we deserve the credit. Harlequin knew nothing about publishing. They were marketers. They said that books could be sold like soap. But books aren't soap."

Larry Heisey recalls, "Mrs. Bonnycastle in the early days, and then Judy Burgess, her daughter, had decided on a sort of decency code for our readers. And they failed to keep up with the readers. And Alan Boon knew, because these books were selling well in England." While Boon was carrying on his campaign to have Harlequin use the better books, he invited Dick Bonnycastle to his first-ever lunch with an author. In preparation Bonnycastle read his first-ever romance novel – actually, just the first chapter –by the writer in question, Anne Hampson. Afterward, at the races at Newmarket, Boon asked Bonnycastle if he was going to use Hampson. "Yeah, let's go for it." Boon immediately went to a phone to confirm the deal. Meanwhile, Heisey had arranged to test-market 400 copies of each of four gamier titles to a random selection of North American readers. Judy Burgess had already chosen two of the books as Romances but rejected the others as too sensual. "Well, by golly, if the rejected books didn't score better than the accepted books," Heisey says. "At that point, we had three authors who had been regularly rejected but had written a lot of books." Among them Hampson, Mather, and Winspear had a backlog of at least 50 titles that became the spine of the new series. As Heisey confessed to *Publishers Weekly,* their supposed worldliness was relative.

The first Presents was Hampson's *Gates of Steel:* "Helen Stewart was a woman disenchanted with love. . . . Leon Petrou was a man with no need for love. He used women merely to satisfy his own desires." The blurb was hyperbolic: the English heroine and the Cypriot hero get married, anyway, but in the only bit of real lovemaking, no one's desire is satisfied, including the reader's. Other titles, however, did introduce a fresh sensuality: Anne Mather's *Devil in Velvet* has André's hand sliding under Harriet's dress "to find the taut nipple outlined against the cloth" and his hard fingers "caressing, arousing her to the realisation that she wanted him to lose what little control he had" – all in all, a Nureyev-like leap from the offstage sex of the Romances.

Mather was among the new breed of provocative authors who would sometimes visit Toronto. Larry Heisey once took her cruising aboard his 42-foot Bertram yacht on Georgian Bay in Lake Huron, which inspired her to use the setting for a novel, *The Spirit of Atlantis* ("her geography is kind of screwed up," he notes). Another British visitor was the outspoken Roberta Leigh, among the early Presents authors, who had a commanding personality. She accused her publishers of being "a bunch of men climbing to success over the frail shoulders of a cadre of women authors." By the mid-1970s, the prolific author, who also wrote as Rachel Lindsay, Roumelia Lane, and Rozella Lake, was earning well over $100,000 a year. The middle-aged Leigh, who loved dining out at good restaurants, was at dinner one night with Larry and Ann Heisey when she mentioned that a man had recently made advances to her, which she had repulsed.

"You have an affair," the romance writer observed, "and the next thing you want another affair, and another."

"It's just like peanuts, isn't it?" Ann Heisey remarked dryly.

If the Boons were unhappy with the North Americans' heavy-handed editing practices, a newcomer in the Toronto headquarters soon became the fiercest critic of Mills & Boon's sheer lack of editing. Fred Kerner, 54 at the time, had a distinguished record in publishing when he joined Harlequin as vice president and editor in chief in 1975. Natty, wearing a trademark bow tie, he was as lean and as smart as a whip; he also had a tongue that could wound like one. Born and raised in Montreal, he was one of many Jewish kids, the children of eastern European immigrants, who attended Baron Byng High School, satirized as Fletcher's Field in Mordecai Richler's *The Apprenticeship of Duddy Kravitz*. Kerner's teachers told him to be a writer or editor; after getting his arts degree at Sir George Williams University, he became a sports writer for the Montreal *Gazette*, an editor with the New York bureau of Canadian Press, covering the United Nations, and then a news editor and roving correspondent with Associated Press. While at A P , Kerner learned the book business on the side, freelancing as a proofreader, editor, and ghostwriter for Prentice-Hall. In 1957 he joined the house as a senior editor for its Hawthorn Books imprint, where he wrote the bestselling *10 Days to a Better Memory*, the first book by Dr. Joyce Brothers of TV's *$64,000 Question* fame, as well as the psychologist's syndicated column, a twice-daily T V show on A B C , and even her record album. (If anything, Kerner proved protean in his career, editing a men's-magazine anthology titled *Love Is a Man's Affair*, and writing *It's Fun to Fondue* under the cheesily punning name of M. N. Thaler, a booklet that sold 1.1 million copies.)

After two years, he went to Fawcett World Library as executive editor and editor in chief, building it into the leading American paperback house over half a decade. Once, negotiating with G. P. Putnam's Sons to buy the paperback rights to *Lolita*, he knew the two colleagues accompanying him would bid well into six figures for Vladimir Nabokov's hugely successful hardback. He preempted them by bluntly asking Putnam's president, Walter Minton, how much he would accept for the book. Minton blurted out, "I'll take the first bid over $100,000." Kerner replied: "Fine, you've just sold it for $101,000." Kerner left Fawcett in 1964 and, with $850,000 of borrowed money, bought Hawthorn Books, which he ran successfully for five years. But he was ready to leave New York when the deep-pocketed Reader's Digest Association (Canada) came a-courting for the second time, offering him the hands-on post of publishing director for its books and educational divisions in his hometown of Montreal. The Canadian subsidiary had an ambitious large-format hardcover program, which he oversaw. Until 1974, when, flying back with Dick Bellringer from a seminar in Edmonton, the Harlequin vice president (at Larry Heisey's prompting) invited Kerner to join their leanly run but rapidly expanding company.

He was given 5,000 shares in stock options and carte blanche to fire all the people working for him in editorial, production, distribution, and public relations – all five of them. Among the three he did let go was art director Harold Boyd, who had designed the Harlequin Presents cover but who (among other indiscretions in Kerner's hard eyes) would argue with the Reader Service people over what constituted good marketing art. One of the two he kept was editor Alice Johnston, who had been with the *Toronto Star*. Kerner's sharp green editing pencil would become legendary: Toronto literary agent Helen Heller, an editor at Harlequin in the early 1980s, says, "He ran a good and tight ship with the highest editorial standards of any house. He was hyper-careful about editing and proofreading. He would never countenance more than two typos in any book." Actually, it was no more than three every 100 pages. Kerner cared about the distinction between "drapes" and "draperies," "career" versus "careen," and the proper use of "run the gantlet/gauntlet." He would even check airline schedules to ensure a character could fly the route mentioned in a novel. A younger editor of that decade told me that "Kernerized books were generally a joke. Sometimes there *were* terrible mistakes, but sometimes he was really being fussy. He'd get very upset about 'that' and 'which' and 'further' and 'farther.'" Yes, exactly.

Mills & Boon, meanwhile, was still supplying all of Harlequin's books – supposedly edited – but Kerner wasn't impressed with much of the British handiwork. He knew the Boons, liked them, had even bought their nonfiction books when he was at Fawcett and Hawthorn. However, at a meeting infamous in Harlequin history, he confronted the brothers with examples of their editorial laxness.

"Alan," he said, "your people don't edit books."

"What do you mean?"

"When two people get into a canoe and the guy drops the paddle, it *sinks*. Paddles *float*. I have the book right here. And when the heroine goes for a walk down to the beach on the Pacific every morning from Pasadena, it's *16 miles*, for crying out loud."

As Alan Boon reddened, brother John got angry.

The most disturbing item Kerner presented them with was a misogynistic book reflecting the new permissiveness in which the hero beats the heroine numerous times and holds her head underwater until she is blue in the face. "At least give her mouth-to-mouth resuscitation!" he said.

"They never read the book," Fred Kerner told me. He mentioned the prolific Roberta Leigh, who might write a book in 18 days and then not bother to look it over again until after publication. "She complained bitterly to me – that's how I realized eventually that Mills & Boon was botching the editing. She said, 'You know, a name changes in the middle, and if my secretary doesn't catch it, the editors don't catch it. I want somebody to edit the goddamn books. I don't even think they are read.' And she was right. They weren't read."

You might consider yourselves British subroyalty, and I'm just a colonist, Kerner thought at the time, *but I'm working with you guys, and we're the bosses.* Over the next few years, he would work to shift the balance of editing power from London to Toronto.

Before coming to Harlequin, Fred Kerner had already had a couple of encounters with the company. While at Fawcett in 1964, he went back to Montreal for a visit and spotted Harlequin Romance novels on the newsstand. Impressed by their potential, he returned to New York recommending that Fawcett buy Harlequin Books, a proposal that was rejected – "Fawcett thought they could do it better" (but didn't). Eight years later, when Kerner was at The Reader's Digest Association, Chris Ondaatje approached him during a sales meeting in Toronto and promoted "this great company here called Harlequin." Dick Bonnycastle was obviously losing interest after only four years as an owner; as Larry Heisey reflects, "Dick believed you shouldn't fall in love with businesses, and, because he doesn't have a lot on his plate at the time, I guess, he's constantly thinking about how to enlarge his empire by exploiting Harlequin." Bonnycastle had asked Ondaatje to find him a buyer or a significant investor in the company. Kerner told the investment dealer to send research material on Harlequin to Digest chairman E. Paul Zimmerman. After Zimmerman sent the research report on to Kerner for comment, they met with the Digest's treasurer and marketing director, who agreed with Kerner that the company should make a bid for Harlequin. About 10 days later, Zimmerman decided on his own that the two publishing houses were not a good fit editorially. Kerner tried to persuade him, unsuccessfully, that Harlequin's mind-set – "everything always works out in the end, if you are good people" – was a perfect match for the Digest's "Pollyanna approach to life." Zimmerman disagreed; the irony is that within a few years, he would be president of the relentlessly Canadian company that would buy into Harlequin and benefit so mightily from its financial strength.

By 1974 Dick Bonnycastle had decided to sell Harlequin. He hated flying into Toronto, even as little as he did, and he hated the fact that his money was

Fred Kerner, a masterful editor and a terror with a green pen, throws out the bouquet at a Harlequin readers' party on Vancouver Island in May 1981. FRED KERNER

tied up in a company based in that city. Nor was he sure of his company's growth prospects on its own, and there were few businesses it could buy for expansion purposes that would offer as good a rate of return. It was time. He put out the word to his friend, Chris Ondaatje: find a buyer. An obvious one was Maclean Hunter, the Toronto communications conglomerate that owned media giants such as *Maclean's* and *The Financial Post* as well as a bevy of business publications and the book publisher Macmillan Company of Canada. But Maclean Hunter's president and C E O, Donald G. Campbell, had already been burned in one potential business involvement with Harlequin.

That story begins in the early 1970s in St. Louis, the home turf of a major American wholesale periodical distributor, the notorious Molasky family. The middle-aged father, Allan, and a son in his mid-twenties, Mark, descended from the founder of the business, William Molasky, whose office was reputed to be bulletproofed behind steel doors and his desk drawer to hold a gun or two. At various times, his son and grandson ran more than half a dozen news-distribution companies in the United States as well as the substantial Metro Toronto News. They had bought other distributorships in cities near Harlequin's home base, closed them down, and served those markets with truck deliveries. "My flesh crawled to be near them," Larry Heisey recalls. Aside from the fact that they were always pleading for bigger discounts from Harlequin, they had a reputation for dishonesty and strong-arm tactics. For instance, they pleaded no contest in 1975 to a federal suit alleging the use of coercion in buying a Gulf Coast competitor. Although the offense was technically a misdemeanor, they were fined $50,000 apiece, and Mark Molasky got 30 days in jail and two years' probation. There were many other suits against father and son, one of them by Curtis Circulation for failure to pay $1 million for books and magazines; when a spiteful Mark Molasky started burning magazines in his warehouse, Curtis had to get a restraining order to stop him. He would later die in prison after being convicted of molesting his own child.

Heisey was at a periodical distributors' convention in New Orleans when he heard that the Molaskys faced a new charge. This time it related to the buying of counterfeit paperback covers that a crooked printer had run off and sold to unscrupulous wholesale distributors who would return them to publishers for credit. Harlequin wasn't among the publishers being ripped off, but Heisey was so angry with such deceit that he convinced both Simon & Schuster in the United States and his current Canadian distributor, Har-Nal (jointly owned by Harlequin and New American Library), to join him in boycotting the Molasky distribution companies. A few months later, the beleaguered Molaskys put Metro Toronto News up for sale. Because Dick Bellringer had been pressing him to find a good acquisition, Heisey suggested with sweet irony that Harlequin buy Metro. It turned out to be too big a deal to handle alone – more than $5 million – so he approached a possible partner, Don Campbell. The Maclean Hunter president was interested and had the company researched – "we were suspicious it was Mafia-controlled," he recalls. But the day before the purchase offer was to be presented, Heisey and Bonnycastle went to his office to announce that they were backing out of the venture.

What had happened is that although Heisey thought Harlequin could own Metro with integrity and make some money, Bellringer was uneasy: "I don't like the smell. My nose is twitching."

"Fine," Heisey said, "but don't harass me over acquisitions!"

Don Campbell says, "We were so intrigued, we went ahead on our own." A few years later, he and the chief financial officer of Maclean Hunter personally faced criminal charges for distributing pornography, which is what the government was calling magazines such as *Penthouse* at the time. Although they plea-bargained to have the charges dropped, the company had to pay a $100,000 fine. It then sold Metro Toronto News to former employees. Campbell says, "We got out at the first opportunity. . . . We didn't make any money." Heisey says, "Maclean Hunter lost millions. They poured more and more money in it. In subsequent chats, Campbell has said, 'There've been times when I wished I weren't in the province the day you called.'"

Well before that, Don Campbell was not happy about his involvement with the periodical distributorship. Almost from the first, it proved to be a wretched investment. So when approached by Chris Ondaatje to consider buying Harlequin, Campbell was perhaps not as receptive as he should have been. Although he knew something about the company (and his wife had read some Harlequins), he concurred when Maclean Hunter's principal owner, Donald F. Hunter, wanted to pass on the investment. He recalls that Bonnycastle was asking for a price based on 16 times after-tax profit. "Why pay that kind of multiplier?" Campbell thought. "We could get General Motors for a few times that." Today he admits how wrong he was: "We made a bum decision."

Another conspicuous contender to buy Harlequin was Canada's largest newspaper, the *Toronto Star*. Roy Megarry, who would go on to become a respected publisher of the *Globe and Mail*, was the new vice president of corporate development and a director of Toronto Star Limited, soon to become Torstar Corporation. Its chairman and president, Beland H. (Bee, or the Bee, or the Beast) Honderich – the equally respected but much feared publisher of the *Toronto Star* – had asked him to set out a strategy for diversification. Megarry recommended that the company go after both Harlequin and Western Broadcasting, a conglomerate involved in four TV stations and five radio stations, which he found now owned 35 percent of the romance publisher. "Nobody believed Harlequin could continue to grow at the same rate," he recalls, but he also knew that Western president, Frank Griffiths, "did things for sound economic reasons and had picked up a lot of [Harlequin] stock cheap." In fact, Western wanted to buy the rest of the company, Bill Willson says: "Western took a run at us. Bonnycastle told them to go to hell. He wouldn't let them sit on the board. They had driven the stock up. We were laughing."

Megarry, meanwhile, was ready for a question from Ruth Atkinson

Hindmarsh at a meeting of the newspaper's board. Then in her early eighties, the daughter of the *Star*'s founder, Joseph E. Atkinson, and the widow of its former president, Harry C. Hindmarsh, asked him, "Mr. Megarry, have you read any of these books?"

Having devoured Harlequins for a couple of months, he could honestly answer yes.

She and other directors expressed their fear that the books might contain too much . . . well, *sex.*

"There's nothing in these books that anyone could object to," Megarry assured them, in spite of the sexual assertiveness that Harlequin Presents was then displaying.

The newspaper went after Western first – "which pissed them" – taking a 15 percent position in the Vancouver-based company, which owned radio and TV stations and had ambitions to become a big player in the sports arena (which it did, acquiring the NHL's Vancouver Canucks). Although the *Star* soon had a third of Western, Megarry realized the broadcaster didn't want to be acquired. "They started doing nasty things," he says cryptically. So he went to see Larry Heisey at his office.

"We'd like to buy Harlequin," he said without much walk-up.

"Well, it's not for sale." (Tell that to Dick Bonnycastle.)

"If it *was* for sale, what price would you put on it?"

"You'd never pay the price it's worth," Heisey said, "because you'll never believe our forecast of future earnings." Which broke the ice.

Assuring Heisey that the *Star* was serious, Megarry went off to spend a week or so working out a proposal to buy 51 percent of Harlequin – more than $29 million worth of cash and securities – through a stock market transaction. (Chris Ondaatje, helping to structure the deal for Bonnycastle, met once with Bee Honderich – "and I got a commission from both." Ondaatje also paid $25,000 to buy back the 25 percent of his Pagurian Press that Harlequin then held: "I didn't want to be controlled by the *Star*.")

As it transpired, the deal that Megarry fashioned would include an earn-out provision in which the newspaper company would purchase any shares held by Harlequin's senior officers that were not picked up under the initial offer; at the time, Bonnycastle held 15 percent. Based on multiples of earnings, the earn-out formula offered the officers a multiple that would be 50 percent more than the basic multiple if Harlequin achieved certain financial goals over a five-year period – "and then you'll really make a killing," Megarry told them while bargaining. Meanwhile, Bee Honderich told him that he wanted to protect the minority shareholders. "We had a plan (which nobody knew about) that after the deal closed, if we had to we would support the price of stock by buying more shares on the open market to prevent the minority shareholders from being hurt. Whatever it was [that Toronto Star Ltd. did have to buy additionally], it was peanuts." Of course, the deal made sense for Star, too: the generous earn-out incentive would ensure that the entrepreneurs who had built the business would continue to make it grow. When a Star director asked Megarry, "What happens if we have to pay this high multiple?" he replied: "Well, that will be good news. It would mean they were making money."

The negotiations were nerve-racking and broke down at one point, but the earn-out provision was just too sweet for Harlequin's major shareholders to ignore – for Bonnycastle in particular, who had got a management contract based on a percentage of the profits, which had him earning about $2 million a year for a few years. "It was a very imaginative deal," Larry Heisey says. Not that he was in love with the new partners. "I could have featured people that I'd rather have had in it, on the same basis. It concerned me that it was Torstar. Torstar was not, it probably is not now, a fun company. I mean, being a newspaper and people with a mission and an obligation to the original owners, to which they are committed, is kind of irksome. It doesn't allow for a light touch on anything."

If he was crying, it was all the way to the bank. "Heisey and Bonnycastle had a lot of shares left and made tens of millions of dollars," Megarry says. But the day the deal was made in 1975, "my elation was mixed with fear. I knew the statistics: 80 percent of [the situations of] one company managing another are failures. If this one fails, *boinnng!* there goes my reputation. If this doesn't work, I'm washed up."

As it turned out, Roy Megarry had no cause for concern. To this day, healthy, expansive Harlequin Enterprises continues to save the beleaguered Torstar Corporation's assets.

6

The Realms of Gold

HARLEQUIN HEADS OVERSEAS

The little village of Champeix lies below the ruins of a feudal chateau in the
Auvergne, the volcano-strewn center of France. Its gentle croissant of a main
street backs on to the river Couze, which has a bad habit of flooding the lower
village come spring and autumn. None of the buildings rises more than four
stories. Beneath the flower-bedecked, wrought-iron balconies of shuttered
apartments are the facades of five bars, two hotels and grocery stores, a *patis-
serie* and a *charcuterie,* and several other shops that offer a rural French community the necessities of life – including a stationery store and newsstand
called La Maison de la Presse. Every two weeks, a 70-year-old village woman
visits the newsstand and heads for two racks of paperbacks. She ignores the
contemporary softcover fiction and classic novels by the likes of Victor Hugo
that are virtually hidden away in the back of the shop. The books she wants
are the only ones displayed front and center amid the magazines and hardcover tourist books running the length of one wall. Inevitably the woman
picks out two or three new paperbacks in the Croix Blanche series – the nurse-
and-doctor romances. Sometimes she browses through Les Historiques and
Les Best-Sellers, by authors named Bronwyn Williams and Jayne Ann Krentz,

and she often buys the Collection Horizon, three novels for the price of two, at 32 francs.

Here in the heart of the country, *la France profonde,* as in much of Europe, Harlequin rules the paperback racks. "We sell a lot," Roger Marin, who owns La Maison de la Presse, told me in the fall of 1995. He had only been selling them for a year. "I regret I didn't start carrying them from the beginning, because from time to time women came in, looked around, and said, 'Do you have Harlequin?' Tourists. People from the village. Some older ladies and young ones, 25, 30. I should not have ignored them." Now, on the 15th and 30th of every month, a truck from France's major publisher and distributor, Hachette, delivers enough Harlequins to stuff 16 pockets with series called Amours d'Aujourd'hui, Collection Azur, and the more sensual Collection Rouge Passion. "How can they come out with so many stories and so many books?" Roger Marin wondered aloud that autumn day. The twin racks are labeled with the French corporate name – as synonymous there with romantic fiction as it is in North America.

Harlequin had come to Europe two decades earlier, in 1975, establishing a beachhead in Holland with a series called Bouquet Reeks (which sounds better in Dutch, in which it means "bouquet of flowers"). West Germany followed, with novels in magazine-style format, and in 1978 France, which would become the second largest operation outside North America. French adaptations of Mills & Boon romances began turning a profit the following year. By then, its 30th anniversary, Harlequin was also publishing on its own or in joint ventures in Scandinavia and Greece, south of the American border in Mexico and Venezuela, and across the Pacific in Japan. Larry Heisey's embryonic campaign to expand internationally was part of the appeal the company had for Toronto Star Ltd. By decade's end, the overseas division would show an impressive increase in revenues and profits.

Before 1975 Harlequins had appeared in several other languages, but the company simply licensed the rights to the books to local publishers who released them under their own imprints. The Boon brothers were handling these sales in their usual fusty way. About sales to publishers in France and Holland, Heisey says, "We were getting one percent of the cover price or maybe two percent of the wholesale price. That's all. If we published the books ourselves in Canada, we could make a margin of 10 to 13 percent on the retail price. So it didn't make a lot of sense to me to pressure other people to publish them. And when I was at the Frankfurt Book Fair, I wondered why I didn't have my Paris office" – thinking back to the boy who saw the globe-trotting label on his mother's perfume bottle – "and why we couldn't do it ourselves. It's a perfect product. It travels everywhere."

It was Dick Bonnycastle who pushed for Harlequin to have either its own presence or engage in joint ventures in Europe. Finding a first foothold was happenstance. A Dutch publisher had approached Harlequin to get the rights for Holland. "He could really drink Scotch," Heisey remembers, "and ultimately he fell ill and couldn't go on with the plan." At Frankfurt Heisey had met a tall, slender Dutchman in his late twenties who also wanted to license the rights. Klaas Koome (pronounced *Koo*-may), charming and enthusiastic, could speak half a dozen languages and had already been distributing English-language books in Spain. Now he wanted to publish romances in Dutch. After the book fair, he received a letter from Harlequin's president inviting him to work for the company instead and to set up the company's first wholly owned, stand-alone foreign operation, in his home country. "Klaas fixed on me. We bonded well," Heisey says. "I never had such a personal impact on a person, in the sense that his own father had left his mother, and he was always trying to show his father that he was a better man than he was." It was a relationship that would end in bitterness for Koome and sorrow for his mentor.

In Holland, for the first time, Harlequin was spending true investment money rather than operating from cash flow. Koome hired eight people for the Amsterdam office, including an editor in chief who worked with a team of local translators. He launched the Bouquet Reeks line of four titles a month amid a blaze of television commercials, within a year had introduced a second line, and expanded further over the next two years, releasing as many as 50,000 books a month. Holland soon shared with Canada the company's highest per capita readership rate for women over 15. "He lost a lot of money in the first year, which we accepted," Heisey says of his protégé, "the second year he sort of broke even, and in the third year he was very flush. It was a classic case of how to introduce a brand."

Over the following few years, Koome worked with Dutch-born Jake Van Ginkel, Harlequin's director of taxation and then controller, who was eventually funneling about a third of the company's income through a branch set up in Switzerland to reduce taxes. "We paid just under 10 percent tax this way," Van Ginkel recollects. "In Canada we'd have paid 50 percent tax and 45, 46 percent in the U.K. So the authors got paid from a Swiss bank. A big chunk of the value of that company to Torstar was created through the tax structure."

West Germany was the next international target. Mills & Boon already had a relationship with Axel Springer Verlag A G, the nation's dominant newspaper and magazine publisher. Again it was a licensing arrangement. In the late 1960s, Springer had set up a new division, Cora Verlag, to explore opportunities in mass-market publishing such as comic books, true-confession magazines, and romantic fiction – to some dismay within the company. "There were two concerns," says Horst Bausch, a former foreign editor with *Der Spiegel* who was then acquiring novels for the Springer group to be serialized in magazines and newspapers. "The top editorial echelon in Springer were really quite snobbish. They simply didn't like the romance genre. And others said, 'Well, if you do this, you will fall flat on your nose.' . . . The idea was to do it with German authors, but they weren't good at writing romance – what the Germans call trivial literature." Early in the 1970s, the Cora Verlag people negotiated a highly favorable two-year rights agreement with Mills & Boon. They had no idea that Harlequin was now running the show: at a meeting in Frankfurt, the Boons simply introduced Dick Bonnycastle and Larry Heisey as "our Canadian cousins." Nor did they know that Heisey intended to use Cora's experience with the books as a test run for Harlequin's own entry into the German market (Alan Boon even gave the operation a code name: Tristisolde, for Tristan and Isolde, the star-crossed lovers of Wagner's opera).

Cora released two novels every two weeks in a digest-sized magazine format under the Julia imprint, with color photographs on the covers instead of illustrations. Such frequency astonished the industry, recounts Ralf Kläsener, then the division's editor. "People said this can't work. Then a year later they said, 'You've had the idea of the century.'" Because the company controlled the country's newsstands, positioning and distributing the novels like magazines – and ignoring the bookstores, which demanded higher margins – was a brilliant strategy that led to instant success. It also meant German romance readers were about the same age group as magazine consumers: "Our target group is roughly 10 years younger than in the United States," Kläsener explains. "So we may have them a little longer."

At first, worried about readers' response to these bracingly British stories, the company had Germanized the names of some of the characters and even the authors – until deciding that readers didn't care about their patrimony, in fact enjoyed their foreignness. Within three years, "English romance" was such a generic trade term that competitive publishers sometimes anglicized the names of their German authors.

Before the licensing deal had expired, the Springer people finally learned who Larry Heisey was. He met with them to propose buying half of the German company's mass-market division and operating it as a joint venture. The response was curt: Dr. Axel Springer never sells anything. Would it hurt to ask him? There would be no point, they retorted. Well, Heisey said, in that case he'd be back in a month to discuss a new royalty rate with them. Two weeks later, he heard that Dr. Springer, who never sold any of his assets, had sold half of Cora Verlag to a comic-book publisher, an old friend. Heisey had a delicious return engagement with the German executives: "Well, I have some good news for you. You've got a while to run on this inexpensive contract, and I'm not going to raise the royalty rates. The only trouble is, at the end of that period, I'm not going to sell you any books at all." Don't be too hasty, they replied. He wasn't being hasty: they still had several months left on their contract. If they would now like to talk to Dr. Springer about his proposal, please do.

"Well, my goodness, if the sale wasn't reversed and they sold it to us," Heisey says now, still delighted. "It was a terrific deal." In 1976 Harlequin paid $2.1 million for a 50 percent interest in Cora Verlag, which distributed the romance novels to the German-speaking populations of Austria and Switzerland as well as Germany. Backed by brand-awareness promotions, the joint venture was profitable from the first year on, with sales of up to 160,000 a title, and soon it added two biweekly romance series, Romana and Bianca (with hospital settings), and a romantic-suspense line, Baccara.

The slight and gentle Horst Bausch became Cora's editorial director, working in Berlin with a base of more than 100 freelance translators. "At that time, many of the professional translators wouldn't touch a Mills & Boon," he says. "We got journalists and secretaries, anybody, and trained them. We had male journalists who thought they could do it with their left hand" – mistakenly, as it turned out: almost all his translators were women. Because so many

Germans learn a British English as their second language, idiomatic expressions weren't a problem until Harlequin began exporting some of its American-written romances in the 1980s. "But English has so many more words than German," Bausch notes, "and it can be rather monotonous if you go from English, where you can use four or five verbs, to German, with one or two." He met with the translators once or twice a year to keep them current with English idiom. Pleased with the success that Bausch helped to fashion in Germany, Harlequin would later recruit him to run its editorial operations in London and Toronto.

Ralf Kläsener, now international affairs director for the Springer group that includes the joint venture, says Cora's total readership of eight million women today represents a much higher penetration rate than Harlequin has in the United States or Mills & Boon has in Britain – "Germany is still 40 percent of the total European business of Harlequin."

Unlike Germany, France had a long tradition of romantic fiction before Harlequin arrived in 1978. Over the last two centuries, authors such as Magali and Delly (brother and sister), Berthe Bernage, and Max de Vieuzit (a woman despite the name) wrote the equivalent of what the French call *le roman rose* or *le roman à l'eau de rose*. More recently Anne and Serge Golon conceived the Angelique series that transcended French borders. Yet Harlequin's initial foray into France ended in failure. It had sent an ex-Catholic priest there on a fishing expedition; his major credential for the task seemed to be his knowledge of French. He did find Maurice Dumoncel of the Tallandier publishing house (now part of Hachette), who was publishing a native variety of the romance novel. Heisey and Klaas Koome negotiated an agreement with Dumoncel, but despite their best efforts, he never did manage to publish a single Harlequin. He benefited from the relationship, however, when Harlequin later paid him about $1 million to tie up the rights to French authors whose romantic-suspense novels it published in German and English in a series called Mystique Books – which failed miserably.

Harlequin had a hard time interesting French publishers in its product. Heisey quotes them as saying, "Our women don't read these kinds of books." To which he responded, "Well, the reason they don't read them is that they've never been offered them." A publishing consultant did a market survey and came to the overwhelming conclusion that the North Americans shouldn't brave a venture in France. Undeterred, Heisey and the Boons decided to go it alone as Harlequin had in Holland. They hired Christian Chalmin, who had operated at an international management level with French publishing houses. "He was a pistol. Very bright and aggressive," Heisey says. "A very handsome Gallic individual who spoke English with a Boyer accent and had a beautiful wife – quite an elegant man." How elegant? He had a brand of perfume, Chalmin, manufactured especially for him. "He wore a lot of it, too." In 1977 Heisey finally had his Paris office. Within a year, his new managing director had convinced the giant Hachette communications group to distribute Harlequins through newsagents, supermarkets, and bookstores, and a year later was selling 140,000 apiece of six monthly titles. Three other series appeared early in the 1980s, when annual sales reached 30 million books, and despite new competitors, Editions Harlequin had three-quarters of the French romance market. It was the leading paperback publisher in the country.

As the representative of a North American company in his chauvinistic homeland, Chalmin spoke a good game: "We see ourselves as a French publisher because we choose what we want from the Harlequin backlist. And our expansion will be in the direction of French originals." Actually, 10 percent of the books were commissioned French originals, love stories with an adventurous flavor in the vein of *Gone with the Wind.* The rest were reprints, translated from English, although often adapted and heavily rewritten. Heisey says, "We had a bad period in France, when the business got soft, somewhere in year three, and we found out that our editor in chief was taking all the spice out of the books. She was the most wonderful déjà-vu kind of blond, looked a little worn, but a lovely woman. And she was getting all these books tamed down. Alan Boon was very stressed that you had to keep up with the authors and understand 'steam,' and if they were writing 'steam,' that's what women wanted."

Adaptation still happens today. Claire Ulrich, a translator of 40 Harlequins, satirically spells out some of the guidelines she assimilated: "Don't forget to shave the bearded ones; it looks dirty to French readers. . . . Be careful with erotic passages. . . . The kiss: three pages, it always lasts three pages." As the magazine *Madame Figaro* reported not long ago, French translators might have to "latinize" a crude love scene – "by replacing a detailed anatomical evocation, too sordid for us, with a description of strong feelings – or to take out some shocking scenes." It gave as an example "a young armless man, who has his stumps gently caressed by the heroine: spicy detail for the Americans, but in France he has to get his arms back."

A spin-off from Harlequin France was the Canadian company's reentry into Quebec, which the Bonnycastles had pioneered for a few years, beginning in the late 1950s, with translations of Mills & Boons bearing titles such as *Docteur Ruth Prescott* and *L'Infirmière Amoureuse*. About two decades later, the success in France prompted Harlequin to print M&B titles in French on Canadian presses, which made them cheaper than other French-language books from overseas being distributed in Quebec. Collection Harlequin, with four titles a month by old faithfuls such as Violet Winspear, had a promising reception in the province. Larry Heisey's pride played a role in the decision to publish them: "It really tickles me to be an English Canadian and have a successful publishing venture in Quebec." And perhaps a touch of hubris, too: "We may have set in motion a minor revolution in the Quebec book business," he predicted a little optimistically.

In 1985, when annual sales in France were $24 million, Harlequin sold Hachette half of its operation there – "our pearl," in company parlance – for $5 million U.S. The joint venture would cement Harlequin's hold on the marketplace, although John Boon has since said it was a mistake to sell to the French communications giant: "They are so difficult." The following year, the partnership bought out its only real rival, an imprint called Duo published by J'ai Lu. The acquisition, along with promotions such as distributing thousands of free books on Métro stations with links to suburban trains, led to an increase of one million readers. Now Editions Harlequin enjoyed a market share of about 90 percent. Discovering, however, that its slogan, "Harlequin, a whole world of escape," was being perceived negatively, the Paris office hired a new ad agency, Résonnances Ayer, which conceived a campaign to reduce the guilt feelings readers have in purchasing the romance novels. The idea was to position Harlequins as recreation rather than reading. Creative director Claude Magnin explained: "There is, between recreation and reading, the same difference there is between a light comedy and a play performed at the Comédie Française. We go back to the roots of the name: wasn't Harlequin, in the commedia dell'arte, the go-between thanks to whom love always triumphs?" The new slogan, introduced with a 12-million-franc budget in 1992, was "Let yourself be taken in by the game of love" (*"Laissez-vous prendre au jeu de l'amour"*). A typical ad had a woman seated between two darkly handsome men and the line: "Harlequin books are like men – it would be too bad to try only one." The campaign was a run-up to Harlequin's 15th anniversary in the country, in 1993, when it hired good-looking young men to hand out 45,000 roses to women on the main streets and in the malls of large cities.

Harlequin had a less expansive experience in Scandinavia. In 1978 Larry Heisey hired a 35-year-old Swede who had successfully represented the major Swedish publisher, Bonnier, in a bidding war with Harlequin for the Chris Whittle/Phil Moffat 13-30 Corporation of Tennessee, whose ad-sponsored publications targeted college and high school students. Staffan Wennberg spent a few weeks in Toronto, boning up on the corporate marketing and editorial styles, before going home to establish a start-up operation. He hired an editor (a young woman with a marketing-magazine background who is still there today) and four others to publish romances in Sweden, Norway, and Finland – in which, as the only Scandinavian country with T V advertising, expansion was quick. Harlequin broke a Finnish distribution monopoly by introducing its own racks in supermarkets. In T V -commercial-free Sweden, Wennberg launched women's magazine ads and billboards in Stockholm and adopted Heisey's beloved sampling technique, in one autumn alone giving away about 250,000 books taken from the returns pile. Denmark proved a trickier market to crack because major magazine publishers controlled delivery channels, and Harlequin was reduced to third-rate distribution. So Wennberg licensed Harlequins to the largest of those Danish publishers (which is still distributing a couple of hundred titles a year). Norway was almost an afterthought, he says, but with its tax-free books, low costs, and high margins, it was "fabulously profitable." As in West Germany, he found his readers younger than those in England and North America; half the Swedish audience was teenagers. Meanwhile, his aggressive mail-order business was marketing half a million books a year (now doing at least triple that).

Still, it took four years before the Scandinavian operation repaid its borrowed investment funds – substantial for a Swedish company, he notes – and turned a small profit. His best year was about $1 million. Larry Heisey, who calls Wennberg "a very nice, decent man," adds that "he was not very profit-oriented, and we finally pointed out to him that he had to raise his prices." Although Wennberg greatly admired Heisey, he did prefer his fellow

Europeans' overall approach to the North Americans': "John Boon was always extremely supportive and positive. It added a nice touch to the pushy Canadian marketing people." By the time Staffan Wennberg left in 1987 to run a major Swedish book club, Harlequin had sold 25 million books in the three countries where it ran its own show.

In 1979 Harlequin moved into Greece under the name Harlenic Publishing of Athens, a small joint venture with local partners, run by a Scotsman. The company had a team of skilled translators working on the initial lines of two Greek-language Arlekin Romances a week and two historical romances a month. The operation prospered, expanding with a series called Bell Bestsellers that featured popular American fiction, acquired at low cost because there had been no history of selling such rights to Greek publishers. Greek readers proved a more purely romantic breed: they like the Bianca line of sensuous romances, and, as editorial director Marina Kouloumoundra has pointed out, "North American women will accept more real-life issues in the books than Greek readers."

Publishing in Spanish was a special case. Harlequin first published in the language in Mexico on Valentine's Day 1979, in a joint venture with the Dearmas Group, a leading publisher and magazine distributor in Central and South America. Two Mills & Boon titles appeared in paperback every month under the name Jazmin, and in less than a year – when the enterprise was already declared profitable – the series was introduced in Venezuela, Colombia, and Costa Rica. Meanwhile, Harlequin had given licensing rights to a Brazilian company to publish in Portuguese. But allegiances in these countries ebbed and flowed – Mexico devolved to a licensing arrangement – and Alan Boon said not long ago that "the whole relationship with Spanish is difficult." His brother says the lesson they have learned is that "where there are difficult currency problems – with inflation and currency control – the licensing approach is the best. As we've done in Brazil, as in Turkey and Israel."

As in Spain at the start. Harlequin has operated there since 1980, stepping into the country gingerly, by the back door, because a holdover law from Franco days forbade foreign companies from publishing in Spain. Although it collaborated with a local company with a license to publish paperbacks, its annual reports from that decade fail to mention any activities there. Yet an article on Harlequin in a recent Spanish magazine points out that "in record time, the newcomer had replaced its rivals." The company has since established its own profitable presence in the country, with a dozen staff; the magazine says Harlequin Spain's annual sales now range up to 3.5 million copies. And it quotes general editor Maria Teresa Villar, a native of Cuba, on the cast of characters that appeal to Spanish readers: "In these novels men are invariably rich and handsome and the women are from the middle or lower classes. For many pages the woman hides her feelings, but suddenly her life is absorbed with the man with whom she has fallen in love."

Harlequin's biggest leap, culturally speaking, was across the Pacific, into Japan. Like their French counterparts, Japanese publishers who were approached in the late 1970s to form a joint venture decided that that sort of book was not read by their female readers. The cultural differences *are* huge: as John Boon said a decade ago, before Harlequin had gone into China, "I think of all the countries in which we publish, or to which we sell books, probably Japan's social background differs most from that of the United Kingdom. Traditionally the Japanese like unhappy endings in which everybody parts in sorrow and tears but having done their duty, whereas we have happy endings." The Japanese publishers' negative response actually encouraged Alan Boon. He accompanied his brother, then president of the International Publishers' Association, to a convention in Japan. "Alan drank quite a bit of beer," recalls Larry Heisey, who was along to lend moral support, "and he did a lot of judging of people and decided that they'd love his books." Harlequin, resolving to do it on its own there, first hired a local consultant who was a national distributor of English-language publications in Japan. Two years of market research, including a test sampling of 1,000 women who read Harlequins in Japanese, convinced the company that foreign romances were a viable product for the Asian marketplace. Among the readers' comments: "The book size is handy"; "I always buy a couple at a time"; "The stories should be made into movies."

Harlequin Japan's first manager was Henry Tamaki, who had been raised by a German mother and a Japanese father in Japan during World War II. Tamaki, who had worked for Lufthansa, was a charming representative for the

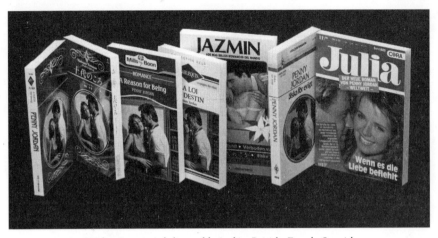

Harlequins around the world: Arabic, British, French, Spanish,
Scandinavian, and German editions. HARLEQUIN ENTERPRISES

company in his home country, but head office felt that his marketing skills left something to be desired. In the summer of 1979, it sent in marketing director Dave Sanderson, who took his wife and two children. He fashioned a large advertising and promotional campaign for the September launch of a series of four Mills & Boon titles a month with North American covers. He was in a survival mode the first few weeks, dealing with culture shock in general and Japanese office employees in particular. As he wrote to a friend, "Japanese white-collar salarymen *have* to be the *least* productive collection of humanity on the face of the planet. JEEE-SUSSS, they are *slow* and contrary and stubborn! . . . just like you said." Soon after arriving, he met an elderly gentleman in the American Club in Tokyo, an American with a Japanese wife, who told him: "Young man, Harlequin has been a success everywhere, but you'll be a failure in this market; the Japanese are far too literate to read that crap."

The warning was all the inspiration Sanderson needed. Working with the national distributor Yohan, he targeted kiosks in the busy subway systems as key points of sale, suspending small spinner displays that held 100 books. Initial distribution decided, he placed TV commercials on prime-time programs and soap operas, and ads in women's magazines and on subway trains. All that, combined with print-media promotion of "the American invasion" variety, kick-started Harlequin into turning over 1.2 million books in the first half year. But the momentum was never maintained, and over the years distribution problems arose – supermarkets were particularly difficult to educate about the rewards of selling romances. As John Boon says, "we still haven't broken through in Japan."

There were other concerns: Harlequin had to make certain concessions to Japanese taste. Henry Tamaki had assembled a group of female translators who would meet Friday afternoons to discuss all the baffling English passages they had saved up all week – phrases such as "I'm over the moon with you!" Covers showing a man and a woman kissing were generally unacceptable, while those featuring high technology such as the Bullet Train – perhaps symbolizing dependability and/or virility – were most popular. And as John Boon has remarked, "You do have to make alterations in the dialogue. For example, I was talking to a Japanese editor a week or so ago, and she said that no Japanese man can say 'I love you' to a woman. I asked what does he say instead, and she replied that he *shows* his love. A smile crossed her face, but I couldn't get any more out of her!" That was in 1989, but recent surveys have shown that Japan's romancing quotient remains low in real life: the ratings that Japanese men and women gave to each other in love and romance were the lowest among the 14 industrial nations polled. Only a couple of years ago, Boon mentioned that Harlequin was still getting "a lot of fan mail from Japan from women saying they wished their husbands would be more like our heroes."

Heisey sent Canadian Glenn Johnson, who had run Scholar's Choice, to set up operations in Australia and New Zealand, which Mills & Boon had been servicing from England. "One of Glenn's great moments," Heisey says, "was when he was in New Zealand negotiating with a distributor who shouted at him: 'You damned Australians are all the same!' And he realized he'd arrived."

As foreign activities flourished for Harlequin, Christian Chalmin's star continued to rise. In 1981, the year Dave Sanderson returned to Toronto, Larry Heisey named the head of Editions Harlequin a vice president of Harlequin Enterprises and president of its overseas division. Chalmin, living in London, was put in charge of distribution in more than 90 countries and became the effective overseer of book publishing in Japan, Australia, the Spanish-speaking countries, Holland, West Germany, Scandinavia, Greece, France, and the United Kingdom. His appointment was unwelcome in two quarters. John Boon, who had the title of Chairman, Overseas, disagreed with the selection, arguing that Chalmin didn't have enough experience. "John never entirely embraced any foreigners," Larry Heisey comments, "unless he thought they were desperately loyal to his side." (Chalmin did leave eventually and ended up working for Harlequin's competition in France, J'ai Lu.) But the reaction to his appointment as overseas president that proved more painful to Heisey came from his protégé, Klaas Koome, who felt he should have got the job.

Reminiscing, Heisey says of Koome, "I just adored him, and we got along like a house on fire. Until about five years later: I promoted another man over him and broke his heart. A decision had to be made, and Chalmin was the better man for that job at that time. And Klaas just lost his will to do things. He couldn't seem to focus on anything anymore; or he was perverse and didn't want to. But I know it was deeply personal. I've only spoken to him a couple of times in all the intervening years, but I think of him often, and I have such an affection for him."

One consolation for Larry Heisey was the general success of the overseas operations. It proved what he had known in his heart: that Harlequin would translate, if with some alterations, anywhere in the world. Translate into and, as happened, transform, take over, those other cultures in the area of light reading – as it did in France, whose own healthy tradition of *le roman rose* continues to be supplanted by the North American interloper. In an article about Harlequin, the conservative daily *Le Monde* suggests plaintively that the romantic-fiction genre is "the victim of a kind of racism, a contempt that inevitably includes its readers. That obviously explains why there are almost no authors in France. For the most part, those books are today translated from English, mainly from the United States, even though this type of literature was born in Europe, and France had well-known authors such as Delly, Max de Vieuzit. . . ."

This is the best job in the world. We get paid to tell lies and
don't have to put on makeup or panty hose. I could be
scrubbing toilets or selling toasters.
  – American romance writer Nora Roberts

7

The Pleasure and the Pain
THE WRITERS

The year Harlequin invaded Europe, launching its own company in Holland, another North American presence was making a quiet assault on the Anglocentric ramparts of Mills & Boon in London. In 1975 the unsolicited manuscript of a first novel by a 31-year-old secretary from small-town Iowa arrived at M&B. Her name was Janet Dailey, and she would transform the character of contemporary romantic fiction. No longer would the Harlequin fiefdom be the preserve of Commonwealth writers. Of about 140 then writing for the company, most lived in the United Kingdom, although there were many resident in Australia and New Zealand, a few in South Africa, and a mere three in Harlequin's birthplace, Canada. "There was a myth that you couldn't get others to write them," Larry Heisey recalls. "Janet Dailey *smashed* that." She was the first American that the editors of Mills & Boon deigned to publish and the first of their authors to treat American locales as exotic backdrops – so consistently that she decided to make *The Guinness Book of World Records* by setting a book in every state. If anybody kept track of the speed with which series romances were written, Dailey might have vied for that record, too: she claimed they never took her more than 20 days, although

Heisey says "she never publicly said she could do one faster than five days because she felt four days was obscene."

Janet Dailey, who insisted on writing under her real married name and never a pseudonym, added another twist to the then-orthodox enterprise of romance publishing. Following her second book, her husband – 15 years her senior – retired from his successful land-development business and devoted himself to her career. A handful of other romance authors had similar arrangements: for instance, Fred Greiveson, an ex-factory worker, managed the affairs of wife Mildred, who wrote from the north of England as Anne Mather. But perhaps no husband threw himself into the role with such abandon as Bill Dailey. He became Janet's full-time manager, researcher, stylist, and even chauffeur. In the late 1970s, the couple decided to become purposeful vagabonds and voyage over several years through each state, digging up background for her books, in a 34-foot-long, $30,000 Silver Streak trailer behind a $22,000 Mark 5 Lincoln. "I used to look down on the husbands who lived off their wives like that," Heisey says now. "But I realized they took care of the women's emotional needs. Alan Boon had spinster authors who leaned on him and needed constant consolation." (Perhaps that is why *Romantic Times* now has a regular feature of emotional support called the "Husband's Column.")

The Daileys' working relationship may not have been a feminist's dream: Janet would begin writing at 4:00 a.m. and serve Bill coffee and juice in bed when he awoke at 7:00. It did work well enough, however, that she had written 53 Harlequins that sold 80 million copies by 1980, when she was all of 35 years old. Although the books broke no social or sexual barriers, Dailey – inspired by the more liberated British authors such as Mather and Violet Winspear – did write a heroine with a certain American-style spunk, a Katharine Hepburn sparring with a Spencer Tracy. Typical was *Valley of the Vapours,* one of her first seven, all of which Harlequin published in the fourth year of the Presents series. Originally released in England as a hardcover, the text was untouched for its North American debut in paperback. From the title on, the spellings were anglicized (cars had "tyres," for example), and even the British-style single quotation marks around dialogue were left the same. But the setting is the Ozark hills of Arkansas, and the 19-year-old heroine, Tisha (or Red, as the hero prefers), drives a Mustang, pursues a career in art, knows her Shakespeare, and says things such as "Sometimes I wish I'd been born a man. . . . A woman is controlled by her parents until she marries. Then she's a slave to her husband's whim for the rest of her life. I think I hate all men. The way they've tried to convince us that they're so much better than women is sickening. We are the weaker sex because we were given less muscle and more brains. A woman can outwit a man any day." Except, perhaps, in the game of love. All her fiery words go up in smoke when Tisha is forced to marry the man she thinks she hates, gets carried off to their marriage bed supposedly against her will, and ends the book with nary a thought of any career but wife- and motherhood.

Janet Dailey was five years old, the youngest of four sisters, when her farming father died. She was a book-loving, bully-bashing tomboy growing up in the hamlet of Early, Iowa, until her mother married the supervisor of a mental health institution across the state in Independence. After high school, she took a secretarial course in the Omaha, Nebraska, area and went to work for a man she had met on the street who had a construction and land-development business with 100 employees. Bill Dailey also had a wife and two children. "Bill used to call me Sam," Janet Dailey once told a colleague of mine. "That was so he would think of me as one of the boys and we wouldn't fall in love." The ploy failed, and after what was apparently a less than bitter divorce, he married his young secretary one afternoon, after which they returned to work. She was five foot three, a brunette with green eyes and a great smile. Bill was no romance- novel hunk: well below six feet, weighing in at about 130, with glasses and a well-lined face. He had been a carnival barker and fire-eater and still had hearts and snakes inscribed on his arms from his time as a circus tattoo artist. She once described him to *Forbes* magazine as "blunt, adventurous and domineer- ing." But he was supportive of her wish to be a romance novelist, a wish nur- tured since the time she'd read her first Harlequin, Nerina Hilliard's 1969 *Dark Star*. Dailey's first, written over a year and a half, was *No Quarter Asked*, about a self-sufficient, virginal heroine and a gorgeous, imperious hero in an untamed slice of Texas. "I would still be agonizing over each word if Bill hadn't put his foot down and insisted that I send it off to a publisher."

A little naively, she sent it to a house that had never published an American romance author. "It took months for Mills & Boon to answer her," Larry Heisey says. After dithering, the Boons decided to attempt their first American romance. It appeared as a Harlequin Presents in January 1976. North American readers took immediately to Dailey's relatively independent-spirited heroines and their recognizable, if romanticized, surroundings. The novel, for which she got advance royalties of $12,000, attracted 1.5 million buyers. Fifty-six other books followed in that series, as Bill Dailey sold his business for $4 million – about what his wife would earn in the next four years – and they and their German Shepherd, Dreist (German for "bold"), traveled the states to background titles such as *Dakota Dreamin'* and *That Carolina Summer*. At times Janet turned out 7,500 words a day over eight arduous 12-hour days, always stopping on the 20th page, even in midsentence (so that "when I put in that first sheet in the typewriter the next morning, I already have something to type"). Her husband, meanwhile, was researching the local facts she needed to make the novels' settings sound authentic.

Dailey was learning the business as she went along. Editor in chief Fred Kerner tells the story of receiving one of her early novels from the Boons for publication in North America and discovering it wasn't even 160 pages, much less the 192 that Harlequin Presents required. When he called to tell her, she apparently said, "I didn't know that! England never tells me. What do I do?"

Kerner took the book home and then suggested a few places where she could expand it. He says she took his advice and remarked, "No one ever told me this before." Several years later, after she had been handled by other North American editors, Dailey would tell *Publishers Weekly*: "Let's be honest – there are some poorly written, grammatically incorrect, weakly plotted romances on the shelves. I don't blame the writers. Speaking from experience, a writer only learns, improves and grows if there is someone – an editor – telling or showing her what she did wrong and making her correct it."

Janet Dailey, closer at hand than the Mills & Boon authors, occasionally came up to Toronto with her husband to visit the Harlequin offices. The executives were always pleased to play the New World equivalent of the Boon brothers, romancing writers over tea and leisurely lunches. Larry Heisey recalls planning to take the Daileys to one of the city's poshest restaurants, Winston's, and finding Bill Dailey in a western jacket and tieless. Heisey had to borrow a tie from another executive and put it on his guest.

Dick Bellringer, who remembers Janet as "a beautiful lady, half Cherokee," got a call from her husband one day saying she was leaving for Simon & Schuster after the next two books. Bellringer flew down to see them and, over a three-hour dinner, convinced them to finish the 50-state series. But Dailey was wooed away from Harlequin by the beginning of the 1980s. Her departure prompted Larry Heisey's successor, David Galloway, to speak publicly about the hurt he felt. *His* successor, Brian Hickey, didn't let any lingering wounded pride get in the way of quiet discussions in 1995 to try to lure her into publishing with the company's new Mira mainstream imprint.

Dailey had long since graduated to bigger, more sensual and complex books, with subplots and many secondary characters – Pocket Books published her Calder series set in Montana, and Little, Brown published hardcover mainstream novels such as *Rivals* and *Masquerade*. Her editor at Simon & Schuster's Poseidon Books, Ann Patty, groomed her for the *New York Times* bestseller list, where Dailey regularly appears. The Daileys also got her one of the better agents in the business, Richard Curtis of New York. The author of about 50 books of nonfiction and fiction – including *Beyond the Bestseller*, now a standard text about the business of books – Curtis has been president of the Association of Authors' Representatives, an organization of 300 agents, and an informal advisor to the Romance Writers of America. His five-person agency handles up to $8 million a year for its authors, 15 percent of which it takes as commission. Among all his authors, including the 40 or so writing mostly mainstream romance novels, his star client is Janet Dailey.

Bill Dailey called him one day in the early 1980s, well after his wife had left Harlequin, saying they had heard about an article Curtis had written about publishers cheating writers out of royalties. "I don't know if you put your money where your mouth is," he told the agent, "but if you do, we'd like to talk to you about representing us." Curtis took her – them – as a client. "Bill still manages much of her career," he explained to me. Although her husband doesn't tour with her as much as before, "he's helped design her clothes, her image, her hair – he's an obviously great stylist – and he produces promotional material for her." Curtis moved her to Little, Brown, "a highly classy, old-line Boston publisher that was looking for a commercial author." Seven books there put Dailey on the bestseller lists, but he says diplomatically, "I think she's disappointed that they really couldn't put her on the list as high and as long as had been hoped." Recently he brought her to HarperCollins with a three-book contract worth $4 million, for which she wasn't asked to present even a word of outline.

Some claim that Dailey is now among the world's five most popular living authors. She, her husband, and their extended family have settled down in Branson, Missouri, a mountain town of 4,500 that attracts 5.5 million people a year as the capital of the country music that the Daileys love. Belle Rive, their 12,000-square-foot home, sits on a hill amid a 20-acre estate like an antebellum mansion out of one of her books – in fact, right out of *Masquerade*.

Janet Dailey, at 52 typically clad in blue jeans and cowboy boots, and writing of modern heroines who bed their lovers unblushingly in the reader's view, represents a contemporary reality of the romance writer as superstar. Barbara Cartland epitomizes an old-fashioned, popular image of the breed: at 95 she is costumed in pink coat and pink high heels, oozing with pearls, lavender makeup layered on her lashes, what looks like a white fright wig haloing her face, and she is still writing of historical heroines who remain unswervingly virginal until the book's sweet end.

The two do have things in common, even if the younger is as down-home as country singer Dolly Parton and the elder as caricatured a creation as T V drag queen Dame Edna – Cartland herself now being a real Dame Barbara, as Queen Elizabeth II dubbed her in 1991. Cartland has her own place in *Guinness,* as the world's bestselling author, with about 600 million copies of her books published. Obviously she can also compose as swiftly as Cupid's arrow, dictating to two of her three secretaries one full chapter in two hours a day, a complete novel in two weeks. Like Dailey, she has made romance writing a family business, employing one of her two sons, the never-married Glen McCorquodale, as a literary consultant and the other, the divorced Ian, as an agent/manager who also helps with her styling on the road (Ian doubles as chairman of *Debrett's Peerage and Baronetage*). Cartland, too, has a mansion, hers being the stately, four-century-old Camfield Place with a 500-acre farm in Hertfordshire; her extended family is Romany gypsies living at Barbaraville, an encampment that the large-hearted woman set up three decades ago so the gypsy children could legally attend school. And what's not commonly known is that Dailey and Cartland share a little history as well: Harlequin has published them both. Although corporate legend has it that Barbara Cartland was never a Harlequin author, her books did appear under the imprint during the 1980s in both Holland and West Germany.

Not that she needed any help: she has operated as an entity virtually coequal with the world's leading romance publisher. As 58-year-old son Ian told me one afternoon in New York, speaking as if she were General Motors rather than his mum, "There was only Mills & Boon and Barbara Cartland around. And Barbara Cartland was still writing the same book and was still just as popular as she used to be. Not so much, I have to think, in English-speaking parts, but in Europe she's still immensely popular, particularly in France and Germany, and now in the Far East. And of course in eastern Europe she's selling very well in Poland. The Czech Republic pretty good. Hungary, we've had a few problems there – difficult place. Russia has been very, very good. They have been publishing two books a month, printing and selling 120,000 copies of each book, which is not bad for the old books."

The old ones read much the same as the new, with sweet young things in love with titled or well-positioned chaps during Regency, Victorian, or Georgian times. Cartland appears the apotheosis of Prim. However, what critics overlook is that while her heroines must be fresh-snow pure before marriage, the bad girls in the books can occasionally be scandalous. As in this scene from *Stand and Deliver Your Heart* (1991):

> Her gown slithered down onto the floor.
> For a moment she just stood there naked and looking in the light of the candles like a statue of Aphrodite.
> Her skin was dazzlingly white and her necklace glistened iridescently.
> Then before the Earl could speak or move she flung herself against him.
> Her arms were round his neck, her lips on his and he felt the fiery passion of them seep through his body.

Cartland's son and I were chatting at the Rizzoli Bookstore in Manhattan, where his mother was signing copies of a book called *Apocalypse of the Heart*. She had dictated it, although the supposed author was Marcus Belfrey. Its launch, and the revelation that Belfrey was really Cartland, was the centerpiece of an elaborate promotion by MCI Telecommunications Corporation, the long-distance carrier and Internet data-communications provider. A series of its TV commercials and Internet ads had featured the soap opera shenanigans of the fictional Gramercy Press, publisher of *Apocalypse*, which was actually a nationwide release of Random House's Value Publishing imprint. Now the real-life author was meeting the press as MCI milked publicity from the ad campaign.

London Weekend Television, doing a Cartland documentary, was filming long-haired romance-cover model John D'Salvo as he tried to cream off some of the media attention. He presented her with a poster of himself as bare of chest as he was in person. Unrolling it, the image-conscious Cartland tsked: "Another naked man. I'm not going to be photographed with naked men." Rerolling it, she gave a little laugh and said: "Thank you very much."

Wheedling, D'Salvo protested, "I have my pants on. I just don't have my shirt on." Then he kissed her hand for the camera as she lectured him in her plummy, word-swallowing accent.

"Sex . . . nasty . . . love is completely out. . . . What we've got to try now is to get rid of all sex, sex, sex . . . everlasting sex." After he left, she continued to talk to me about the emphasis on sex: "It really is silly."

Failing of eyesight, plagued with arthritis, Barbara Cartland has endured on estrogen-replacement therapy for the last few decades, a diet heavily laced with honey and ginseng, and something called Flame vitamins for her complexion. She founded England's National Association for Health, which promotes alternative medicine and fronts for a health-food business with sales of about £650,000 a year. Cartland has outlived at least two husbands. Her first was Alexander McCorquodale, a former Highlanders officer with titled relatives, whose hand she accepted after 49 earlier proposals (of course, she has said that "I would not allow any young man to kiss me unless he had formally made me a proposal of marriage"). Their daughter's second marriage was to the eighth Earl Spencer, whose own daughter was to become the Princess of Wales, Lady Di. Barbara Cartland, after being divorced, married another McCorquodale with a Highlander background: Hugh, who fathered her two sons. A friend, *Romantic Times* publisher Kathryn Falk, believes she was married a third time, for only two years.

Falk tells the story of lunching at Claridge's in London with Cartland, who was touting her Flame vitamin pills by showing off the firmness of her flesh. "My breasts, they're so full I can nurse a baby."

"Barbara," Falk replied, "don't you think that would be the Immaculate Conception?"

Cartland went on to talk about her jewels, which she was about to sell at a Sotheby's auction: "I just don't wear them out anymore, people are always robbing them." Then, noticing her wristwatch was loose, she called over

Claridge's maître d' and asked: "Luigi, would you fix this? My lady's maid never does it properly."

Barbara Cartland's first novel appeared in 1923. Entitled *Jigsaw*, it has been described as "Mayfair with the lid off." As I write this (slowly), she continues to dictate a chapter a day of her outdated yet still curiously popular romances. As for her major corporate competitor, Harlequin, she has been gently dismissive: "Nice stories," she once told the *New York Times*. "But you get the feeling that their authors never experienced really passionate love. As I have."

The clichés about writers of romantic fiction are many, a predominant one being the belief that they are ill-educated secretaries or loveless spinsters who write to escape their humdrum lives. While some do spring from those backgrounds (Dailey was a secretary, though life with Bill was far from routine), others in fact have had careers that belie the myth (few, however, with biographies as sumptuous as Cartland's). The name that used to be trotted out as evidence of the rich life histories a romance writer can have was Ida Cook – the nom de plume of Mary Burchell – whose *Hospital Corridors* had been the first novel Harlequin bought from Mills & Boon under their agreement of 1957. Cook, who died in 1986, was an English civil-servant-turned-magazine-writer who so loved opera that she and her sister traveled the Continent and North America to see their favorite singers. Through their music contacts in the 1930s, the sisters almost casually began helping Jewish families to emigrate from a darkening Europe. They used Mary's romance earnings and their cover as ardent operagoers to keep revisiting Hitler's Germany and arrange to bring 29 Jews to London before World War II began.

Other Mills & Boon authors have been journalists (Sara Craven and Anne Weale), servicewomen (Rosamunde Pilcher, who was with the Wrens in Ceylon), and teachers (Anne Hampson and Sara Wood). In North America, a recent survey revealed that the most common previous occupation of romance writers was teaching, and I have met Harlequin writers who were once lawyers, successful businesswomen, and college grads with advanced degrees. However, a reality on both sides of the Atlantic is that a disproportionate number of the authors have been housewives and readers of romances who saw the writing of them as a possible part-time occupation they might squeeze in between husbands and children. Women such as Lancashire-born Mary Wibberley, who has written scores of M & B romances, the first at age 30 after telling herself, "Mary, you're a happily married wife and mother, but you're totally bovine, drifting around in a haze of gripe water and little bootees."

Another instance: half a century after Barbara Cartland's first novel, and three years before Janet Dailey's debut, Charlotte Lamb published her first Harlequin, *Follow a Stranger*. Lamb is Sheila Holland, the archetype of the bored, romance-loving English wife and mother who decides to write her own novel. Urged on by her journalist husband, she finished it in a mere three days and nights while her trio of toddlers fought and danced naked on the windowsill to a neighbor's disgust. To Holland's own disgust, her agent – picked randomly from a list by her husband – sent the book to a publisher other than Mills & Boon. The British house of Robert Hale paid her £120 and released it in 1970. M & B, whose books she had grown up with, published their first Lamb title three years later and more than 100 of her books since. From the first, the convent-educated author's subject matter was seldom tame: the 17-year-old heroine of *Forbidden Fire* falls for and marries her twice-as-old stepbrother; *The Long Surrender* may well have been the first M & B to feature a fully described female orgasm, not to mention a heroine's rape by her stepfather.

By 1978 Sheila Holland, realizing the British tax system would eat up her burgeoning profits, fled with her husband and three of their five children (she has since had twins) to the Isle of Man, a tax haven in the Irish Sea. A good move, since by some reports she was soon earning £250,000 and more a year. There the Hollands now have a 22-room Gothic stone mansion, Crogga, with stained-glass windows, oak fireplaces, and perhaps 20,000 books. The mother is big and round-faced and bespectacled. One of her three daughters, who is as shapely and vivacious as a Charlotte Lamb heroine, took up romance writing in 1980 at 18, after epilepsy shattered her acting dreams. When her mum criticized her first imitative attempt, Sarah Holland wrote a second novel in her own style, *Too Hot to Handle*, and sold it to Mills & Boon; three years later, the publisher's youngest author wrote six highly sensual books in a single year to earn more than £100,000 (the publishers, punning bilingually on her mother's pen name, privately refer to the daughter as Mouton Cadet.) She writes with much of her mother's speed, finishing a 55,000-worder in two weeks, and while realizing it's not high art, she takes it as seriously as her mother does when she writes. The Hollands reflect a theme I heard from many romance authors when Sarah says, "you must believe every single word."

Or at least suspend *dis*belief. An American named LeAnn Lemberger – pen name Leigh Michaels – is a Harlequin author who has thought hard about the genre. Describing the romance heroine, she says, "she has to be interesting and someone the reader can picture as her friend – not a plastic doll who's incapable of thinking for herself. She has to be like a real person – though perhaps not too real. Have you ever noticed that when a romance heroine is disappointed in love, she always stops eating and loses weight?"

Lemberger lives in Ottumwa, Iowa, the home state of Janet Dailey, another farm girl and the writer who inspired her. She wrote her first romance at 15 but didn't burn it until graduating from journalism at Iowa's Drake University in 1975. The next five novels also met the flames as she worked in radio and public relations and got married. With the last of them in ashes, she discovered Dailey's American stories and wrote one of her own, a sweet contemporary romance set in Iowa "with a different feel to it than anything else I'd ever done." Recalling the feeling as she wrote the final page, she says, "I was laughing and crying all at the same time – it was about two in the morning, and I had the typewriter balanced on the coffee table." She mailed it to Harlequin in Toronto, which sent it on to Mills & Boon. One of several thousand manuscripts that landed there each year, it was picked from the slush pile by an editor who wanted something to read on her tea break; four months later, Lemberger received two single-spaced pages of advice on rewriting the book. In 1984 Harlequin released the prophetically named *Kiss Yesterday Goodbye*. About 50 Leigh Michaels have since appeared, averaging about four a year, which has made her among the most published writers in the Romance and Presents lines. And on a day her success was toasted with champagne in the Palm Court at the London Ritz, she would have met Dame Barbara if only Cartland hadn't had a cold and stayed home at Camfield Place.

Nora Roberts also wanted to write for Harlequin, but the company rejected two of her novels during the early 1980s in letters that essentially said: "This manuscript shows promise, but we already have our American writer" – Janet Dailey. Silhouette, just created by Simon & Schuster and looking for home-grown authors, took her on instead. Roberts had started writing while stuck in a Maryland snowstorm with her two young sons. "Every morning the radio would come on and say there was no kindergarten. And I would cry. And I contemplated murder/suicide, but that didn't seem like the right thing to do, so I thought, *I will just take one of these stories out of my head and write it down.* That book was really terrible: it never got published. I piled every stock element of every category romance I'd ever read into that 55,000 words." Several other contenders were rejected before her first sale to Silhouette. Titled *Irish Romance,* the novel reflected the author's family heritage, itself mirrored in her fair complexion and long, curling red hair. Harlequin inherited her after buying Silhouette, and she still writes category romance for the company – as well as mysteries under the name J. D. Robb and fatter hardcover mainstream novels for other publishers, which keep appearing on bestseller lists. "Mainstream is the lights and costumes on a huge stage," she told me. "Category is Swan Lake in a phone booth." In March 1996, she marked the publication of her hundredth novel, a hardcover called *Montana Sky* published by G. P. Putnam's Sons; by then she had another 17 books waiting in the wings.

Her method of writing gives comfort, if not much guidance, to those hopefuls who come to hear her advice at seminars. "I don't have any plotting strategy," she tells them. "I don't outline, either, and Al [Zuckerman, founder of The Writers' House literary agency] is very big on outlines – Ken Follett [the thriller writer, another client] does 100-page outlines. I have a situation, and I have a cast of characters, which sometimes changes or evolves. I don't think I plot very well. My books are character-driven, and the plot just comes along with it. I *hope.* I don't know sitting there writing this paragraph what the next paragraph is going to be. Toward the end of the book, I hope to have a better idea, especially if it's a mystery, how I'm going to solve this crime. . . . I get the story down as quickly as I can, then I go back to page 1 and start fleshing out and filling in – and I go back to page 1 as many times as it takes." In summary, she says, "I don't have any training, and I don't have any answers."

Asked the inevitable question, usually from a wife and mother in the audience, she responds: "I write every day, six to eight hours a day. When my kids were little, I wrote when they were in school, so I got into the habit of working from about eight to four. Now I write more like nine to five because I work out for an hour in the morning [with a NordicTrack, weights, and her indoor pool]. And I cook dinner; I don't want anyone to forget that."

Pacing themselves physically as well as mentally like the professional Nora Roberts can be difficult for new writers, eager to build their reputations by producing as many books as possible in the shortest period. As an example, Laura DeVries of Grand Juncton, Colorado, wrote five Harlequin Intrigues in two and a half years, working so steadily on her computer that she got carpal tunnel syndrome, the painful wrist nerve condition. To prevent the strain of such repetitive stress injuries, Joe Schuler – the husband of another Harlequin regular, Candace Schuler – has been offering romance authors a technological innovation called the Handwriter. The $280 system includes a cordless pen and thin tablet matched with handwriting-recognition software that lets a writer compose on her computer without using its keyboard and mouse. The handwritten words appear on screen as ordinary type. Because the tablet is linked to the computer with a 10-foot cord, the writer can work in almost any position – perhaps even while jumping through hoops held up by finicky editors.

Mary Schaller of Burke, Virginia, might have found a Handwriter handy for her first romance novel, given the number of times she had to revise it and the number of hoops she had to leap through before getting it published as a Harlequin Historical. She had sore wrists and started taping them, and she had to stop writing for a month going into rewrites. Her heroine is a goddaughter of Queen Elizabeth I and the hero the court jester. Schaller, a Shakespeare buff who has written and directed scores of children's plays, is a Living History actress at the Folger Shakespeare Library in Washington, D.C. Working on her debut novel over 18 months, she spent 745 hours in front of the computer. The manuscript was rejected by eight agents and seven editors. She entered it in seven contests. She prayed for a year: "If it isn't too much trouble, I would dearly love to be published." And, she adds, "I also ate a lot of chocolate." The book that began as *Fool for Love* in July 1993 finally appeared as *Fool's Paradise* in March 1996 under her pseudonym Tori Phillips. She has recorded the long, soul-draining process, her biography of a novel, in a timeline that becomes a cautionary tale for the neophyte romance writer. It begins on July 4, 1993, "Outline story in longhand. Title *Fool for Love*," and is followed by a July-August entry, "Write 1st draft on PC."

Over the next couple of months, she wrote her second draft and shipped a partial manuscript to an agent she hoped would take her on as a client. She also sent a query letter and the first three chapters to Fawcett, Avon Books, and HarperPaperbacks. In early December, Avon was the first to send a rejection form letter. The agent then sent a checklist of suggestions and corrections, to which Schaller replied in mid-January 1994 with a revised third draft, retitled *Under the Greenwood Tree*. Meanwhile, the author was entering various contests.

> Feb. 6: Received personal rejection letter from HarperPaperbacks. "Not right for our list . . . lacks emotional depth." Also receive rejection letter from agent: says book is not sensual enough and characters need more heroic attitude.
>
> Feb. 7: Fired with righteous indignation, send query letter to NAL/Topaz.
>
> Feb. 9: Begin 4th draft.
>
> Feb. 18-28: NAL/Topaz requests complete manuscript. Commence to rewrite like crazy.
>
> March 1: Submit completed 4th draft to Topaz.
>
> April 26-May 2: *Romantic Times* convention in Nashville, TN. Learn the meaning of networking. Get names of agents and editors.

In May, while asking Fawcett and Topaz what they were doing with her manuscript, she queried Warner Books, St. Martin's Press, and Zebra Books. St. Martin's sent her a personal rejection letter, advising that her story was a "tough sell in today's romance market." She also received rejections from Topaz ("Good ear for clever dialogue . . . plot less complex than I would have liked") and Zebra ("Really enjoyed reading the partial but over-inventoried in historical romances"). Fawcett and Warner eventually declined with form letters.

The author was still seeking an agent. One recommended by another romance writer agreed to read her manuscript, liked it, and sent her an agent/author contract to consider. Meanwhile, Schaller had also sent copies to a list of five leading agencies suggested by *Romantic Times*. Over the next several weeks four declined to represent her; the fifth took seven months to respond.

> June 29: Finally sign contract with recommended agent. Wonder what have I just done? Feel relieved and terrified.
>
> Aug. 17: Agent sends note saying she has sent manuscript (4th draft version) to Harlequin Historicals. I try to forget about it.

Sept. 6: Got THE CALL from agent. Harlequin Historicals buys my book. Must cut 100 pages, retitle book [to *Fool's Paradise*] and change my name [to Tori Phillips]. Champagne flows for 48 hours in Burke, VA.

Sept. 9-11: Attend [Georgia Romance Writers'] Moonlight & Magnolias Convention in Atlanta. Meet my editor from Harlequin. . . . Win silver Maggie Award for best unpublished historical. Am an emotional basket case.

Sept. 12: Send letters to withdraw from Emerald City Opener, Silver Heart and Motherlode contests as am now accepted for publication.

Oct. 10: Motherlode Contest official requests that I do not withdraw as book is a finalist. Am stunned.

Oct. 14: Signed 15-page contract with Harlequin. Meanwhile editing manuscript like mad.

Oct. 24: Edited 5th (and final, hopefully) draft sent to Harlequin one week early. Collapse.

Nov. 16: First half of advance check arrives. We recarpet the downstairs.

Dec. 11: Winner of Motherlode 1st Chapter Contest. Can't believe this is happening to me.

Jan. 21: Second half of the advance arrives. Ordered the drapes.

Feb. 8: Editor calls: book gone into production three months early. In the hands of the copy editor. Tentative release date: March '96.

Released that month, *Fool's Paradise* was featured as The Book of the Moment on Harlequin's new home page on the Internet. "My husband really perked up when the first half of the advance check came," the author says. Mary Schaller's second book, *Silent Knight,* was scheduled as a Harlequin Historical for December 1996. On the sale of the first, she rewarded herself with champagne and more chocolates.

Other romance writers recompense themselves in various ways. For instance, Judith McNaught's bestseller earnings have bought her a burgundy Jaguar and a 5,000-square-foot house in a Houston suburb where she lives with her third husband, professional golfer Don Smith. She celebrates each book – even before she receives the check – by going out and buying a pricey piece of Baccarat or Steuben crystal.

At the Booklovers' Conventions, another predictable question concerns where romance writers find their inspiration. When posed by a woman who wants to write herself, the inquiry is a straightforward request for useful information. Heather Graham, who writes for Harlequin as Heather Graham Pozzessere and other houses as Shannon Drake, says she tries to keep fresh by switching between contemporary and historical novels. "And I'm very grateful: I have a huge family, and they're incredibly off the wall. It's like they're always giving me some grist for the mill. Your real-life world, the newspaper, everything going on around you just gives you so much for contemporary work. And then I absolutely *love* history." But when asked by a man, the same question about inspiration comes with a nudge and a wink – as in "you must have fun with your husband or lover researching the sex scenes." Heather Graham can offer public proof that collaboration can be fun: she and her hunk of a husband, Dennis, who helps with her research, have actually posed in historical costumes with full cleavage for photographs that became the covers of books: *Tomorrow the Glory* (Pinnacle, 1994), and *Blue Heaven, Black Night* (Zebra, 1995).

Husbands and wives also *write* romances together. There are a few couples in the Harlequin stable, including former lawyers Janice and Ronn Kaiser also known as Janice Kaiser, who have recently written *Private Sins* and *Fair Game* for the Mira imprint. She had already done more than 30 romances and romantic-suspense novels for Harlequin and Silhouette before he made her a team. And Anne and Ed Kolaczyk of Indiana, who call themselves Andrea Edwards, recently released a Silhouette Special Edition called *On a Mother's Day,* one of their 50 titles. Anne always writes the love scenes, for a very good reason: "The man wants to get to the destination the quickest way possible," Ed explains. "Women like the doing: men just want to get it done."

Harold Lowry – pen name Leigh Greenwood – is among the relatively few men who write romantic fiction on their own (others include Bob Rogers, who writes as Jean Barrett, and the veteran, bestselling Tom E. Huff, a six-foot Texan whose pseudonym is Jennifer Wilde). Married, with three children, Lowry taught music in schools for three decades before becoming a full-time romance writer in 1993. Publishing regularly with Leisure Books, he has to deal with the startled reactions to his chosen field. "A fan from Australia said she told a friend of hers that Leigh Greenwood is a man," he wrote recently in *Romantic Times.* "The first thing the woman said was, 'Is he gay?' And this from a romance reader! You can imagine how the guys at the local beer joint would react."

Marius Cippola was a male romance author who retired from the genre. Under the name Madeleine Ker, he did about 30 novels for Mills & Boon, including *The Wilder Shores of Love,* in which the heroine is addicted to, yes, heroin. A former academic whose thesis at Newcastle University was *Self-Knowledge in Shakespeare's Tragic Heroes,* Cippola thinks he knows women well enough to understand their love stories – as he told another Shakespeare, the novelist named Nicholas, "It concerns the fascination many women have of being physically attracted to someone who's totally unsuitable, either to reform him, or to discover he's not such a stinker. It's Don Giovanni. Women don't seem to be attracted to missionary types. Their sex symbol is Heathcliff. They want to have it both ways. They want to have a demon lover who turns out to be rather angelic."

Politically incorrect as that sounds, Cippola would have no argument from Jayne Ann Krentz, who, under several pseudonyms (Amanda Quick, Stephanie James, Jayne Castle), has written more than 50 series romances for various publishers, including Harlequin. In *Dangerous Men and Adventurous Women,* the intelligent, groundbreaking 1992 book in which romance writers analyze their craft, Krentz defends "the heroes who made Harlequin famous." She asks rhetorically, "Why did we dig in our heels and resist the effort to turn our hard-edged, dangerous heroes into sensitive, right-thinking modern males?" She replies that "in a romance the hero must play two roles. He is not only the hero, he is also the villain."

And from whom is Jayne Ann Krentz defending these alpha males? From "a wave of young editors fresh out of East Coast colleges who arrived in New York to take up their first positions in publishing." They tried to change romance novels, make them more politically correct, respectable – in a movement that she claims has ended in failure. But certainly not for want of the editors' trying.

The writers have felt confident enough to do battle – on this issue and in other arenas – with the editors who control their destinies. Suggesting that this confidence springs from special intrinsic qualities that women bring to their work, Nora Roberts argues, "Most romance writers, because they're women – and that's not a slap against men – are nurturers." In 1980 about 40 of them came together in Houston to form Romance Writers of America (RWA), a nurturing organization that would instill a degree of professionalism the envy of other writers' groups. Two decades earlier, Mills & Boon authors Denise Robins and Vivian Stuart had organized Britain's similarly inclined Romantic Novelists Association, whose long-term president was Ida Cook (Mary Burchell). Early personality clashes there gave way to a solid support network, a model for the American organization. And despite its own continuing internecine skirmishes, the RWA in years to come would do battle with many editors and the publishing houses that employed them. Among its principal targets would be Harlequin Enterprises. An irony is that it was an editor who founded the organization: Vivian Stephens, one of the few black women in the industry at the time, who later became senior editor of Harlequin American Romances.

The featured speaker at the RWA's inaugural meeting was the writer who had introduced American sensibilities to Harlequin's Commonwealth-conceived romances and who was leaving the Canadian publisher for its feisty new U.S. rival. The Iowa farm girl who became one of the world's most popular authors and was proud to say, "I was a romance writer before it was cool to be a romance writer": Janet Dailey.

Half a heart never won a damned thing. Life is not a gar-
den, it's a crucible. What is it that moves men, for God's
sake? Fun? Frolic? Mark, let me tell you, the good life is the
challenged life, not the easy life.
> – Action-adventure writer Don Pendleton, to
> Harlequin editor Mark Howell

8

Strange Bedpersons
OTHER VENTURES

It was, by all accounts – including the federal judge's – an amusing trial. The
witnesses were writers and editors, publishers and pollsters, even professors of
literature. They were testifying with at least a semblance of a straight face about
a fictional creation called The Executioner who had been single-handedly
slaughtering the Mafia for nearly two decades. Mack Bolan is the kind of hero
who totes a short-barreled Colt Commando and says, "Puke it out of your system, soldier, and then get back out there and *fight!*" The defendants in the case
were Warner Books, the Scott Meredith Literary Agency of New York, and the
character's creator, Don Pendleton of Los Angeles. The plaintiff was Harlequin
Enterprises.

How Harlequin the happy-ending publisher came to own The Executioner
line of men's action-adventure novels – and to sue the former author whose
name still appeared on the series – had its beginning 18 years earlier. Pendleton
was a jut-jawed, well-lined veteran of the American antisubmarine service in
World War II who had later worked as an aerospace engineer in the rocket
program while moonlighting as a pulp novelist. In 1968, when Pinnacle Books
of New York asked him to create a protagonist for a new paperback imprint,

he conceived Bolan: a Vietnam vet, a one-man army using paramilitary tactics and weapons to conduct a personal vendetta against Mob rule. The character first appeared the following year in *The Executioner: War Against the Mafia*. Through the 1970s, he blasted a bloody path across the pages of 37 more books and became the most popular series character of the decade in North America. Many of them were set in different states, as Janet Dailey had done with her romances. He also infused them with subliminal metaphysical messages: "Warm sties and safe stables were no place to live the worthy life. There was no cosmic sprawl in such places, no magic worth pursuing."

The Executioner prompted a raft of imitators, including Dell's The Assassin, Lancer's The Enforcer, and a half dozen in Pinnacle's own stable, most notably The Destroyer. But in 1973, Pendleton left the original publisher for New American Library, bringing his creation along. Pinnacle, which had copyrighted the books and claimed to have created the name, sued the writer. Pendleton sued back. In the out-of-court settlement, he received a $250,000 advance for several forthcoming books as well as copyrights to the first 15 in the series and each new one – all to be published by Pinnacle. NAL got nothing.

By 1978 Larry Heisey and his executives were trying to build the value of Harlequin and fatten the coming payoff of their earn-out formula from Torstar. With $16 million in cash and short-term securities to play with, they had the company in a full-tilt expansionary mode. Along with setting up the European divisions, they had embarked on a buying spree in 1977. They acquired Ideals Publishing of Milwaukee, Wisconsin, which produced the treacly inspirational magazine *Ideals* and similarly sappy books as well as cookbooks and greeting cards. They bought one book-packaging company in Canada and started another in London. A year later, Harlequin had 78 percent of The Laufer Company of Los Angeles, publishers of teenage, black-audience, and Hollywood-gossip magazines, and created another magazine division that started a women's monthly in Texas. In its basic paperback business, the company had already launched and killed a science fiction series, Laser, and in 1979 it was planning a romantic suspense line, Mystique, and a mystery imprint, Raven House. So why not try to duplicate the success Harlequin had experienced for so long in publishing romances for women by marketing a line of action-adventure paperbacks for men?

Why not indeed? In 1978 Harlequin quietly proposed buying Pinnacle, now based in Los Angeles, from Michigan General Corporation, a multi-industry company. Before the deal could go through, the U.S. Department of Justice announced that it would challenge the acquisition on antitrust grounds. Concerned with concentration in the mass-paperback industry, Justice officials pointed out that Harlequin already had total rack space of 8.2 percent in the United States while Pinnacle had three percent. "Shocked and surprised," the Canadian company withdrew its offer to buy in February 1979. Instead, Fred Kerner hired Pinnacle's former executive editor, Evelyn Grippo, as Harlequin's West Coast editor. *Quill & Quire,* the journal of the Canadian book trade, called it "a curious appointment considering the firm doesn't have any western book headquarters." That soon changed when she began working under the new editorial director of the new West Coast operations, Andrew Ettinger – none other than the editor who had helped Don Pendleton to develop The Executioner as a series. In 1980 Pendleton was in ill health, and with Ettinger's encouragement, agreed to sell Harlequin the rights to his character, along with his consulting services to a team of virtually anonymous writers who would continue the series under his name. Pinnacle – piqued – again sued, but this time steered clear of the tough-minded writer and went after his literary agency, Scott Meredith, as well as Harlequin and Ettinger. It asked $24 million in damages for their allegedly inducing Pendleton to breach his contract. Once the dust had cleared, Pinnacle settled for having the rights to reissue the old titles and capitalize on its competitor's new advertising campaign.

Harlequin's executives had fallen over themselves to lock in the rights. Dick Bellringer at first was ready to offer Pendleton $500,000. Lou Krupat, now vice president of finance and administration in the book division, said they could probably get him for $400,000. Finally, during the negotiations, an impatient Bellringer volunteered aloud: "We'll give you $200,000 a year for the rest of your life." The deal was based on royalties of two cents a book, but with the guarantee of $200,000. Fred Kerner, knowing writers, felt that if they had let Pendleton name his own price, he might have suggested as little as $50,000: "He never earned out $200,000 a year on royalties. I don't think we ever reached $80,000 a year." As the federal judge was later to remark wryly, "their projections proved overly optimistic."

The only kicker in the deal for Don Pendleton was that he couldn't write a competing series for another publisher. As agent Jack Scovil of Scott

Meredith worded it for him in the contract, "Notwithstanding anything to the contrary in the provisions of Paragraphs 6 and 7 hereof, Pendleton reserves the right to create and/or write works for others, other than works which would compete with the sale of the action-adventure series contemplated in this agreement. . . ."

All proceeded apace for five years. Harlequin begat a Gold Eagle imprint for action-adventure, and the star attraction was The Executioner, who was now fighting international terrorists: "Fed up with America held hostage by the world's crazies? Then set your sights . . . and let Gold Eagle pull the trigger." By now the company had hired Mark Howell in Los Angeles. He was a fair-haired, Cambridge-educated Welshman who had worked in London with the publishing firm The New English Library. The effervescent Howell's mission was to oversee the series and a team of ghostwriters he gathered to maintain it, while liaising with Pendleton. His base was the old Hollywood Athletic Club on Sunset Boulevard. The Executioner's creator had his own dressing room-turned-office there, still bearing Johnny Weissmuller's name on the door. When he wandered in occasionally, he might lecture Howell on how the books should be written – "No more flabby, undirected, unstructured, incoherent thinking! My books do not talk, they *move!*" – help to edit early manuscripts, and write some prologues. But eventually he wasn't much of a presence in the creative process.

Howell found the perfect lead writer for the series in the giant-sized G. H. Frost, whose other job was projectionist in a grotty East Hollywood theater. He took him up to Toronto to concoct a standard-setting Super Executioner in eight days of frantic writing. Mack Bolan, now battling terrorists around the world, became the market-share leader, and Howell became Gold Eagle's editorial director at head office. There he met and married another editor working on the new mystery line, Barbara Gowdy (who would end her relationship with both Howell and Harlequin and become one of Canada's most promising young novelists, a nominee for a Governor General's Literary Award for *Mister Sandman*). Gold Eagle spun off two series, Able Team and Phoenix Force, while the Mack Bolan books continued selling steadily at about a million copies a year.

Then, in 1985, Don Pendleton, healthier and about to remarry, decided to resume writing. As the judge would remark, "his creative urges had again come to life." One creation was *Ashes to Ashes,* the first novel in a series featuring Ashton Ford, Mystic Eye, a detective with psychic powers. Warner Books signed Pendleton to a six-book contract and, oblivious of the author's deal with Harlequin, promoted the debut novel with a cover blurb that trumpeted: "Creator of THE EXECUTIONER – the 57,000,000-copy series."

Whoops.

The subsequent trial was to determine whether Pendleton had indeed contravened the noncompete clause of his contract with Harlequin. Within the company itself, there was no unanimity on the subject. As Fred Kerner remembers it, Harlequin wanted him to testify on the company's behalf. Its American lawyer handed him a copy of Pendleton's first Ashton Ford book and told him to read it. He says that after first refusing, "I read the book, and they said, 'What do you think?' I said, 'There's no competition at all. I told you why I shouldn't read the book.' I was fearful because Don and I had had a long conversation about what he wanted to do, and it didn't bother me in the least. It was a whole new area, and it may work or it may not work, but it didn't conflict with Bolan at all. So I never testified."

Mark Howell also had his doubts about Harlequin's case: "It all depended on proving that Warner's series was indeed action-adventure like The Executioner, when its actual premise about a young detective who has psychic powers seemed to borrow more from the mystery category, or even occult. But Harlequin was my employer, so when all was said and done, I had no choice but to be on their side." In fact, as the judgment would note, Pendleton's agent belatedly offered the series to Harlequin's Gold Eagle line. "Harlequin's editors thought it flawed as action-adventure because of its occult aspects. Instead, they considered it a detective thriller series and rejected it."

The six-day trial was held in the U.S. District Court in Manhattan before Judge Gerard L. Goettel, who was tickled to be adjudicating a quasi-literary case. Married to a novelist, the learned justice was not above mentioning an earlier warrior-hero, the eighth-century paladin eulogized in the *Song of Roland.* Howell testified before him for two and a half days on niceties of language such as the meaning of "nightscorcher," which he said was "a made-up word and must be taken metaphorically. It's like calling the bad guys 'slime buckets.' We don't literally mean they are bucket-shaped, but there are references in the compound word that colorfully describe what you're after." At

Strange bedfellows for a romance publisher indeed: the Japanese launch of Mack Bolan. HARLEQUIN ENTERPRISES

another point, Howell claimed there were only two major branches of fiction: adventure and romance.

Although other editors spoke on the question of reader appeal, and the expert witnesses included publishers and writers, not to mention pollsters and literature professors – much of which caused Pendleton merriment – Judge Goettel found their testimony "contradictory and inconclusive." He would have to decide himself whether the books attracted similar readerships and so could be considered competitive.

His judgment, when it came in the summer of 1986, was in the whimsical form of a mininovel. It opened with epigraphs: "Truth fears no trial" (Thomas Fuller, 17th-century English clergyman), and "Every man stands trial for his actions at one time or another. I have no fear of universal judgment or the verdict that must, inevitably, be handed down" (Mack Bolan, nightscorcher). In a prologue and the first two chapters, Judge Goettel recounted the background to the case. Chapter 3 discussed the trial testimony: the fact that a witness had described the Ashton Ford character as "a California Woody Allen," that he indulged in graphic sex but not flagrant violence, that he was psychically gifted. All in all, the judge reasoned, "the majority of Mack Bolan fans will not find Ashton Ford to be their sort of hero," and "Harlequin bought Pendleton's characters – it did not buy his writing abilities."

Nor did he find that either Pendleton or his agent had any say in Warner's unnecessary trading on the success of Bolan and The Executioner series. In his epilogue, Judge Goettel dismissed Harlequin's claims. The author was free to keep publishing the exploits of his psychic hero. Meanwhile, The Executioner's begetter had made a counterclaim disputing the company's right to use the line "Don Pendleton's Mack Bolan" on the covers of books others had written. The judge rejected his argument: by allowing his name to be used repeatedly over the years, "he does not have the clean hands required of someone seeking such equitable relief." But Pendleton walked away tall, with justice on his side, having bloodied the big Canadian corporation, which had to continue paying him $200,000 a year for not writing The Executioner series – for life.

Don Pendleton died of a heart attack in 1995. He was living in the New Age capital of Sedona, Arizona. Prolific as ever, he had continued the Ashton Ford series and had a new one on the go starring a private investigator named Joe Copp involved in just as much mayhem as Mack Bolan. As *Publishers Weekly* said of *Copp in Shock*, "if his tale isn't very deep ('There are a lot of badass people out on the streets – anywhere, everywhere'), it's still rollicking fun."

Meanwhile, Mark Howell's career path at Harlequin had reached its nadir. During the trial, Pendleton's lawyers had played tapes of phone conversations between author and editor. As Howell recalls, "I had rattled on to Don about the corporate types at Harlequin who were driving me just as bananas as the authors were. I named names and wickedly caricatured my colleagues at work for his amusement. All this was played loud and clear to the Toronto executives assembled in the courtroom."

Howell was relieved of his duties in early 1987. A couple of years later he surfaced briefly as a partner in Palace Books, a packager of an anti-Harlequin series of "adultery romances" or "empowerments." HarperCollins published a handful of them to help launch its paperback line. Their unhappily married heroines have affairs with men who are wrong for them, but with whom they have great sex that opens them up to the eventual men of their dreams.

Although Harlequin's male action-adventure line has never performed up to the original expectations, it has at least survived. Not so Laser Books, the ill-starred science fiction imprint that the company started in 1975. Its life span was about as brief and had about as much lasting impact as a comet streaking across the sky. Barrie Hale, a writer with a national magazine, *The Canadian,* for whom I was working at the time, wrote of the optimism the company was feeling: "This fall, Harlequin is bringing all this marketing expertise to bear on the science-fiction field with a new series of books called Lasers, to be just like Harlequins in their strong series continuity, their product identifiability, and, they hope, their addictive properties." Laser was considered a test run that, if successful, would encourage the company to expand into every genre of fiction with similar marketing approaches.

It hired an American, Roger Elwood, as series editor and Kelly Freas as designer. Both had some presence in their field, Elwood as a writer and anthologizer of science fiction short stories, and Freas as a great illustrator of s f subjects. But as it turned out, Elwood was young and inexperienced as an editor of full-length original manuscripts, and the design of the books around the artist's work was unsophisticated. "They had a great artist in Freas, and the package was amateurish," says Fred Kerner, now distancing himself from the project even though he was editor in chief. "The science fiction reader is not a jerk, he's a thinker, and doesn't want to be seen carrying something that looks like a kid's book." The editing was another problem. Larry Heisey says, "There were sufficient errors – typos – in the first book we used as a sample to cause my head to hang in shame. A woman in the business, Ian Ballantine's wife [of Bantam Books], knew a lot about science fiction, and she went through it and just noted the mistakes."

That first sample book, *Seeds of Change* by Thomas F. Monteleone, was used as an incentive to readers who bought one of the first six Laser titles and returned a questionnaire. Most of the 58 novels were by first- or second-time writers or veterans who hadn't been published recently. Despite an extensive publicity campaign and ads in genre magazines and book-trade journals, they sold no more than 30,000 copies a title, compared with more than 10 times that for a romance novel. When nothing seemed to be working, and after changing the cover design and firing Elwood as editor, Harlequin quietly killed Laser, for a loss of at least $1 million. Kerner says today the company was too hasty: "They forgot that it took years to build Harlequin romances into a line."

An experienced s F editor, Donald Woolheim, attributed the failure to "a complete misunderstanding of the special appeal of science fiction and the nature of its addictive readers. Nobody 'in the know' ever believed this venture would succeed." Perhaps the most devastating critique came from an Ottawa public relations manager who taught a course on science fiction in the media at the University of Ottawa. In an article read by a Canadian business audience in *The Financial Post*, Brian M. Fraser argued that the publisher had underestimated the intelligence of the s F fan, who seeks nonformula fiction. "But perhaps Harlequin could not overcome its image of selling packaged goods, a completely standardized product from cover design to contents. In this respect, if it had labeled the series 'juvenile science fiction' right from the start, it might have made a difference."

During the next decade Harlequin had another run at the genre with an imprint called Isaac Asimov Presents, which showcased new writers under the name of the prolific American science fiction author. The series' life was even shorter than Laser's.

In spite of their disappointing experience with Laser Books, Larry Heisey and his colleagues were still hungry to broaden their base from pure romances. For instance, Dick Bellringer met with Louis L'Amour, the hugely prolific author of westerns such as *Hondo* and *Flint*, with the idea of turning his books into a series. Aptly named as he was for a partnership with a romance publisher, L'Amour declined.

Harlequin tried a field closer to its heart with the Mystique series released in 1978 under a new imprint, Worldwide Books. These were the romantic suspense novels acquired from Maurice Dumoncel of France's Tallandier house – translated, at times rewritten, and packaged with titles such as *Strange Encounter* and *Cruise of the Sphinx.* Heisey picks up the story: "When we had this wonderful machine, we wanted to put more books through it. Once you have the mechanism everywhere in the world, if you can publish more of them, you should escalate. One of the few sources of a lot of books that had some kinship to each other was the Tallandier list in Paris, which had been successfully published in France. They certainly didn't have the continuity and evenness of our books. Dumoncel identified about 20 authors who had a big backlist. We gave him a million dollars to tie up those rights for some brief period of time, and he told me that he gave most of that money to the authors. We published them in German and English, tested them in North America, called them Mystique – and I had to push people to do that. No one had given a strong green light to the editorial. I read a couple of the books and actually enjoyed them. My lips didn't move when I read them. . . . But it didn't work."

Harlequin had not gone into a romantic suspense line blindly. Its research indicated that 63 percent of women preferred the category and that, between them, the separate romance and suspense markets totaled 51 percent of all paperback volume. Mystique was introduced in North America with a $1.3 million campaign, spent mostly on 30-second network T V commercials along with an extensive sampling program and in-store displays built around an Eiffel Tower logo. One Compton-created commercial showed hero and heroine necking in a Venetian gondola as the voice-over intoned: "A couple that met by chance in one of the world's most romantic places. They shared each other's lives and love. Now they are going to share something new: danger." It wasn't enough. Again, as with the science fiction, the marketing people – among them Dave Sanderson and product manager Jay Whiteside – were trying to sell the line like Harlequins, with its own series name and imprint. But they weren't spending enough to justify print runs of up to 200,000 books. Larry Heisey says, "I would think between the million-dollar advance and all the money we put into the various countries, we must have spent $5 million over several years on that project." Not an insignificant loss, but because Harlequin was growing so big, so fast, and the annual report figures looked so buoyant, stockholders failed to notice or comment on it.

Nor did the board of directors or investors get upset at senior management's decision to enter the mystery novel field in 1979. While two attempts at competing in new markets had now failed, nobody with enough clout at the top stopped the marketing-driven mania to repeat the Harlequin success in spite of apparent differences in audiences. Originally to be called Keyhole

Books, the new line became Raven House Mysteries (after Poe's menacing bird). It appeared as numbered, standardized, unattractive, yellow-covered paperbacks in the fall of 1981. The editors, however, had begun acquiring manuscripts two years before with the idea of a launch in 1980. The delay was a symptom of several problems that should have triggered warning bells in high places but didn't.

The first editor on board was Helen Heller, recently arrived in Toronto. An Englishwoman who had worked for the London publisher Cassell, she had barely heard of Mills & Boon but was a passionate reader of mysteries, of which she had about 14,000. Heller, now a successful Canadian literary agent with a reputation for tenaciousness, was blunt-spoken even then. From the first, she wondered at the rationale behind the marketing of Raven House: "To me a mystery stands by itself, and a series is by one author. To do a series by generic line was a little odd. Mystery readers aren't romance readers – and I told them that, but they kept shitting on me." She was in place as an assistant editor when her boss, senior editor Walter Exman, came to Harlequin from Stein & Day in New York. "I don't think any of us had any hopes at all," she says. "We'd all come from a different mind-set, from trade publishing, and we were hitting our heads against this monolithic organization." Wally Exman, though he was known to take a drink, had a good reputation as an editor and impressed Heller. However, she says, he resented her, particularly when she mentioned her heretical opinions even casually, over coffee, to the marketing people: "I stopped saying anything."

But she did have the power to reject the bad manuscripts that flooded in. "Agents and authors simply believed that Raven House was an ideal dumping ground for trunk manuscripts, failed proposals, and any old shlock that they happened to have lying around," she wrote later for mystery fans in a perceptive autopsy in *The Armchair Detective*. Although the quality of those manuscripts improved – "we got some reasonable ones, nothing very good," Heller told me – and the editors found pleasant surprises in the slush pile, they had to deal with an equally disturbing problem: Harlequin's marketing department. The marketing personnel overseeing Raven House kept changing, each of them trying to put his or her stamp on it, which led to delays. "They said our research shows people will look at a yellow cover," and she thought, *Yeah, but then they'll run a mile.* When she was proved right, the covers changed to black with white type.

Deciding to read the mysteries to understand the product, "the marketers turned overnight into editors, and the editorial department was inundated with unignorable 'suggestions' from the boys upstairs." Among them were demands for longer, less violent books, more in the Agatha Christie mode, which led to "a preponderance of overromantic stories with rather silly heroines."

The books sold about the same numbers as Laser science fiction had, 30,000 copies or fewer, with returns of 70 percent and more. Harlequin withdrew the line in July 1982, less than a year after its launch. Editor in chief Fred Kerner, who had also disapproved of the marketing approach to Raven House, says that years later he met one of the marketers involved, Paul Clark (now vice president of marketing for TSN, The Sports Network). He quotes Clark as saying, "I have to tell you that when you criticized the marketing group for not going with what the books were, you were right, and we were wrong. I see it now."

There was a parallel to this debacle in England, where, at about the same time, Mills & Boon was using Keyhole Crime as the name of its mystery imprint. As John Boon sums it up, "it was a good idea really, but we did it the wrong way." A major publicity campaign cost M&B "more than a million quid," and when sales failed to meet forecasts within a couple of years, it killed the line. "We should have given it three years," Boon says now, but he adds, "I'm not sure that with crime readers you get the obsessive reading you get with romance." (However, Harlequin did try again with the 1988 launch of a series of reprints by well-established mystery writers under the Worldwide Library imprint – to moderate success.)

By now Harlequin had two other book divisions. Jonathan-James Books, acquired from a former Harlequin publicist, Allan Stormont, was its entry into the international book-packaging market, creating books on a presold basis for other publishers (the first was *Kain and Augustyn,* a handsome volume about the National Ballet of Canada stars). When it proved unprofitable, Jonathan-James was phased out in 1981. A more rewarding venture in this field of coedition publishing was a start-up by Bruce Marshall, a friend of Fred Kerner, who had run book divisions for Reader's Digest in London and New York. With Harlequin financing his line of credit – which he exceeded before becoming profitable in about five years – he established Marshall Editions on his home turf of London. Its first three nonfictional offerings were typical of the high-quality coffee table and informational books that Marshall would produce: *The Great Chefs of France, The Flier's Handbook* (for air travelers), and *The Hunters* (about predatory animals). Marshall Editions is still packaging about 20 titles a year for publishers as prominent as the Digest. Many have been million-sellers, among them *The 35mm Photographer's Handbook,* released in nine languages. "We're not incredibly profitable," Bruce Marshall says of the wholly owned Harlequin subsidiary, "but they take pride in the prestigious things we do."

At the time, magazines also seemed a logical extension of Harlequin's publishing business. On the surface, the 1977 acquisition of Milwaukee-based Ideals Publishing Inc. must have made sense. "Did you ever see an Ideals publication?" Larry Heisey asks. "Filled with love, the kind of thing you'd think a Harlequin reader might enjoy. Wrong. There are not as many of *them* as there are the Harlequin readers, and not all Harlequin readers like that. If we'd taken more time and actually compared and did some consumer research, we might not have bought it. But it just seemed that they had some skills that were worth exploiting and we had some. I'm not ashamed of that deal. It seemed like a very good fit." Harlequin paid about $2 million for the small, privately held firm that published the bimonthly magazine *Ideals,* abrim with inspirational words and pretty pictures, and like-minded books, cookbooks, and greeting cards. To run it, Heisey hired a 35-year-old American, William (Josh) Gaspero, as president and C E O. Josh Gaspero was a U.S. Peace Corps alumnus from Philadelphia who had worked in marketing for Hershey Foods and Western Publishing of Wisconsin, which produces the evergreen children's series of Golden Books. In his 11 months at Western, he claims, sales doubled to about $10 million. After he left to take over Harlequin's one-year-old magazine division, Ideals was resold following five years of generally unexciting results.

Harlequin was pursuing a different strategy in buying the Laufer Group, the California magazine publisher, in 1978. Charles and Ira Laufer had a stable of teen- and adult-entertainment publications that derived most of its revenue from circulation. The book publisher, although buying at a peak price, felt there was potential for growth in an area that its other properties had no way of tapping: advertising. The major magazines were the *Tiger Beat* group featuring the idols of 10- to 14-year-olds and *Rona Barrett's Hollywood* capitalizing on the gossip columnist's name to spotlight film and television stars. When in-house management failed to produce results, Larry Heisey and Bill Willson (now an executive vice president, as was Dick Bellringer) looked south for experienced magazine management. They went after Carlo Vittorini, a tall, 49-year-old Italian American who had been with *Look* and *The Saturday Evening Post* before becoming president of Charter Publishing Company of New York, whose several magazines included *Sport* and *Redbook*. "They hadn't given it the due diligence they should have," Vittorini says of Harlequin's handling of the Laufer publications. "They found themselves with heavy returns and receivables. They'd made a $13 to $14 million investment and expected a 13 percent return. Instead, they were in the red."

Heading the new Harlequin Magazines Inc. (N Y), he moved swiftly, starting *Texas Woman,* a lifestyle monthly sold on newsstands for a year before it folded, and buying for a few thousand dollars, 57 percent of a Toronto company publishing *Photo Life*; 49.5 percent of *ARTnews* (reflecting Larry Heisey's interests); and 100 percent of *Antiques World*, both New York-based magazines. Harlequin was also publishing *Snow Goer,* a snowmobile magazine, under license from its American owner. The one truly profitable deal was a joint venture with the publishers of *American Baby* to publish *Weight Watchers Magazine* for Weight Watchers International, an existing publication that they turned around, making as much as $400,000 a year in profit. Vittorini left after 18 months, before the company got out of the magazine business over the next few years, to become publisher of Si Newhouse's *Parade Magazine.* Josh Gaspero took over from Vittorini as president of the magazine division and as a Harlequin vice president, trying to stanch the hemorrhaging at most of the magazines. Meanwhile, Harlequin had the management consultants McKinsey and Company study the organization, and McKinsey concluded that the publisher should stick to what it did best: books. With that advice, combined with the drive for consolidation that was soon to overcome any passion for diversification, nobody had the enthusiasm to stay in the magazine business. The partners in the one lucrative publication, *Weight Watchers Magazine,* withdrew from their association with Harlequin. "The decision was taken: why waste capital and energy on magazines?" says Gaspero, who had already moved on to become president of Harlequin's North American book division. Phil Whalen, Vittorini's financial assistant and Gaspero's successor at the magazine division, bought the remaining publications.

No matter which other enthusiasms ebbed and flowed, from early on there was the lure of Hollywood, of transferring the hoard of Harlequins to movies and television and, eventually, video. Harlequin's feature film debut was *Leopard in the Snow*, based on Anne Mather's bestselling romance, but it was a dog on the screen. Critics universally panned the $1.3 million movie, which surfaced in 1978 with unstars Keir Dullea and Susan Penhaligon, and the dismal box office returns sent the company again scurrying back to its expertise in print.

In spite of himself, Larry Heisey had been seduced by the prospect of Harlequins on film. "I feel that the books are so internalized. It's a private act, reading, and what fantasies you bring to it yourself and how you embellish what you're reading is a very private matter. But there's been lots of romantic films that have [succeeded] – George Cukor's *An Affair to Remember* – and I felt that if anyone could figure out what we did, and did it, then they might take our business away from us. So we had to try and find out. . . . We got the best we could organize to put that movie together – and it wasn't good enough. The production values were good, but the emotional content wasn't there."

Nor, as it turned out, were the audiences. It had all begun optimistically, with the company deciding to be the first Canadian publisher to become a movie producer. An Anglo-Canadian venture, *Leopard* was coproduced by 31-year-old investment counselor Christopher Harrop of Toronto, who spent half a year on the road selling distribution rights in a dozen countries. Shot in Ontario and England, the low-budget production had problems from the first day, when Peggy the trained leopard of the title shredded Keir Dullea's parka; from then on, the actor demanded a stand-in for animal scenes. The feature premiered in Manitoba, the province where Harlequin was born and still had some of its most loyal readers. The producers decided to "four-wall" the film in small towns throughout Canada: sell it with saturation TV and radio spots targeted at specific markets and then rent whole theaters and retain all box office receipts. The idea behind the technique is to move quickly through a region before filmgoers have a chance to advise their friends that a movie is dreadful. As the critics were soon doing. A typical review appeared in *Maclean's*: "The script itself is a collection of one-line clichés. . . . The acting by 42-year-old Keir Dullea and British actress Susan Penhaligon has the resilience of petrified wood."

The movie reputedly made back its investment but little more. Harlequin's plans for two more features hard on *Leopard*'s heels, and perhaps a television series, came to naught – as did its hope of becoming to women's film what the Disney name is to children's. It was, however, The Hope That Would Not Die: many years later, it would resurface to tantalize a new crop of expectant company executives.

Halfway through the 1970s, the president of Harlequin produced a classic Heisey quotation expressing his boundless expectations for the company. "I feel like it's 1880 in Atlanta, Georgia," Larry Heisey told Barrie Hale of *The Canadian,* "and I have just been approached on the sidewalk by this local pharmacist. He says to me, 'I have this wonderful drink that I make at my soda fountain. *Everybody* seems to like it, young kids, older adults. I call it Coca-Cola. . . . I wonder what I should do with it?'"

Unfortunately by decade's end, many of the ambitious things Heisey and his colleagues had done with Harlequin had gone flat. One of the few exceptions was romance publishing, which they had expanded in 1978 with a series of one-a-month historical novels in North America and two a month in Britain. But during the 1980s, as they overreached themselves again, their core business would also begin to lose its fizz.

We knew how to distribute these books, and Harlequin didn't.
  – Dick Snyder, chairman and CEO of Simon & Schuster

This is war.
  – Attributed to Dick Snyder, *Publishers Weekly*

War of Love

9

SILHOUETTE VERSUS HARLEQUIN

If Larry Heisey were to write a book about his career with Harlequin, he would end the story in 1980. In fact, that was the instruction he gave to a Toronto writer he commissioned three years ago to recount his authorized version of the corporate history, a project that – for various reasons, including the existence of this unauthorized book – was never completed. The cutoff date he proposed is perfectly understandable given the tumultuous years that were to follow it and the events that would unalterably change Harlequin from an entrepreneurial, expanding enterprise at the summit of its industry to a cautious corporate subsidiary besieged by competition, bleeding tens of millions of dollars, and being forced to dismiss more than 100 employees. Heisey would have to call in reinforcements to help him run the company – David Galloway and Brian Hickey – and, in doing so, he would be removed from much of the day-to-day drama on which he had feasted throughout the previous decade. Even his earnout from Torstar was a double-edged sword: although he profited handsomely, he would no longer have any ownership position in the publishing house when the parent company exercised its option to take 100 percent control. And in the battering Harlequin then sustained, the fun that defined his job was to disappear

153

like an ice-cold Coke on a scorching summer day. "As I've been heard to say," Heisey told me with a smile, "I believe in free enterprise. I *hate* competition."

What triggered the five years of turmoil was a classic error in judgment prompted by the overconfidence, if not the arrogance, of Harlequin's senior management in the last half of the 1970s. Because the company's principal publishing specialty continued to grow in spite of ill-fated diversification, Heisey and his associates came to believe they were, or could be, experts in every facet of their business – including distribution. They were mistaken. Their second major error was to underestimate the power of a potential competitor that had been discarded like a worn-out lover.

The aggrieved party, Simon & Schuster, had maintained a reasonably respectful relationship with Harlequin for a dozen years. The s&s Pocket Books division was the reigning expert in mass-market book distribution in North America. Its system of supplying paperbacks to wholesale distributors servicing retailers of magazines and out-of-town newspapers relied upon a specialized sales team. Harlequin's growth in the United States had largely been dependent on the efficiency of that Pocket Books pipeline and the strength of its representatives in the field.

Yet as early as 1976, Heisey and his managers were seriously wondering whether the arrangement was mutually beneficial. They figured that although the two companies had virtually equal volumes of product in the pipeline, Harlequin was financing considerably more than half of the distributor's sales force. And because series romances sold so predictably well – as opposed to Pocket Books' own ever-changing books, which had to be promoted anew each month – they felt they weren't getting the sales reps' full attention. Another consideration was Harlequin's decision to diversify into genres beyond pure romantic fiction that would demand more focused selling and stricter supervision, possibly by its own people. Finally they convinced themselves that Pocket Books just wasn't doing the job on the Harlequins they were already handling.

Order regulation is the phrase for a system in which reps keep track of the rate of returns on each title by each retailer; if the rate is very high, too many books are being unnecessarily printed and shipped; if very low, retailers might not be getting enough books to sell. Reviewing the order regulation process for Harlequins, Larry Heisey found there were about 400 distributors, each carrying Romances and Presents. "That meant we could have had up to 800 changes in order positions per month as wholesalers fine-tuned their demands to optimize our return rates. As I recall, there were only about 23 changes per month in the time period we checked. The Pocket Books sales force simply wasn't managing the situation the way they should have been."

Rather than trying to improve the existing situation, Harlequin management generally agreed that setting up their own network of salespeople was the answer. Fred Kerner, for one, felt that American wholesalers would not care who was distributing the product: "They're not going to stop buying Harlequins because Simon & Schuster isn't selling it anymore. You could come in with Hunky Dunk and Shlunk, and they'll buy it because it's a big seller for them." Heisey says now, "It was everyone's view, with one exception who wasn't there to vote, that we would do better to do our own distribution – we could afford it, and we would have more latitude as to what we could distribute." The exception was John Boon: "When he heard about it, he was scandalized."

In deciding to give notice to Simon & Schuster that they were severing their ties with Pocket Books, they either ignored or never really entertained three crucial factors. With a prevailing air of infallibility in the Don Mills offices, no one at Harlequin seems to have weighed the possibility that the lost revenue might seriously hurt s & s. And if it did, that s & s might want to create a competitive line of romances. And if *it* did, that the powerhouse Harlequin would have something to worry about.

It was 1976, and the new president and publisher of Simon & Schuster had been in place for one year – ever since the grand old publishing house became part of Gulf + Western, the giant conglomerate that later metamorphosed into Paramount Communications, Inc. and wound up owning properties such as Madison Square Garden, New York's pro hockey and basketball teams, Prentice-Hall, and Paramount Pictures. The aggressive parent corporation had an equally aggressive – some would say offensive – leader of s & s in Richard Snyder, who had been part of the firm since the early 1960s. He once expressed a key tenet of his philosophy in the saying: "Any book, no matter how bad, is better than no book." Like Larry Heisey, he believed in books as products, but Dick Snyder pushed his editors and salespeople to produce and sell them with a ferocity that became legendary. A former s & s sales rep once said, only half humorously, "Simon & Schuster runs a sales contest every year. The winners get to keep their jobs."

In nearly 20 years at the helm of s&s, where he became chairman and chief executive officer, Snyder would turn a $40-million-a-year company into one grossing $2 billion. In the doing, the *New York Times* reported in 1994, shortly after he was fired, "he developed a reputation as a sometimes cold-blooded manager who dismissed people when he felt that they had outlived their financial use." Among his victims was Ann Patty, Janet Dailey's editor at s&s's Poseidon Books, and Joni Evans, who created an independent imprint for him, married him, and lost both jobs in a nasty divorce. Brash and temperamental, Snyder was not a tiger to trifle with.

Fred Kerner, for his part, maintains that the biggest mistake Harlequin made was giving Snyder three years' notice – in essence – of its decision to pull out of the distribution agreement. It hadn't intended to continue the arrangement beyond the few months remaining of the deal in 1976. But when Heisey, Dick Bellringer, and Bill Willson met Snyder in New York, Kerner quotes the trio as saying, "he ranted and raved and chewed the carpet and foamed at the mouth, so we gave him three more years."

Kerner: "You've now set up the best possible person to go into competition with us."

Heisey and Company: "Oh, he wouldn't do that."

Self-serving as the story sounds, it rings true. As Heisey told me, "I don't think any of us perceived that Simon & Schuster would come into the business as effectively as they did. If I had anticipated that future, I would have given them the profits they would have made just to stay out of it." Chuckling, he added, "You can desperately ignore that remark."

In fact, Snyder seems to have used the three-year extension of the distribution deal to plan a launch of his own product line of romances. According to Kerner, he had some unwitting help from Harlequin during that time. As the company's publishing director, Kerner wanted to create a series of American romances that more closely reflected their readers' lives and interests. He tried at least twice, and each time he was stopped – by the Boons, who were smarting from Kerner's criticism of what he considered their nonediting of books. His understanding was that Dick Bonnycastle Jr. had given them a handshake agreement when buying Mills & Boon that the North Americans would never interfere with their editorial practices – "they were the Motherland." But in 1977, Kerner convinced Heisey, Bellringer, and

Willson to let him try an American line. He had already hired his own art director, Charles Kadin, who would bring a level of sophistication to cover design and illustration. New York agents whom Kerner approached were soon sending him their clients' manuscripts. Meanwhile, he was training his staff to edit them under a new editorial manager from New York. George Glay, a Canadian by birth, was editorial director of Universal Publishing and Distributing's Award Books and had run his own literary agency. A former true-confessions writer, he was the author of two well-received novels, *Gina* and *Beggars Might Ride,* which the Bonnycastle family had published in 1949 and 1952 (and a third, *Oath of Seven,* that he later wrote for the money in three weeks). Before arriving, Glay read about 100 Harlequins and showed Kerner a chart he had made that essentially reduced them to a formula, as most critics do. At which point Kerner advised him to read another 100 – "and he fully agreed, there was no formula there."

In 1977, the first time the Boons killed the idea of a line to be written in the United States and produced in Canada, Harlequin edited more than 50 manuscripts for which it paid $4,000 to $8,000 apiece in advances. The authors kept the money when the publisher sent their work back to their agents to be resold, if they wished. They wished. Josh Gaspero, then heading the North American books division, had been given a couple of pieces of wisdom from Heisey: "Run the business. Don't ask me a lot of questions. If you do, you have to be prepared to heed my answer. And don't screw it up, kid!" Gaspero also wanted American authors, but at one meeting of the board in London, the Boons convinced Torstar's Bee Honderich otherwise. "I walked out of the boardroom and had a drink at Claridge's," Gaspero remembers. "Larry said, 'There are ways to do it,' and we reinstated it a month later." Kerner received a second go-ahead to attempt developing a New World line; again the Old World rejected it. Harlequin was left with scores more of unusable manuscripts to be returned to authors and agents for resale. And, as it happened, someone was secretly buying them.

In early 1979, with Harlequin's contract with Simon & Schuster's distribution division scheduled to expire at year's end, Dick Snyder called Larry Heisey to ask what his intentions were. "Dick, let me think it over. I'll talk to the boys." Then the boys sat around deciding who would go to New York to give Snyder the bad news. Heisey recalls: "Bellringer, who took his title of president of North America very seriously, said, 'I'll do it,' and I guess I – chickenshit – said, 'Well, yeah, you can do it.' And I thought he would go down there. But Dick, for reasons I'll never understand, asked Snyder to come to Toronto. That was very bad judgment, which just made Snyder hostile as can be. That was offensive to him." In fact, the story goes, Bellringer actually read a written notice of severance to Snyder.

It was all too easy. Dick Snyder went away obviously agitated but making no threats. As it turned out, he had not been sitting passively by, waiting for the distribution deal to die. Harlequin had underestimated how much the loss of revenue – a reported $45 million a year – would hurt Simon & Schuster. There was talk that Snyder himself would lose $90,000 in bonuses. Anticipating Harlequin's nonrenewal of the agreement, he had been covertly laying the groundwork for a massive campaign to launch a Pocket Books paperback line called Silhouette Romances. s&s had long since signed up Janet Dailey to a multibook contract (for a reported $2 million and twice the usual royalty rate), and, as Fred Kerner was about to learn, Snyder had a slew of other American authors with which to slay Harlequin.

In the summer of 1979, Kerner had a call from a contact he knew at Pocket Books, wondering if he would be interested in a job down there to run a new paperback line. He didn't think so, but he did want to know what the competition intended. A private plane from New Jersey fetched him in Toronto, and a limousine took him to the Simon & Schuster offices, where an elevator was waiting to take him to Dick Snyder's office. He knew the man from his days in New York in the 1960s, when Kerner was buying Hawthorn Books. At the time, Max Schuster, a principal shareholder in s&s who was retiring, had a buy-sell agreement with Snyder but wanted to do an end run around him and so suggested that Kerner buy his piece of the company. The figure was $5 million, Kerner says, because Schuster did not believe that Snyder could come up with that amount; unfortunately Kerner could raise only $3.5 million himself. But in discussions of the possibility, he says Schuster told him: "Fred, if you get the company, the first person you fire is Dick Snyder." So why didn't *Schuster* fire him? Kerner quotes him: "Too much politics. Family. But *you* can."

Kerner spent a day with Snyder that summer in 1979, listening to him describe the birth of Silhouette Romances the following year. Playing along, Kerner pointed out that s&s would need a year's supply of publishable books before launching. They had more than that, Snyder said. From where? From all the unused American manuscripts that Harlequin had been returning to their authors. Silhouette had a stock of about 180 titles.

That settled, Snyder asked Kerner what it would take to lure him to Silhouette. Thinking he was aiming high, Kerner presented a package worth roughly $1 million. "You buy me a house in Westchester. I want a chauffeured car to take me back and forth – I don't commute normally – and a second car for my wife, in-house help, and a salary of close to half a million dollars."

"You don't think big enough," Snyder retorted. "That's peanuts."

I wouldn't work for you if my life depended on it, Kerner said to himself.

Telling Snyder he would think about the offer, he flew back to Toronto and announced to his colleagues that Snyder and Pocket Books president and publisher Ron Busch were primed to take on Harlequin. All their new competitor needed was a president. It got one by year's end: P. J. Fennell, senior vice president of marketing and sales in Harlequin's book division, reporting to Dick Bellringer, with whom he seldom got along. Fennell, 36, formerly with General Foods and PepsiCo in Toronto, had been at Harlequin only a year. He was one of the most recent proponents of having the company set up its own dedicated distribution force in the United States. At a board of directors meeting in March 1979, he presented his case, with Bellringer's backing, and the board agreed it should happen. There were no dissenting votes, Fennell says now, "although a lot would deny that meeting happened."

The same summer Snyder talked to Kerner, he also called Fennell to invite him to join the new imprint. Fennell refused, but he changed his mind in November. By then the Harlequin Sales Corporation was operating out of Tarrytown, New York, with about five of its 60 people stolen from Pocket Books. At a meeting of the reps in Miami, Fennell announced his decision to an angry Bellringer. Harlequin paid for his airfare home. P. J. Fennell says today that "Snyder, to his credit, never asked me to disclose anything about Harlequin." Fred Kerner disagrees: "Six months after Fennell was there, he was fired. Six months later, we discovered he had taken our five-year plan. Snyder sent it to rub our noses in it."

That was but the start of the nose rubbing. Silhouette's initial $4 million TV and print campaign had Latin film star Ricardo Montalban as the spokesman and "It's your own special time" as a marketing slogan (salting the wound, ads would soon jeer: "Sorry Harlequin, millions of American women are being unfaithful to you"). Just before Mother's Day in 1980, 200,000 copies apiece of nine Silhouette romances appeared on the racks. The first was *Payment in Full* by none other than veteran Mills & Boon author Anne Hampson, who was to upset her former publishing house even further within a few years over payments that it had not made in full. Not only was the new line brimming with ex-Harlequin writers, but the cover style was virtually a dead ringer for the Harlequin Presents approach. So much so that Harlequin pursued a lawsuit against Simon & Schuster in which the district court judge noted the startling likeness: both companies used glossy white covers with similarly designed color illustrations; the same placement of series number and identifying trademark, which was also flanked by the series name below a scrollwork design; and the identical positioning of the author's name in large letters above the smaller title. Harlequin won an injunction against any further release of Silhouettes with that design. The competition's covers went from all white to white with purple borders and spine. As late as spring 1981, Heisey was still promising to go after Simon & Schuster for "continuing infringement of our cover design, misappropriation of confidential information, and use of Harlequin display racks."

In tone the romances from s & s /Pocket Books were the same as the more pure Harlequins, with sex play forever suffering from premature interruption. The second monthly batch of six books was pretested by readers. P. J. Fennell authorized sending copies of edited manuscripts to 200 American women for their appraisal of plot, characters, and overall quality. One book rejected because of a "bizarre" plot had already been returned for re-editing. The unusual system was not to survive – nor was Fennell, who found Dick Snyder a smothering employer: "When he tried to lure me to Simon & Schuster, he was absolutely charming. But the first day of the job, the rules were absolutely changed. It was like a cash register on his desk to check the pound of flesh." Fennell was replaced by John Gfeller, previously senior sales and marketing executive for Gulf + Western's consumer product division and vice president of marketing for Madison Square Garden. Gfeller oversaw Silhouette's phenomenal growth to 60 million copies worth $100 million in its second year. He also toyed with the idea of capitalizing on the company's new young-adult line, First Love, by marketing lingerie under the same name.

Silhouette's first editor in chief, Kate Duffy, handled the sweet, safe manuscripts by American writers that Harlequin had rejected. Her successor,
Karen Solem, reacted to market research and the prevailing mood of the
decade to introduce more complex, sensual, and slightly controversial
romances under the name Special Editions early in 1982. Heroines were older,
had careers, and sometimes escaped from bad marriages. Solem also had
Harlequin superstar Charlotte Lamb writing for Silhouette under the pseudonym Laura Hardy. Meanwhile, Mills & Boon's editors pooh-poohed the
Silhouette product as "writing by numbers" (although David Galloway has
noted that "even today, Silhouette outsells Harlequin").

By then Harlequin had already launched its own Superromance line featuring "a contemporary love story with spice." It ran about 100,000 words, with
more than the usual single plot and two fleshed-out characters. Fred Kerner,
using what he called his research and development budget, had surreptitiously
worked with a Toronto ad copywriter named Barbara Browse to develop her
more complex manuscript as a midlist book, rather than the typical category
romance. When it was ready, he printed 1,000 copies and only then showed
one to a surprised Dick Bellringer, asking him to take it home to his wife,
Alma. She loved it, and when the book became the first Superromance in late
1980, selling for $1.95 rather than the Presents price of $1.50, the author earned
about $100,000 from *End of Innocence*. "It was Mills & Boon's end of inno-
cence, too," Kerner remarks, although the Boons did insist that the new line
have a name other than Harlequin – which is why it came to be called
Worldwide Superromance. Within a year, the company was releasing two titles
a month in the series. It also increased the price of its Romances to $1.50 and
Presents to $1.75, a strange move in such a competitive time.

In 1982 the Canadian publisher faced an American rival that was spending
about $22 million in advertising and promotion, which Harlequin began to
match. s&s was running network TV ads 21 days a month. Both companies
were fine-tuning their television spending. At the time, Joan Schulhafer was
doing publicity for Pocket Books and later for Silhouette. "Some of the first
television advertising went on soap operas," she says, "and people thought this
was a wonderful idea. And it was absolutely the wrong thing, because people
who were watching soap operas were not reading romances. I'm sure there's
overlap somewhere along the way, but you've got X amount of leisure time." A

better idea proved to be advertising to romance readers on evening news shows.

The two competitors were soon having to fight off interlopers as other publishers, seeing the blossoming market for romances, leapt in. Harlequin had already beaten back Bantam's Red Rose Romances, which limped along through much of the 1970s. Another attempt had been choreographed by Ted Scharien, once general manager of Harlequin's consumer sales division. He became vice president of House of Romance Publications, a Canadian firm that claimed to want only a small piece of the romance reader's heart. It was aiming at an American audience for its British novels, where it felt its competitor was not as deeply rooted as in Canada. Advertising in *TV Guide* and other popular magazines, House of Romance soon died for lack of deep pockets.

Another two rivals had reared up in 1979. Richard Gallen Books began packaging four sexually charged and more complex historicals and contemporaries each month for Pocket Books. Fawcett Books announced that it would be publishing a historical line called Coventry Romances using the same brand-marketing techniques as Harlequin, a $1-million ad campaign with cents-off coupons, and, initially, commercials on soap operas. A year later, Dell launched Ecstasy Romances, a contemporary-romance spin-off of a line called Candlelight Romances that it had been publishing since 1967. With the creation of Vivian Stephens, one of the few black editors in the industry, Ecstasies placed the reader firmly in the bedroom and reputedly were the first to offer straightforward sexual consummation without the usual bothersome interruptions. By the end of 1982, Dell had sold 30 million of these sexy, slender, single-plot romances under titles such as *Gentle Pirate* and *The Tawny Gold Man*. Jove, soon to become part of the Berkley Publishing Group, was next with a series called Second Chance at Love, portraying more mature heroines, and later To Have and to Hold. Over the next couple of years, four other publishers tried the market and failed: Bantam Books' Circle of Love and New American Library's Adventures in Love were doomed sweet-romance lines; Avon's Finding Mr. Right had heroines shopping around for lovers; and Ballantine Books' Love & Life offered psychological realism. Editor Carolyn Nichols had shaped Jove's successful Second Chance line, which would sell 200,000 titles a month, but even she couldn't help Bantam's bland Circle of Love series she was enlisted to save.

The writers' guidelines about handling sex for Second Chance demonstrate how far romances had come from kiss on the last page, if not how desperately their publishers were trying to differentiate them in the marketplace:

> The hero and heroine make love even when unmarried, and with plenty of sensuous detail. But the explicit details will be used only in foreplay, and the fadeout will occur before actual intercourse. The setting and circumstances of the lovemaking are also crucial and should contribute to a slow buildup of sexual tension. The hero and heroine should not make love too early in the plot. In the Regency novels the sex can stop before intercourse, since the lack of birth control devices creates an element of worry that isn't present in the contemporary romances.

As Dick Snyder said, "Some who seek gold will find ashes." Among those left blackened were his company and Harlequin; the two companies met fire with fire. On the stiletto heels of Dell's Ecstasy, Silhouette had brought out a Desire line, with a label warning readers how sensual they were, and later the longer, plot-busy Intimate Moments. Harlequin took a while to counter with Temptation, but in the meantime hired Ecstasy creator Vivian Stephens to fashion a new line titled American Romances that focused more on the authors than the brand name; it was launched with a $5 million ad campaign. Silhouette went into the direct-mail business, offering four free romances to new book club members, one more than Harlequin did. Silhouette's first sale of foreign rights was to Holland, where Harlequin had made its significant European debut; within three years, Silhouettes were selling in 17 countries, including digest-sized Romances in Germany and steamy Desires in Japan with tamed-down covers.

A bemused observer of the hostilities was Andrew Ettinger, Don Pendleton's former editor and ex-Harlequin editorial director who was now an agent and publishing consultant in Los Angeles. "After so many years of no real competition," he told *Publishers Weekly,* "Harlequin felt they were beyond anyone's reach. . . . The Pocket Books/Simon & Schuster sales force had been selling Harlequin's product for many, many years. They knew where the profit areas were. If Silhouette could determine what women readers really wanted to read, and put it in a bright new package, they could succeed. They did it and they did it brilliantly. They did it fast, with a lot of intelligence and a lot of investment. The timing was perfect."

While this war was being waged, the directors and shareholders of Torstar watched in appalled fascination. The Toronto communications conglomerate had been buying up shares of the romance publisher since 1975. Six years later, it owned 100 percent and was wondering, with some justification, if it had bought a pig in a publishing poke. Or (to continue the porcine metaphors) whether Harlequin's management was making a sow's ear out of a silk purse.

Torstar had not bought all the remaining shares in 1979, when Harlequin was seriously, if secretly, contemplating its own distribution system in the United States. Dick Bonnycastle, although largely an arm's-length chairman, had been privy to the deliberations about cutting the cord with Pocket Books. He had disagreed with the idea, arguing that the powerful American company – expert in both publishing *and* distribution – should be kept happy. And he had asked Heisey not to back out of the deal without informing him. However, Heisey told me, "I never felt I had an obligation to report that to him before we did it." When Bonnycastle did find out in 1979, he knew there was a potential for disaster in the value of the shares that Torstar had yet to buy, which would affect stock that he, Heisey, and other senior officers still held. He warned Bill Willson not to bring Harlequin's disappointing first-quarter earnings to the next meeting of the board of directors. He had to convince the parent company to go through with its proposed stock purchase.

Harlequin was about to have its annual board meeting outside Canada. Some of the corporate fun sprang from bringing directors, officers, and their wives together in exotic parts of their publishing world. Places such as Paris and Frankfurt and Amsterdam, where they had canal tours and dinners in windmill restaurants. For this conclave, they took over the 13th-century Leeds Castle in Maidstone, Kent, the typical moated palace of romantic fiction. Dick Bonnycastle was walking the grounds with Torstar chairman Bee Honderich when he mentioned, casually he hoped, "You know, it's not quite the same, not being in control. *You've* got it. You should probably have it all." Then the Harlequin chairman went into the meeting and, to his horror, heard Heisey talk about a possible decline in profits resulting from the decision to drop Pocket Books as distributor. Among the well-informed directors was Bonnycastle's racehorse partner, George Gardiner of the Gardiner, Watson investment house, who

(Heisey says) "wants to evidence that he has read all the material in such depth that he can find a typo on page 26 of the material." (Harlequin's managers would sometimes even plant an error or two, hoping Gardiner would find them, and then correct the mistakes at the beginning of the meeting before he had a chance to point them out.) Fortunately at this meeting, neither the sharpest-eyed directors such as Gardiner nor the three Torstar people paid much attention to the downside of the new distribution plan or other omens of disaster. After all, even investment dealer Midland Doherty proved sanguine about the scheme, noting that "the full-time efforts of [Harlequin's] own sales force and the still large potential opportunities to broaden market penetration in the United States augur very well for future prospects."

Bonnycastle's friends told him he was crazy to sell out his holdings in Harlequin. In fact, he had been unloading shares even before then. He was much more interested in his Cavendish Investing Group – of which he owned 75 percent, his sister 18 percent, and management seven percent – and its over $100 million in assets, including 30 American high-tech companies and Rupertsland Resources, a junior oil and gas exploration venture. Bonnycastle resigned from the Torstar board as the parent corporation paid $153 million for the remaining 25 percent of Harlequin stock over the next two years to take full ownership of a company whose continuing prospects appeared to be golden. The Boon brothers still express disappointment about Bonnycastle's decision to sell to Torstar. "I thought Dick was interested in building a publishing company," John Boon says. "He was only interested in making a business."

The departure of Richard Henry Gardyne Bonnycastle's son signaled the end of an era. Ruth Palmour had already retired as corporate secretary in 1977. And although his sister, Judy, would stay on as a Harlequin romance editor for a while, the Bonnycastles had handed over the family business to a media conglomerate after more than three decades of mostly successful operation. Dick Bonnycastle Jr. walked away without a backward glance, hoping to build a second venture that would flourish like Harlequin. Although he has had his successes over the years, with his ranches and petroleum plays and a pharmaceutical company, none would quite equal the publishing phenomenon. "I always wanted to come up with another world-class company," he told me, almost plaintively. "Lots of guys can do it once – but can you do it twice? And so far we haven't done one. And maybe we won't."

Within three years, Judy Burgess retired as the longtime liaison with the sweet British novels of Mills & Boon that had fueled the North American company for so long. Its first editor on this continent, Mary Bonnycastle, had been living in Toronto since 1980 to be near her two daughters. Neither Judy nor her mother had any great illusions about the work they had done at Harlequin. Years later the outspoken daughter would upbraid her mom for having wasted her intelligence, for staying home and doing only volunteer work instead of pursuing her gifts in a career.

"What about Harlequin?" Mary demanded in her own defense.

"Mother," Judy replied, "you could have done more than that."

"Too true," her mother said.

Mary Bonnycastle died in July 1995. A brittle socialite at the funeral in Winnipeg remarked to Judy on Richard and Mary's great romance, "Wasn't it wonderful how they adored each other?"

For Harlequin in 1981, much of the original romance was over, with two-thirds of the original management triumvirate on their way out. Bill Willson, uneasy with the new owner, cashed out that year ("definitely a mistake," he admits) to become executive vice president of Dick Bonnycastle Jr.'s failing Rupertsland Resources. He was supposed to start in the fall, but Larry Heisey asked him to stay on for six months; by the time he came on the scene in the spring of 1982, Rupertsland was going belly up. Bonnycastle still sounds upset when he recalls that Willson demanded $3 million or so in cash for the stock that Bonnycastle had given him. Meanwhile, Dick Bellringer was displaying no intention of leaving Harlequin. But after McKinsey & Company had evaluated the company in the late 1970s, Heisey realized the need for reorganization at the top: either he or his executive vice president had to go. "They took me through my foibles and slowly revealed how I wasn't managing the company well," he says. "I realized: Dick wasn't doing well. I had to replace him or myself." Early in the new decade, when Bellringer refused to handle other, lesser duties – "I'm not a good operator, I'm a keen builder" – he and Heisey worked out a generous severance deal. Bellringer was already wealthy: "Larry and I invested heavily. When Harlequin needed money, we'd borrow from the bank and put it in."

He retired well to dabble in real estate, limited partnerships, and the odd publishing venture with financier and frustrated publisher Chris Ondaatje.

Bellringer's replacement was David Galloway, who was put in charge of all operations. The *Globe and Mail*, mocking the romance jargon, once described Galloway as square-jawed and handsome. He is that and, as a recreational runner and tennis player, was fit and fighting trim, if prematurely balding, at 37. His management-consultant work as a partner in the Canada Consulting Group had led him to the vice presidency of corporate development for Torstar in 1980. In that position, he had stood before its board of directors and told them: "If we don't buy Harlequin today, we will not be able to afford it later." The truth was, the romance publisher was making more money than the flagship newspaper, the *Toronto Star*, and in holding only about three-quarters of Harlequin's stock at the time, Torstar had no access to its copious cash flow. The following year, when Larry Heisey himself invited Galloway to become executive vice president of Harlequin, the parent company was pleased to have the safety net of one of its own people running the day-to-day operations of the subsidiary.

David Galloway was a refined-looking, impeccably mannered local product of University of Toronto Schools and, like Heisey, of Harvard's M.B.A. program. He and his wife of 15 years, Judy, had a son and a daughter. Sophisticated and outgoing, he was as globally minded as his boss, the president. But wholesale corporate expansion was not an immediate option as Galloway took over management of a company suddenly toe to toe with its first real competition.

True, certain divisions were doing well. Overseas, Harlequin was now in Italy through a joint venture with the country's dominant publisher, Arnoldi Mondadori Editore, which had a potent system of 5,000 or more kiosks to distribute their new Collezione Harmony series. It would do well for both partners; John Boon recalls a Mondadori executive later telling him at a party: "*Harlequina* – a jewel, a little jewel!" Foreign sales generally had become significant: the company was selling about 120 million books outside North America to 100 million within. In 1980 Harlequin had paid $34.5 million U.S. (plus the book value of net current assets) for Miles Kimball Company of Oshkosh, Wisconsin. The 46-year-old mail-order business distributed moderately priced giftware and household goods, books, and cards to one of the largest established catalog lists on the continent. After a faltering start, it flourished as a complementary Harlequin subsidiary and continues today with kitschy products such as Easter doormats, pet car seats, and corn-relieving toe separators (among its most popular items are pencils and calendars personalized with customers' own photographs).

That was the good news. The very bad included Scholar's Choice, the learning-materials division suffering from a drop-off in demand from educational institutions. A little desperately, Harlequin had gone into the retail business with 10 stores in Canada and 11 in the United States, which were currently on life support. The Laufer magazines were also hurting, and Galloway was sure the Raven House mystery line would soon be losing hundreds of thousands. The potential for translating Harlequins into films seemed poor; a licensing arrangement with Torstar subsidiary Nielsen-Ferns to produce romantic TV movies would lead nowhere. In England Mills & Boon sold off the less than lucrative general and educational book division that had been John Boon's love.

Then there was Dick Snyder and Silhouette – and a small horde of other publishers elbowing into the field. In 1981 there were 30 romance titles being published each month; two years later, there were 100 more, 22 of them published by Harlequin, whose market share had sunk by half to 41 percent. Many rivals did drop out, as Snyder had predicted. In the shakeout, however, two competitors stood firm, their success based much less on big promotional budgets than on reader word of mouth: Dell's Ecstasy, and Bantam's newest, an author-driven brand called Loveswept, created by ex-Jovian Carolyn Nichols. A customers' poll released by a panel from Waldenbooks, B. Dalton, and independent bookstores named the three top sellers as Ecstasy, Second Chance at Love, and Loveswept. Harlequin and Silhouette had not made the cut. David Galloway had to swallow this, along with the fact that industry returns were running at the extraordinary rate of 60 percent – some within Harlequin have since claimed it was as much as 70 percent.

Two, three, four years had passed, and Heisey and Galloway were being forced to cut costs severely and refocus on their basic business. Harlequin was embattled everywhere it turned. Even a renewed concentration on its cash-cow mail-order business, in which it offered more discounts and free books, was met by fresh competition from new players in the field: Dell, Berkley, and New American Library (only Bantam's Loveswept stayed out of the book club market, which endeared them to retail booksellers). On the retail side, Harlequin reached a low point in promotion when it placed sample books in Hefty trash bags and tried to ignore the resulting cheap jokes. Larry Heisey sounded poignant when he told *The Wall Street Journal*: "It's not as much fun."

It wasn't for Dick Snyder, either. Silhouette announced a salary freeze for its employees, and Pocket Books disbanded a special sales force it had created for the line. The most embarrassing moments came when Silhouette had to admit that it was losing money on its retail operation and, in a private session with New York literary agents, threatened to shut down the company if they and their authors pushed for larger royalties. Galloway was not reassured by these signs of weakness: by then Simon & Schuster was a large educational as well as trade publisher, and its parent, Paramount, was a colossus that, if it chose, could afford to continue to lose millions of dollars a year.

By 1984 it was a time of decision. Larry Heisey and David Galloway had communicated with Snyder in the intervening years. In his first year at Harlequin, when Galloway tried to argue with him that there wasn't room for two big players in the market, Snyder told him to go to hell. Once, the three of them met in New York over the Silhouette cover dispute, and the Simon & Schuster president presented them each with a crystal sculpture in the shape of an *S* (they don't know whether it stood for Silhouette or Snyder). Heisey in particular was not in a gift-getting mood; when he and Galloway came back across the Canadian border and the customs officer told them they would have to pay $600 in duty, Heisey told him to take the sculptures. No, he really couldn't. Heisey held them over his head as if to drop them, and the officer hurriedly agreed to hold the sculptures for safekeeping.

Well after Snyder had fired P. J. Fennell, Heisey sent Snyder a news clipping about the first Silhouette president's new position in Toronto, along with the comment: "Richard, we didn't agree on a lot of things, but I think we agree on this chap. Hope you're keeping well." Amused, Snyder made contact, and they had breakfast in New York, during which Heisey said Harlequin was interested in buying Silhouette and giving Pocket Books the distribution rights again. Snyder rejoined that Harlequin should just let Pocket Books do the distribution, no strings attached.

Galloway followed up, bucking opposition among his own managers, most of whom disagreed with him and Heisey about taking over Silhouette. He had six months of difficult negotiations with Dick Snyder. Yet he diplomatically recalls him in words that some others might have trouble uttering: "I became friends with Snyder. . . . His bark was worse than his bite. . . . Dick was a man of honor." Heisey admitted that too much blood had been shed for him to have done the deal. "There was no pride on my side," Galloway says now. "*I* hadn't taken away the distribution."

The antitrust division of the U.S. Department of Justice, which had warned Harlequin in 1979 not to acquire Pinnacle Books, decided this time that it wouldn't oppose the Silhouette takeover. As for Snyder, he went on to earn the mocking title of "warrior-king of Simon & Schuster," which he built into America's biggest publishing house. He maintained his bellicose management style until 1994, when he himself faced a humiliating public firing when Viacom took over Paramount and forced him out. A year later, he bought Western Publishing (where Josh Gaspero had worked), the owner of the children's line of Golden Books, and announced to the world a kinder, gentler Dick Snyder: "This is not the same person you saw after I was fired."

Nor had he been the same person at the time he took on Harlequin. *Publishers Weekly* summed up the five competitive years as the Romance Wars and, with a homer's instinct, gave the victory to Simon & Schuster/Pocket Books: "After heavy losses on both sides, the Americans, primarily under Snyder's leadership, would ultimately regain control of the U.S. battlefield." Showing equal chauvinism, I would suggest that while the Americans had their distribution deal back in place, the Canadians, in fact, came out on top by regaining their virtual publishing monopoly on the lucrative category romance market – however costly the war was.

And high-priced it was for Harlequin. It agreed to pay $10 million U.S. for money-losing Silhouette and a variable amount not to exceed $25 million, depending on earnings over the following seven years. But there were other costs to be tallied. Galloway reckoned later that between 1981 and 1984, corporate earnings in the $20 million range could have been twice that high without the Silhouette competition.

David Galloway has used the word hubris to describe the company's prideful decision to do its own distribution. Not long ago, I asked him if, between his estimate of lost revenues and the princely payout to Silhouette, the overall price of Harlequin's hubris might be somewhere approaching $100 million.

"It's not a bad number," he told me. "It was a big mistake."

10

The Men Who Changed Everything

GALLOWAY AND HICKEY

A year after taking over, while still under siege by Silhouette, David Galloway saw an overseas opportunity he felt his company could not ignore. Foreign operations were among the few bright lights on Harlequin's dimming horizon. With most of non-Communist Europe Harlequinized, perhaps there was potential in the Arabic nations of Africa and southwestern Asia. The only way to justify the venture was to have a single print run for each title to blanket the entire region. The proposal was to print romance novels in the Arabic language with different prices on the back cover for each of the 13 different target markets. In Egypt the price would be the equivalent of about $1, and in oil-rich Saudi Arabia $4. The key to the project was, in fact, the potential revenue from Saudi Arabia, which had a population of 10 million vastly divided between the minority of rich Saudis and a huge pool of immigrant labor.

The first hurdle was to have the Saudi government approve Harlequins for sale in the country. The ruling House of Saud dynasty had been in full control for half a century. It wielded power using the *Shari'ah*, the Islamic code of civil and religious law, which regulated the society with a thicket of orthodox religious restrictions. This was a country, perhaps the most fundamentalist of all Islamic states, that prescribed the whip for drinking alcohol and amputation of a hand for theft. Women were constrained in public, fearful of the state-financed religious police who enforced the dress code with clubbings. A few years earlier, a Saudi princess and her commoner lover had been executed for committing adultery, an offense that generally brought only 100 lashes. Other factors to be considered were that in the early 1980s, Saudi Arabia's oil wealth was in decline and, as Harlequin was to discover, corruption was rife.

Surprisingly, getting into the country in 1982 proved no problem. The ministry of culture, says David Galloway, "thought they were funny little books, so they let them in. And we found, like everywhere else, they became a bit of a phenomenon. The books sold very well." For this 13th of the languages Harlequin published in, concessions were made: foreign settings and non-Arabic heroines were fine, but characters could not drink alcohol, and the spicier prose had to be tamed. What most intrigued the Harlequin people was that their research showed fully 40 percent of their readership was male, a curiosity duplicated nowhere else. One explanation was that the men were interested in Western culture; another might have been that sweet as they were, Harlequins were still the sexiest paperbacks widely available to Saudi readers, male or female.

The Arabic experiment proved to be a nonstarter. Lebanon, originally a major importer of the books, became even more of a battle zone. Harlequin's 1983 annual report announced that "Arabic-language operations are being written down largely because of unsettled conditions in the Middle East." Another reality intruded: Saudi Arabia, the pivotal market, soon declared the romance novels a corrupt influence, after all. That was the official government line – and the story that the company told publicly at the time to explain why it was no longer operating in the country. According to John Boon, "the Saudis decided we were corrupt." In truth, David Galloway says, "after two years, some government official it was important for us to have approval from came back saying we had to pay a bribe." The blackmail threat eventually worked its way up to the desk of Galloway, along with the belief of at least one middle manager that the bribe should be paid. "It certainly would have paid us to pay it," Galloway says. When he refused – "it wasn't something I was going to do, *period,* and it's not Torstar's style" – the government official banned Harlequin. Larry Heisey says, "The distributor was even afraid to talk to us over the phone until he had left the country." And without Saudi Arabia, the Arabic edition was no longer viable. Interestingly Harlequins continued under a licensing arrangement in Israel, where the company had some difficult dealings but enjoyed among the highest penetrations of any country in the world. In recent years, however, Hebrew has become one of a couple of languages that are no longer part of the Harlequin world – the other being Welsh.

Saudi Arabia might have been the least of David Galloway's problems in those first few embattled years. He had come into Harlequin with several strengths, chief of which is that he knew exactly what he was selling. As well as graduating from the University of Toronto and the M.B.A. program at Harvard Business School, he also worked one summer at Heisey's other alma mater, the Toronto office of Procter & Gamble. It was there, more than anywhere, that he learned the same lesson his predecessor had: that truly to succeed as a marketing company, you need a good product. And he also recognized Harlequin was all about the marketing of a gilt-edged consumer packaged-goods product.

After graduation Galloway wanted to join P&G for the same reason Heisey didn't want to stay there: the possibility of working abroad. While Galloway hoped for international experience, his only choice was England – but drab Newcastle, not dramatic London. Instead, in 1968 he went into marketing for three years with General Foods (Maxwell House Coffee, Minute Rice, Tang)

Alan Boon and David Galloway (right), *the man who now heads Harlequin's parent, Torstar.*

before becoming a founder of the Canada Consulting Group. Among his six partners in that well-connected firm of management consultants were Jim Coutts, who became chief adviser to Prime Minister Pierre Trudeau, and David Jolley, a classmate at University of Toronto Schools, who became the *Toronto Star*'s publisher while Galloway was C E O of Harlequin. At Canada Consulting, where Galloway specialized in the communications industry, his industrial-strength clients included the Canadian Broadcasting Corporation, Maclean Hunter's *The Financial Post*, and Toronto Star Limited.

His first day on the job at Harlequin in 1981, Galloway felt at home when called in to review some new ads; as a General Foods product manager, he had routinely evaluated advertising campaigns. Within his first six weeks at the publishing house, he felt less comfortable when called upon to decide the fate of the new Raven House line of mystery novels. He didn't believe the research figures showing that at the rate Harlequin's mysteries were to be released, they would soon account for 85 to 100 percent of the current volume of that genre on the market. "And there was nothing magical about the Raven House product," he says. Despite his reservations, he told Bee Honderich, "We've just taken over this company, they put in all this work, and if I turn this thing down now, I'll get the whole place saying Torstar is heavy-handed and won't do anything. But I just want to tell you, Beland, I think we're going to lose a million bucks, and I think it's worth losing a million bucks." Which they did.

Larry Heisey, who kicked himself upstairs as chairman, made Galloway president and C E O in 1982 and allowed him to control the day-to-day activities. For Heisey it was a depressing era as he sat on the Torstar board and listened to the reports of an embarrassing decline in profits. A problem, in Torstar's eyes, was that it had paid too much for the romance publisher. In its first year of full ownership, when all the book returns were tallied, the parent company discovered that earnings had been overstated by $7 million. Galloway, who had recommended that Torstar buy Harlequin, gave Bee Honderich a running account of the dramatic downturn as the weeks progressed: "It's not a $2 million loss but $4 million," and a few weeks later, "It's a $5 million loss." Honderich, he says, was sympathetic: "He gave me time and had big shoulders." Because the buyout was mostly financed through short-term borrowings, Torstar's debt-servicing costs had risen to $34 million in 1981 from $6 million the year before, soaking up 67 percent of pre-tax operating profits.

The first operating plan for 1982 that came across Galloway's desk optimistically forecast that the volume of all Harlequin's lines would increase. But
at the same time, he knew that five competitors' lines were being introduced.
Where was all the volume going to come from? he wondered. *Unless market
growth is phenomenal,* their *sales are going to come at* our *expense.* He also knew
that Harlequin's corporate culture had been nurtured on 20 percent annual
growth, and even to talk about a decline in sales volume was heresy.

Yet it was already happening. Before his arrival, the McKinsey & Company
report on Harlequin management had proposed a back-to-basics approach. It
was left to Galloway to manage it. One step was divesting the magazine division:
the Laufer group of California teen and adult entertainment publications, and
the New York-based art and antiques periodicals. Phil Whalen, who had come
out of the mining industry to be finance director of the division, was now its
acting president. He wanted to acquire *Antiques World,* which was performing
well. "You can buy it," Galloway said, "but if you sell it in the next two years,
you must give us back 50 percent over what you sell it for. And you have to buy
Laufer for a dollar. As a small company, *you* can shut it down. It's different for
us. That's the deal. I'll put *Antiques World* at auction unless you agree."

Whalen and a partner agreed and flew to California to shut down the magazines there. That month Michael Jackson appeared on the cover of the division's flagship teen publication, *Tiger Beat.* Sales began soaring in sync with
the singer's popularity. The surprised new owners kept the suddenly profitable
group, selling out a few years later. The magazine Phil Whalen had originally
coveted and acquired, *Antiques World,* went bust.

The other life-sucking liability in the Harlequin portfolio was Scholar's
Choice, the amalgamation of the Jack Hood and Nor-Ed school-supplies ventures. In 1981 its after-tax losses more than doubled to $2.5 million. As school-
board business dried up, Scholar's Choice went into the retail trade, opening
stores to sell learning materials to teachers and parents. The first one was in a
heavily trafficked, upscale mall in Toronto, where it succeeded. Emboldened,
management believed they could take a cookie-cutter approach and launch a
chain across North America. When Galloway arrived, 40 stores were operating in Canada and the United States, and there was a plan for 200 in all.
Martin Catto, a vice president of finance (who is still with Harlequin in 1996),
blew the whistle on the empire building: an investment in that number of new

stores would take virtually every available penny of Harlequin and Torstar over the following five years, and Scholar's Choice would presumably become larger than either company. It was a Pollyannaish plan, in light of the fact that only seven of the current 40 stores were profitable. Having no retail background, Scholar's Choice had no clout with mall landlords and was paying top dollar on its leases.

The stores had to be closed down and the division wound up. To do the deed, David Galloway enlisted Harlequin's new vice president of corporate marketing and development and a Toronto-bred friend who had shared a piece of his history: Brian Hickey.

Galloway had been Hickey's first boss at General Foods when the 25-year-old was fresh from his M.B.A. at the University of Toronto. Between undergraduate and graduate schools, where his high standing earned him awards and scholarships, Hickey had spent a year designing new insurance policies at Confederation Life. In his master's program, he focused on finance – "it's a brilliant background to bring to marketing," he says, "because they can't screw you with the numbers." He was even then, with his plump face and glasses, beginning to look a bit like that fallen cherub, media satirist Stan Freberg (who might have a field day sending up Harlequin commercials). Still in business school, Brian married an effusive nurse named Wendy, who became pregnant with the first of their two sons. Although facing fatherhood and repaying student loans, he turned down a Montreal brokerage firm, offering him 60 percent more money, to join General Foods in Toronto. If his three years with the company were his Ph.D. in marketing, the next eight with S. C. Johnson & Son of Racine, Wisconsin, were his postdoctorate. The family-held marketer of home and personal-care products – many of them household names such as Johnson's Wax – has its Canadian headquarters in Brantford, Ontario. *The Financial Post* has declared it, like Procter & Gamble, one of the 100 best companies to work for in Canada.

Early on at Johnson's, Hickey had challenged a pet project of the Canadian president, who wanted to build the personal-care business in Canada along the successful American model. Hickey test-marketed relevant products in Alberta, and as early as 1973, he was analyzing results with a modem linked to a main-frame computer in Racine. His conclusion: major competitive categories such as antiperspirants returned almost no profit; they were used as a lever to sell other high-return products. He decided that rather than developing its own personal-care lines, the Canadian Johnson's should be capitalizing on the research and development programs of the parent company. (For years Harlequin thrived on a similar philosophy of "let Jack do the pioneering.") When his group product manager heard his first pitch and expressed doubt, Hickey made his case to the equally dubious regional vice president of marketing. Frustrated, the 28-year-old upstart presumptuously booked a meeting with the Canadian president. "You're in your twenties and think you're pretty good and take a chance, right?" he recalls. "I was pretty sure I was right." The president was impressed enough after half an hour to call Racine on the spot and ask the head of Johnson's interna-tional operations and the international marketing vice president to hear the pre-sentation. One long grilling later, Hickey had convinced everyone, including the president whose project it was, that R&D in the personal-care field was not a suitable venture for the Canadian subsidiary.

He had so impressed the Americans that within weeks, the Hickeys were liv-ing in Wisconsin. But about 60 percent of Johnson's sales were outside the United States. Working out of head office, Hickey traveled extensively throughout Asia for two years as a marketing support manager and then moved to the Philippines for another three as the company's Asia Pacific area director.

"You wake up every morning there knowing that something new, strange, and different is going to happen," he recalls. For example, the company required a supply of kerosene or diesel to manufacture its Johnson's Wax, but the Philippines was a total importer of petroleum products. At a local service station one day, Hickey asked the owner if he could buy his allotment of diesel gas. When the man refused, Hickey decided to buy the man's whole business. "And then I had to notify head office we'd bought a gas station. But you got an assured supply" – just as Harlequin had in buying Mills & Boon. "You had immense independence out there. You've bloodied your nose all over the place – learning how to manage managing directors, those sorts of things – and no one else has to know about it."

In the summer of 1981, Hickey was back in Racine as director of strategic planning – while being sized up by owner Sam Johnson – when he received a

Saturday-morning phone call. In a replay of Larry Heisey's experience, it was the same Chicago headhunting firm on the line. Hickey, on his way to play tennis, gave the man short shrift when he mentioned that the Canadian publisher Harlequin was interested in talking to him about a position. "I just thought Harlequin had these funny little romances, and I didn't know what else it was, and I didn't really have a whole lot of interest in it." Not until a follow-up letter arrived with an annual report did he realize that Harlequin's executive vice president was old friend David Galloway.

Hickey had been in touch with him the year before, when Galloway was still a partner in the Canada Consulting Group and Hickey testified in Ottawa about a project the group was evaluating on the creation of a Canadian-style multinational state trading company. Now Galloway was telling him to take Harlequin's approach seriously: "The reason I had the headhunter call you is because I don't want it to look like I'm bringing friends in here." After interviews in Toronto, Hickey told his wife he hoped Harlequin wouldn't make him an offer. He was comfortable about his future with Johnson's Wax, and he liked where they lived: "I always say John Calvin's alive and well in Wisconsin. People work hard. They're responsible."

The offer was too attractive; with built-in bonuses, he would one day (at least briefly) be earning more than Torstar's top executives. The Hickeys returned to Toronto, and he walked into – "Absolute hell. Everywhere you went in the organization, they just wanted nothing to do with you because you were 'corporate.' They didn't see any benefit to you being there. They just made it very, very difficult. In fact, I started wondering if it was me. I started on September 28, 1981, and by December 15, if I could have gone back to Johnson's Wax, my old job" – and here he whispers – "I would have gone so fast."

Perhaps his lack of appeal had something to do with the other executives' fear that he was the corporate hatchet man. When Hickey called the president of Scholar's Choice, "he forbid me to set foot on the sixth floor, where it was located, and then said to me he would be available in two days' time or something. I'll never forget – he came up, and I was sitting in the boardroom here, where we'd agreed to meet, and I was just sitting at the head of the table, which in Johnson's Wax terminology or culture, the head of the meeting sits on the side of the table in the center. Sitting down at the end is nothing. I remember he walked in, he had two guys with him, took a look at me, and proceeded to walk to the far end and sit at the head of the table at the other end. It's a fairly long board table. So I got up and walked down and sat down beside him and started asking him some questions, and he was just totally obstreperous. I went back to Galloway and said, 'I don't know what you want me to do here, David, but the guy just won't give me access.' So they did terminate him, and then they put me in as *acting* president of Scholar's Choice, which was – in that Ronald Reagan was president of the U.S. at the time – probably not the best title. So I called a meeting, the thing's hemorrhaging, we got inventory in some things with 10 years' supply. So I remember saying to the guys, 'Look, come up with some creative ideas.' One guy said, 'Why don't we just put' – this is late November – 'why don't we just offer 30 percent off everything in the store?' I said, 'That sounds like a good idea.' Then immediately he backs off. He'd just been a smart-ass. He was head of store operations. I was stupid enough – I didn't know anything about retailing – to think, *Why not. . .?* We went ahead and did it. It was the most amazing thing. We started in early December. If you went around the stores six days after we started it, 12 days, there were signs everywhere: *Half Off.* That was the year of atrocious retailing, and by a complete fluke, we ended up 10 days ahead of everybody else because they had this know-nothing who made the decision. We sold so much inventory that we had to actually repurchase some stuff to keep the stores in inventory. And we got better than dollar on the dollar for the inventory – that was the most amazing thing about it. And then we just started negotiating out of the leases and closed it down."

In May 1982, Hickey began traveling to Southeast Asia, ostensibly seeking new markets but really learning the book business "without looking like a complete idiot" – and away from the heat of head office. Today Galloway recalls the dilemma he faced then: "How do you work Brian into Harlequin without getting everyone's noses out of joint? He'd worked in the South Pacific before, and so he took over that, based out of Toronto."

Within six months, Hickey had taken over Josh Gaspero's job running the North American books division as an executive vice president. Gaspero had left to become a Broadway angel, investing in *Sophisticated Ladies* (Heisey took half his share) and trying to produce something called *Captain America.* He also kept his link with Harlequin in a failed attempt to license its name on perfume, collectors' plates, and the like. Eventually he acquired *American Baby*

A meeting of corporate minds: Brian Hickey (left), *Anne Heisey, and Larry Heisey.* HARLEQUIN ENTERPRISES

magazine, which he had worked with at Harlequin, and started a successful children's book-packaging company, Joshua Morris. Reader's Digest bought the company in 1991 and made it part of a children's publishing program called Reader's Digest Young Families, of which Gaspero was cochairman. He resigned in 1996 to become chairman of Best of Times Productions, a film production company, and of Joshua Lockhart, a direct-marketing ad agency.

As Gaspero's successor, Hickey faced another bad time: "People just wouldn't give me information. It was just amazing. They saw me as someone who had nothing to contribute because they thought they knew what they were doing. A bunch of them were gone in the next four months or so."

A bunch: fully 25 percent of Harlequin's staff lost their jobs, and Brian Hickey was the hit man. Galloway had posed the question: would he and Hickey run the business any differently if they owned it? Of the many ideas that surfaced, the most obvious was that the company could be much less bureaucratic – which translated into fewer people. By the late 1970s, Harlequin had become plump with employees, especially at the midlevel. The guest list of a dinner meeting at the time numbered nearly 60 managers, of corporate planning, market analysis, acquisitions, inventory control, order processing, production, public relations, finance and administration, corporate tax, credit, internal audit, and film marketing, among others. The vice president stratum had also bloated, although the lone woman at that level was Roberta Steinberg in personnel. In 1982 Galloway decided to become a low-cost competitor and cut the fat. He lopped off $3 million in corporate overheads by skinning back management layers in the P R, legal, acquisitions, financial, and marketing departments (marketing alone dropped from 21 to 11 people).

A year later, with the Silhouette battle still raging, he had Hickey trim 20 percent of Harlequin's overhead across North America. Over four months, about 100 employees, from editors through salespeople, were let go – most with reasonable settlements, but fired all the same. Hickey professes great pain in the deed: "It's the most god-awful experience you'll ever go through in your life. To this day, I am a real bugger for getting approval to add bodies. And it's got nothing to do with being cheap. I never want to be in a position to have to do that again. In fact, the toughest time to manage is when things are good. Because that's when it's too easy to get lazy and allow that to happen. And there's nothing redeeming in the process: it's just an ugly, ugly experience. You're hurting people desperately." The consolidation continued in 1984 when the overseas operation shifted its base from London to Toronto, saving about $1 million a year in overhead.

Along with getting internally lean by shedding staff, the company also became outwardly meaner. Hickey had come out of the aggressive Johnson's Wax environment with a taste for competitors' blood. At Harlequin he insisted that in any proposal recommending a particular course of action, the proposers must add a section to the usual risks-and-benefits analysis that predicted the impact the action would have on publishing rivals. "So we got much, much tougher," he says. For example, Harlequin's sales force (shrunk to 60 from 100) warned that if overburdened distributors wanted to cut back on its product, they would have to reduce the competition's volumes, too – or, to quote Hickey, "we'll just jam it down your throat again if that's what you want." Harlequin did decrease its shipments by 28 percent in 1983, primarily to lower the company's mounting return rate. In doing so, it squeezed the wholesale distributors to pull back on the numbers that Silhouette and other competitors were shipping into the marketplace. A major wholesale distributor described to me Harlequin's tenaciousness in maintaining its market share of the retail display space: "If they continued to add titles to their series, they would automatically get more space on the fixture. So that's what they did – even though their sales didn't warrant the amount of display space they were getting. They were squeezing out the available space that other people could have sold product in. They rode off their reputation a lot." Carolyn Nichols, then an editor with Jove and Bantam and now with Ballantine Books, still talks about Harlequin's "sharp business practices."

If the company had to ship fewer books to retail customers, it would compensate by beefing up its mail-order business. As Galloway had discovered, the same romances selling at retail for $1.95 demanded a 50 percent discount to the trade, as well as advertising, sales-force, and freight costs. Sold through the mail, each book returned $1.95 – double the wholesale price – and subscribers would have four to 12 books delivered to their doors each month. "No wonder Harlequin is willing to pay the mailing costs," Galloway says. Over two years, he quadrupled the investment in the Harlequin Reader Service, which now carried the internal name of Direct Marketing Department. Operating under executive vice president Michael McSweeney, from the prominent U.S. direct-mail specialist Metro Mail, the division eventually included Reader's Digest alumnae such as Heinz Wermelinger from Switzerland and John Biagini, who would leave Harlequin and launch his own direct-mail romance service.

By the mid-1980s, Harlequin's book club became increasingly sophisticated in its marketing, no longer offering only free books to lure customers. For joining they could get any of 45 different inexpensive premiums offered during a year as signing bonuses. The incentives have ranged from a hand-painted porcelain trinket box to "an exquisite stickpin accented with a glittering Austrian crystal." One solicitation of the time promised a mystery gift if the recipient scratched off the correct boxes in a tic-tac-toe game card to reveal three hearts. Of course, every box contained a heart, although the customer wasn't to know that, having been warned that the card was "not valid if more than 3 boxes have been scratched off." Gradually the stakes got higher as Harlequin offered big-screen T V s, Bermuda cruises, and B M W s as prizes.

The company was late in entering the sweepstakes draws that are a favorite of magazine publishers. But it went into them with a vengeance, dangling the promise of $1 million jackpots to bring in mail-order business. In 1990 Bob Massie, then executive vice president of direct marketing, told Harlequin employees: "Five years ago, we were asking ourselves whether we should even get involved in sweepstakes. Now we can't imagine *not* doing them." The in-house newsletter went on to report: "The aim of these contests is to increase awareness, to sell more books, to keep existing customers and to win back old ones. And it works: from our 1990 Sweepstakes, we will gain approximately four million new customers." That sweeps promotion actually ran for two years, pulling in about 200 million entries from 50 million respondents. Harlequin's overseas subsidiaries in Britain and France have used similar contests to build book club business (now the company also has direct-mail operations in Scandinavia, Holland, and Australia, which it is centralizing with an in-house software system in London). Most sweepstakes prizes are modest in value. "Thank you for the Sunglasses of the Stars that I won. . . . I think I may be the only person in San Saba with 'star' sunglasses," a woman in Texas wrote recently to the Reader Service's monthly newsletter, *Heart to Heart*. The publication, only two pages to minimize mailing costs, is an economical tool to cement subscriber loyalty through readers' letters, author profiles, and a pen-pal column – while plugging the five dozen titles available in the following month's shipment of books.

This focusing on the book club, pressuring the distributors, and slimming down the staff all began to pay back when Harlequin – a year after celebrating its 35th anniversary in New York and its birthplace of Winnipeg – absorbed its competitor. A relieved Beland Honderich restructured Torstar's management into two new operating divisions. Galloway became president of the book-publishing and direct-mail division, while old friend David Jolley was named president of the newspaper and printing division. The book publisher's profits doubled in 1985 to $42 million from the previous year and were $10 million higher in 1986. They were contributing roughly half of Torstar's profits. Harlequin now had another brand to sell in North America and overseas, sales costs decreased in the new distribution agreement with Simon & Schuster/Pocket Books, and the folding of Silhouette's book club into Harlequin would increase revenues while cutting expenses. In 1987 cover prices rose by 25 cents. During the last half of the decade, Harlequin regularly posted record returns.

David Galloway is sensitive about the criticism lodged by stock analysts that, with the Torstar takeover, Harlequin lost much of its entrepreneurial energy. When Dick Bonnycastle and Bill Willson left to build Rupertsland Resources, he says, they attracted the money of a bevy of Harlequin employees whose small stakes in the company had grown over the years. "A lot of people in the company made a lot of money on Harlequin shares. [They] made $100,000 because they had $5,000 in Harlequin. So what did they do with their money? They could have left it in Torstar, but they took it out and followed Bonnycastle and went into Rupertsland" – which, of course, went broke. "So I used to listen to these analysts and say, 'Well, you've got yourself a choice here, you can put your money into Rupertsland, or you can put your money into Torstar.'"

Silhouette may no longer have existed as a competitor, but its influence lingered. A significant fallout of its explosion on the scene was the segmentation of the romance market, which resulted in so many more novels being written for so many tastes by new authors and being handled by new editors – most of them North American. As Galloway noted in a 1983 speech, "Our main editorial department historically was in London. It did not occur to them or to Harlequin management that product development on this side of the Atlantic could pay dividends. We should have produced our own competition." The shell burst of Silhouette and other competitors forced Harlequin to do just that, and the editorial balance irrevocably shifted from London to Toronto and New York.

When Silhouette came on board, suddenly the
company lost its focus.
  – Harlequin vice president Star Helmer

II

A Place of Storms
THE EDITORS

For Harlequin's newly appointed vice president of romance, editorial, the Silhouette takeover meant little but trouble. Although the rival had been swallowed up, it would continue as a separate brand, and its editorial office in New York would survive virtually intact – an acknowledgment that Silhouette had fashioned product at least equal in quality to Harlequin's. True, Star Helmer now had a fancier title, but she wielded no power over the editors she had been competing with during her past year and a half at Harlequin. Not only that, she had just been told that her colleague Richard Lawson, vice president of North American publishing services, would be taking over her copyediting department. While Silhouette's editors would continue to do the major structural editing on their authors' books in New York, the copyediting – fine-tuning for grammar, spelling, house style – would be handled in Toronto. And management had thought the Silhouette editors might feel uncomfortable if Harlequin's editorial chief had a chance to second-guess their work.

Sitting in her seventh-floor Toronto office – its door emblazoned with silver stars and the office settee stuffed with various subspecies of cuddly teddy bears – Star Helmer was not happy. She found the decision insulting, as if they were implying she would somehow forsake her personal integrity to short-change or even sabotage Silhouette's books. Certainly she bore no great love for the line. Before coming to Harlequin, she had been editor in chief of Richard Gallen Books, the packager that started creating long historical and modern romance novels for Pocket Books in 1979. Their contemporary heroines were often independent, sexually knowledgeable women, and the subject matter was mature enough even to allow a homosexual affair between minor characters. Jude Devereaux and LaVyrle Spencer were among the Gallen-nurtured writers who would become superstars in romantic fiction. And as Gallen began collapsing around Helmer, Pocket Books and Silhouette went after its highest-profile names. Now the accomplished Karen Solem, editor in chief of Silhouette when it competed with Harlequin, was still there, running the office in New York.

"In some very subtle ways and not-so-subtle ways," Helmer recalls, "the two editorial departments were never allowed to be brought together. We were supposed to be developing an air of friendly competition, but it didn't work." If a writer being published regularly by either Harlequin or Silhouette had a work rejected by one of them, she could now quietly submit it to the other. Agents began to play the two offices off one another on issues such as the size of authors' advances against royalties. Problems also arose when the small Harlequin staff in New York – set up by Vivian Stephens to start American Romances – had to share new offices at 300 East Forty-second Street with a Silhouette staff about four times the size. "Supposedly Harlequin bought Silhouette," Helmer says, "but *they* were acting like *they* were in charge. A lot of the Harlequin editors in New York definitely felt uncomfortable: nobody wanted to talk to them. They felt that they were being shoved into a corner."

Single, in her mid-thirties, standing nearly six feet, the big-boned Helmer had a physical presence and a personality whose sheer force sustained her through conflicts with her peers, particularly Dick Lawson, as well as through dealings with her staff of about 32 (half a dozen fewer when she lost the copy editors). When she arrived in January 1983, "they had an incredible number of editors for what they were producing – as originals, anyway. Not only was it glutted, but then I found all kinds of little stories: that some of the editors had formed their own freelance company, and they were being permitted to assign things out to themselves. . . . They were all entitled to get overtime, as well. Harlequin salaries for editors tend to be higher than at other publishing houses." Among other perks of a generally generous employer were lavish Christmas and golfing parties and financial support of up to several thousand dollars for editors who wanted to better their education. "Back in the mid-eighties," one editor of the time told me, "they had the best benefits of any publisher. They were paranoid about getting a union into the company." And for a while, David Galloway brought a new openness to the operations. Associate editor Brian Henry describes the change: "In the Galloway months – a very short time when he was hands-on in charge of Harlequin – he had a series of meetings with everybody who worked in the company, with catered lunches and 10 people or so around the table, and he made decisions. The change – and it was a very significant change – is that we were actually talking to the people who were running the company."

In 1983 Mills & Boon was still editing all the Romances and Presents novels in London, Harlequin's U.S. office was about to launch its American Romances in New York, and Wally Exman was running the Raven House mystery brand. Star Helmer's immediate responsibility was the Superromance line, whose sales were slipping. Fred Kerner and his editorial manager, George Glay, had developed this series of four longer novels a month. Through Judy Bonnycastle Burgess, a Toronto advertising copywriter named Barbara Browse had submitted a raw manuscript that excited Glay. As Kerner tells it, "George said this woman had a sense of what a novel is. It's not two characters and they meet in the first chapter and they marry in the last chapter – she *understood.* It was mostly his doing that got Barbara over the hump of making her into a serious novelist. The book was called *End of Innocence,* which was a very appropriate title. She came up with a subplot love story, and we built a 100,000-word midlist novel. Damn thing sold itself crazy. She earned almost $100,000 in royalties." Kerner called it his R&D novel.

Superromance's midwives were on their way out by the time Star Helmer came in. Kerner was about to retire as editor in chief, although he would remain as a consulting editor emeritus until early 1996. Glay was let go in the spring of 1983, after more than six years with Harlequin (he died of cancer in May 1996). He had been hired by Kerner, who knew him in New York as editor in chief at the Macfadden-Bartell paperback house that published genre fiction. The middle-aged Canadian had spent a quarter century in North America's publishing capital. In the 1940s, inspired by his mother's success with true-confession stories, Glay earned the title of the Confession King for selling 50 of the magazine pieces in 52 weeks. He followed up with three novels; *Gina,* the first one, which became part of early Harlequin history, was translated into nine languages and was still in print 35 years later. Seeking more remunerative work, he did stints as a literary agent and as the editorial director of Universal Publishing's Award Books, which specialized in series and category paperbacks. At Harlequin he was responsible for the Superromances, officially described as "contemporary love stories for the woman of today" – in their editor's words, "the Superromance girl might go to bed with her lover, but she thinks she'll marry the guy." The fourth in the series, *Love Beyond Desire,* has this scene set in Mexico:

> Lying sleeplessly in her bed, Robin knew that Ernesto's kiss had stirred feelings deep within her that she had not known existed. The kisses she had exchanged with Fairville boys had been light, casual. They had awakened no sleeping fires, as Ernesto's had done. It's just that Ernesto is older, more sophisticated, she told herself. He's a man of the world. He's not for me. I'm not to blame for that kiss.

Glay was to blame for that and other Superromances. Openly gay, he had sometimes hired male friends to write for the line. While their writing could be equal to the female authors', the men might give the hero a male character as a foil who would then share too much of the spotlight with the heroine. Star Helmer's criticism was that the 95,000-word books were simply extended Mills & Boon titles. She wanted more story, fewer clichés. "I think one of the problems was that the Superromance line was being guided by a man who was not only a man but an older man."

In New York, meanwhile, Harlequin's American Romances were being guided by a woman who was not only a woman but also an attractive young black woman with a wide smile and close-cropped hair. Vivian Stephens was senior editor of the line, a job that Helmer herself had applied for in 1981. Kerner preferred Stephens, based on her track record with Dell's Ecstasy line. That series "had an immediate and lasting impact upon the romance fiction genre," said Vivien Lee Jennings as publisher of the romance newsletter *Boy Meets Girl.* "Its sensual content, modern American heroines and more realistic stories were a clear departure from the pristine Harlequin formula. . . ." The editor also had a superb reputation with authors as the founder of their support group, Romance Writers of America. To Kerner, however, Stephens was "a disaster" – probably because she was soon reporting to Josh Gaspero, the new head of the North American books division, rather than him. "And he gave her her head. All of a sudden, she was a queen. We were just these hicks in Canada. And she didn't last very long."

Long enough, however, to bring a little dose of realism into the old romance, letting a reader fantasize about someone more like her spouse than Tom Selleck. The conflicts were more contemporary: for instance, the heroine of *Tomorrow's Promise* by Sandra Brown falls in love with another guy while her serviceman husband is missing in action in Vietnam. And Stephens revived an experiment she had begun at Dell to publish ethnic romances featuring black, Hispanic, and Chinese characters: although poor sales had killed the idea at Dell, at Harlequin she had author Jackie Weger change the characters in one manuscript from Southern whites to blacks. The bastardized novel sold badly, as did a few later books written originally with black characters, but in recent years, ethnic heroes and heroines by black authors such as Sandra Kitt have reappeared to more success. Stephens, self-admittedly not a corporate animal, was eased out only a few months after her American Romances came on stream. However, most of them sold well: as Vivien Lee Jennings reported, it was "one of the few Harlequin brands that was generally believed to be profitable for Harlequin at war's end."

During Star Helmer's tenure, the Toronto office launched Harlequin Temptations, "sensually charged contemporary romantic fantasies," while the New York editors developed Romantic Intrigues "set against a backdrop of suspense and adventure," Gothic Romances "with [an] element of foreboding or hidden evil," and Regency Romances "set in England between 1811 and 1820." The various strata of editors at the time included editorial assistants who were partly office gofers, assistant editors who were not allowed to sign contracts with writers (but never had to do any more filing), and associate editors who could do contracts. Full-fledged editors had a better title and more money; senior editors had a staff and responsibility for an entire series; and coordinators, a notch above, usually handled more than one series. An editorial director such as Star Helmer ran the department. She was eventually bumped up to vice president, a grander title she claims she didn't want because it would make getting another job more difficult when she left Harlequin.

From a writer's point of view, there are only two kinds of editors that count. In the words of Harlequin author Heather Graham, "there's your line editor and your copy editor. When George has blue eyes on page 3 and then they're green on page 44 and gray on 85, your copy editor helps you think through things like that. Your line editor, which is your house editor, often helps you get into the deeper inconsistencies." Not all of the editors' criticisms are warmly welcomed: "My first book was a Candlelight Ecstasy," Graham notes, "and I had my heroine getting pregnant by accident in the story. And [my editor] wrote me back, 'No intelligent modern woman today would do that' – and of course I was pregnant by accident at the time."

Writers become loyal to editors they trust. But during the first many years when the two North American offices operated independently, it was harder for Harlequin writers to develop such a relationship. Silhouette assigned one editor to remain with an author no matter which type of romance she wrote. Harlequin, determined to keep its different lines distinct, insisted that an author deal with the editor of whichever series her book most suited. One problem of this latter system was that a writer would tend to stay within the same line, and perhaps not develop, simply because she wanted to keep the same editor. Another, more serious concern for Harlequin was that if the editors keep changing, the writer is less likely to retain any loyalty to the publisher. Much later, the two offices blended their operating styles in an effort to keep the authors happy.

Early on at Harlequin, Star Helmer was editing some books herself, including *Double Standards,* the second novel by Judith McNaught, who would soon be well on her way to superstardom. McNaught picks up the story: "She was the new editor who came in and took it over after the first Harlequin editor had bought the book. And she wanted me to do some things I personally abhor the idea of. And her exact reasons were – and I said this in an open speech – she wanted to see them *doing it* on page 249, and forgot the story was about a heroine who convinced herself that this man loved her and realized in the worst possible way that he did not – that it was just a pickup and she might have ended up pregnant. So I withdrew the book, and it was submitted then by my agent to a new line that only had a phone extension, which later became Harlequin Temptation. That editor bought it. . . ." While McNaught had to cut it by a third, she could leave the story as it was. As for Star Helmer's attempt at editing, "that was an irrational and unjust and foolish request – along with 'Move it out of Detroit because it's ugly, ugly,' and she said she'd never been there when I asked her."

Helmer's own writing skills were the subject of some sport among her staff, who would take turns editing her often clumsy memos to editors. She also circulated lists detailing editorial taboos and overworked clichés under various headings. "Conflicts: buying and renovating old inns; being marooned in the wilderness which leads to S.E.X. Careers: politicians; writers of all kinds. Situations: meddling old matriarchs; hero or heroine jumping into a shower immediately before or after sex." Phrases to avoid included "corded sinews, rippling muscles; tiny little fists – often beating against his chest; electrical currents traveling through nerve endings." Sometimes subjects were banned for little reason. At one point, having a hero or heroine with amnesia made the forbidden list – and endured. "They'd done two amnesia stories within a few months," an editor told me, "so somebody said, 'Right, no more,' and somehow the amnesia rule stayed. And they had probably been the two bestselling books of the year – readers love amnesia stories." Some of Harlequin's most recent guidelines, reprinted in a romance writers' journal, say its editors are now actively seeking stories of amnesia victims, along with the "ever-popular" themes of marriages of convenience, secret babies, single fathers, weddings, and bad boy/outlaw heroes.

Helmer's memos supplemented a copy editors' "Style/Procedure Guide (In-house)," which defined niceties such as spelling, grammar, misused words, and what were called dialogue tags – the verbs that doubled for "said." The guide contained a list of 155 alternatives, from "advised" to "yelled," and cautioned especially against the misuse of "hissed." This was an embarrassed reaction to a *Maclean's* article a decade earlier that quoted a classic Harlequin line – "You little fool," he hissed, "you're heading for a fall" – and then twitted: "Apart from the purple prose, have you ever tried hissing a sentence that doesn't have an 's'?" More recently that kind of clichéd writing was the subject of a book by a romance author and a teacher of romance writing – although the authors perhaps planned *The Romance Writers' Phrase Book* as more of an inspiration than an admonition against bad writing. Their collection of 3,000 descriptive tags "guaranteed to stimulate the imagination" includes aids such as "Facial expression: 'His lips twisted into a cynical smile,'" and "Emotions: 'She imposed an iron control on herself.'"

Despite the seeming thicket of shifting guidelines and sheer prohibitions, some editors have been brave enough to write their own romances – Beverley Katz-Rosenbaum, for one. A university graduate, like most Harlequin editors, she had thought of the genre as "sexist and stupid" until quickly boning up on three books before an interview for an editing job with Harlequin. After handling other writers, she decided to become one herself. At 29 she published her first Superromance, *What Friends Are For,* under the more alliterative pen name Beverley Bryan. "I soon realized that I had poured my heart and soul into the first three chapters," she wrote later, "and I couldn't work up quite the same enthusiasm to continue the book." Her editors agreed with her analysis, explaining that the second half of the book "lagged" – a criticism that sent her into "a week-long stupor of self-pity." In all it took two years from synopsis to sale. Rosemary Aubert, a senior editor, had already sold three Harlequins before the release of *Firebrand* in 1986. Its romantic single-father hero was based on left-leaning Toronto mayor John Sewell. Unfortunately Aubert not only modeled a minor character on a neighbor, she also used her name, and when the religious woman threatened to sue Harlequin, the company pulled every copy of *Firebrand* from the shelves and pulped them.

Some authors have protested the fact of editors writing books that compete with their own manuscripts for places on the publisher's list. Author Susan Wiggs noted in 1995 that at least two Harlequin editors were writing for their own line – Julianne Moore (pen name Jule McBride), and Malle Valek. In an article in the Romance Writers of America newsletter, *PANdora's Box,* she raised the issue of an editor/writer's conflict of interest. Supposedly quoting another popular author, she asked: "Are we truly to believe that this editor will be completely objective when she has one slot to fill and one of the submissions is her own book . . . ? I cannot imagine that an assistant editor would reject her boss or co-worker in favor of a 'civilian' writer." Candy Lee, who is currently Harlequin's publisher and vice president, replied that "senior editors have a responsibility to their line and to their author base that far outweighs any private or friendly gesture."

Whether they try writing their own Harlequin or not, the editors I spoke with generally admired their authors' energy, professionalism, and storytelling abilities, if not always their literary skills. Writers such as Judith McNaught, who will work 20 hours a day if necessary and who bought the dress for her daughter's wedding 36 hours before the event after writing for three days without sleep. Or Harlequin author Pat Keelyn, who began her career by typing into her computer two entire romance novels by bestselling Sandra Brown to see if she could absorb writing techniques such as pacing. Or Glenda Sanders, who attended a four-day seminar, led by experts, on bunco crime to research her novel *Gypsy*.

Helen Heller went from editing Raven House mysteries to five months of wading through some of the 5,000 unsolicited romance manuscripts a year that were then flooding the slush piles of Harlequin and Mills & Boon. "It gave me a healthy respect for romance authors," she says. "It's not easy to write a romance. I don't enjoy them, but I'm not going to put down the genre." Today editors take turns reading the slush, the complete manuscripts the company asks first-time writers to send. They remain aware of the fact that Nora Roberts and Janet Dailey were unknowns when they mailed in their first unrequested submissions. The company also realizes that the hopeful writers are usually enthusiastic romance readers – good customers. To help them, it offers general guidelines for all its series. A recent example for the 60,000-word Temptation line:

> This is Harlequin's boldest, most sensuous series, focusing on men and women living – and loving – in the 1990s! Almost anything goes in Temptation: the stories may be humorous, topical, adventurous or glitzy, but at heart, they are pure romantic fantasy. Think fast-paced, use the desires and language of women today, add a high level of sexual tension, along with strong conflicts and then throw in a good dash of "what if . . ." The results should sizzle!

Male editors, like male writers, are rare in the romance field. During Star Helmer's time, Brian Henry was an associate editor dealing with Intrigues and Superromances in the Toronto office, while London had Luigi Bonomi, an executive editor who later went to Penguin. Henry, a University of Toronto arts graduate, began as a freelancer in 1983 by copyediting The Executioner series ("Is 'flesh-shredder' hyphenated?"). The fee was $14 an hour, and the rule of thumb was that an editor could spend about 20 hours per 200-page book. He was grateful to move on to his first Superromance: "The content was irrelevant. I do recall it was rather better written than the action-adventures. You don't ever encounter a page of half-sentences." As a copy editor, he was told to change as little as possible "because these are real authors writing romance, and they care a great deal and don't like you messing around with them." He had to suppress his natural aggression as an editor. "If it's grammatically okay, you leave it. And if you can see a better way of doing it – well, tough. It's not your book."

After two years, he came on staff at about $20,000 a year and went on a night shift of copy editors and proofreaders as Harlequin cranked up to a factorylike frenzy during the first half of the 1980s. Graduating to an associate editorship, he had a stable of about 20 romance authors, a dozen of them regulars. They included Dawn Stewardson, with an M.B.A. and a master's of library science, who eventually became a neighbor of his, and the husband-and-wife team of Dan and Lynda Trent, who write under her name. He would read their submissions for book ideas (two to three consecutive sample chapters and a synopsis), assign the books, edit the manuscripts for sense and substance, and write detailed revision letters. There is an art to such critiques. Judith McNaught remembers the one she received from her first Harlequin editor: "It was a good revision letter, although at the time, I would have fed it to her. . . . Four pages long, single-spaced, small typeface. And for the most part, she was right because I was trying to write the way I'd always seen them written." Professionals such as Heather Graham who acknowledge their limitations come to accept the criticisms with a certain equanimity, even humor. A note about one of her manuscripts came from "an editor I absolutely love and respect, but she must have gotten a little bit weary at the end of it because she said, 'if this heroine bites her lip one more time, there will be blood dripping down her chest.' . . . I've got a thing with eyebrows – people are arching them all the time. So now I'm trying to keep my eyebrows and lips down a bit."

Harlequin publisher Candy Lee told me that, while never a line editor, she understands the subtleties involved in responding sensitively to a writer's work: "It's helping the author figure out in her own voice and in her own methodology how to get to some point that answers all the questions. But to get there in her own way. And to live through that sort of back and forth that's required so you don't overstep the line and the author feels, 'They're making me change my beloved book.' And so the editor doesn't feel, 'I'm publishing a less good book than I really should be doing.' That, I think, is another unique talent, and I don't actually have it."

Harlequin's editors have seldom had to reject outright a veteran author's book – although when Brian Henry tried to pass on one he thought execrable, he was told this was one of the company's most established writers and she would get a second hearing; the novel was published. On the other hand, Helen Heller says she helped to convince Harlequin to decline a Mills & Boon book by a big-name British author, Penny Jordan *(Power Play, Silver)*. "I feel quite proud of it," she says. "The story was so violent. The hero beats the shit out of the heroine and the other woman – a half-sister in love with her half-brother – pushes her down the stairs."

Harlequin editors often have to discuss contracts with writers or their agents – although Henry, who was let go in 1993, says, "Contracts are a joke. There's nothing that's negotiable. It doesn't exactly take much effort." During Star Helmer's time, the usual advance of $5,000 for a novice author did increase by $500 a book, but that generosity ended when sales began to slip during the decade. Recently some new Harlequin authors told me they have been offered as little as $3,500 to $4,000 in advances against six percent royalties and an increment of only $250 for a second book. One of them had done three full revisions of her manuscript over three years. Established writers, of course, earn substantially more per book, especially for the fat Superromances. And a Harlequin author such as Nora Roberts who graduates to mainstream books gets in the middle to high six-figure range for hardcover and paperback rights ("It's like Monopoly money," Roberts told me). A decade ago, as now, the author of the average short Harlequin could eventually collect $15,000 to $20,000 in royalties; prolific writers can do four and sometimes more of those books in a year.

One of the editorial department's tasks is to prepare a report on each manuscript for the art department. It describes the characters physically, perhaps the kind of clothing they wear if it is a period story, the locale, and sometimes scenes that might make a good marketing cover. Obviously covers can be potent selling tools: aside from promoting reader loyalty to an author or a brand such as Harlequin, they play the major role in an impulse purchase of a romance novel.

During Star Helmer's time, Charles Kadin was the graphic-arts director, as he would be until replaced at the end of 1992. The six-foot-three, lean-faced graduate of the art program at Toronto's Central Technical School had spent a dozen years at Eaton's as creative director of the department store's famous mail-order catalog. Fred Kerner hired him as a 41-year-old in 1976, when the only other staff in the department were a couple of so-called mechanical artists who did the physical pasteup of the paperback covers. He took Kadin to bookstores to watch readers selecting Harlequins and ask why they chose one cover over another. "This is a loyal audience. You change things subtly," Kerner says. "We planned six changes. Did one, and 18 months later introduced the second, and no one even knew the covers were changed."

Kadin, with little experience of illustrators, assessed Harlequin's current crop: a prolific, long-running pair in Winnipeg – Bern Smith and Emile Laliberté – and a handful in Toronto. "They were producing covers where everybody looked alike, other than the color of their hair or eyes," he says. "They were working from something out of a magazine or photos of their neighbors." He focused on several Toronto artists, including Will Davies, skilled at creating stalwart Savile Row Englishmen and dark-eyed Latin heroes, who has since done several hundred Harlequin covers in watercolor based on black-and-white photos of models. At the time, Kadin himself would skim a manuscript or galley proof and write a specific art direction for a cover, insisting that the characters look like those in the novel. Later he created a form for editorial to fill in: hair and eye color, heights, settings, clothing, cars, pets. He would hear from readers if a heroine's hair was black on the cover and brown in the book. "The heroines were mostly ingenues, trembling little English girls who were feeling the hardness of his manhood for the first time. When we bought the Silhouette line, there was one fully detailed fuck every 10 or 12 pages."

While Harlequin was competing with Silhouette, Josh Gaspero asked him: "What does it take to get the best illustrators to knock the pants off Simon & Schuster?"

"I need the budget, and I need the access," Kadin said. "You have to be prepared to let me go to New York. The artists don't like working by phone."

Kadin joined the New York Society of Illustrators and started using about three dozen American-based artists, among them Pino Daeni. The recent

Italian immigrant could do five covers a month for Harlequin and its competitors; "he was like a machine, and now. he's a millionaire," Kadin says. Daeni's oil paintings on thin illustration board have a looser style than those of Elaine Duillo, another Harlequin regular whose detailed covers in transparent watercolors made her a popular romance illustrator. Kadin would hire a photographer's studio at $350 to $450 for a shoot, with male and female models charging $150 an hour apiece. If the company was preparing a new line, Kadin or a Harlequin art buyer would be on hand to direct the session with the illustrator – who would then use the resulting photographs to do a sketch for discussion by the buyer, the editor, and the new crop of dynamic young marketing people such as Dave Sanderson. With the concept approved, the artist projected the appropriate photo onto an art board and traced it as the base for the cover art. Today some art directors are using computer graphics to enhance the traditionally created illustrations. Others have introduced covers with eye-catching foil, embossing, die cuts, and even holograms. Meanwhile, as Kadin was commissioning some of New York's best illustrators, Mills & Boon was buying second rights to old paperback and magazine art for its hardcover jackets and paperback covers. Fred Kerner says, "They refused to have our artists supply them with the art we had done for our editions, even though we were buying world rights – and it would have effected a saving for them if they didn't buy any other art." Instead, the London office "bought trashy art with the resemblances to the characters in the books left to chance."

The Harlequin covers of the early 1960s had portrayed the heroine as a sweet, scrubbed young thing, while the hero lurked behind her against a nondescript background. The locales became more definably exotic, but not until the 1970s did the characters share the stage more equally. By then they also appeared more knowing and visibly entangled – although it took the Temptation series of the next decade to have them regularly indulge in the clichéd passionate embrace the industry calls "the clinch." The idea of exposing female skin on the covers of books aimed at women is generally attributed to the fact that the retailers who stocked them were usually men. As editor, agent, and book buyer Denise Little has observed, "Publishers made an amazing discovery. The more female skin displayed on the covers of their books, the more copies these men purchased for their stores." Harlequin's covers were never as flagrant as their bosom-baring competitors'. A typical Temptation of 1987 – Shirley Larson's *Wit and Wisdom*

("He knew too much about the birds and bees") – has the hero with his shirt open, while the heroine, in mild ecstasy as his lips approach her cheek, bares only her arms. In recent years, a move to make romances look more respectable has resulted in what the trade calls step-backs, in which the cover on display is a genteel design of flowers or jewels but opens to a second cover with the familiar clinch. A stock-in-trade that Harlequin has avoided is the use of celebrity models on its covers. Fabio was the first of the breed, appearing on an Avon cover in 1986, and the bleached-blond Italian became so popular that the publisher put his name as author on a series of ghostwritten historical romance novels. Viking Penguin created its own cover personality in Steve Sandalis, the Topaz Man. The closest Harlequin has come to personality posers is occasionally to use Connecticut actress and Ford model Cindy Guyer, nicknamed the female Fabio after appearing on more than 1,000 romance covers.

By the mid-1980s, Charles Kadin was using 56 independent artists as he oversaw the production of more than 450 titles a year. Among them were Gold Eagle's action-adventure novels, which offered him peculiar challenges. He was personally interested in weaponry, and so were the readers. "The yo-yos – the rednecks, the clients – liked our covers. And they wanted to see the hero using different kinds of firearms. The readers had suggestions, and we followed them." Editor Mark Howell also had him fly to England to interview a writer working on a new six-book series called Deathlands about a post-holocaust, radioactive world. Howell had seen only one chapter from the man and wanted to squeeze enough out of him to assign cover art. Kadin sat with the author in Worcester for three days. "He was drunk most of the time, and I couldn't get him to talk about it very much." But the graphic-arts director conceived an effective cover by Michael Henry showing a clutch of daisies beside a pair of feet in battered boots. The boots became a motif for the successful series, which – though the original writer was replaced – is still running today.

And the readers are still fascinated with firearms, often sending editors photographs of their own beloved weapons. Gold Eagle has a club of readers who are finicky about accuracy and consistency. "We do get letters," says the current editorial director, Feroze Mohammed. "We have slipped up in the past. Putting the wrong ammunition in a certain weapon. The writer made the mistake. It passed us by. We do have reference material like *Jane's*, and we do check these things out. We apologize to the readers." Over the years Mack Bolan's fans – among them convicts, survivalists, soldiers, and paramilitary types – have sent voluminous amounts of mail on many subjects, including love notes to April Rose, Bolan's girlfriend, who was eventually bumped off in the series.

Mohammed, an ex-Trinidadian freelancing as a copy editor for Harlequin in Toronto, came on in 1982 as an assistant to Gold Eagle executive editor Mark Howell. At first they were producing 24 books a year, half of them The Executioner series, the others the spin-off Able Team and Phoenix Force. But Howell brimmed with ideas for additional lines that were published for a while – single-title espionage thrillers and SOBs, a series about mercenaries – and some that were never approved, like one featuring western sagas. Among the survivors are Deathlands, The Executioner, and another chip off the Bolan block, Stony Man. That series is named for Mack's command base in Virginia, where he and characters from Phoenix Force and other series might appear ("Satan missiles, the world's most powerful nuclear warheads, are being sold on the Moscow black market. The Stony Man warriors must act with swift and deadly force . . ."). A similar brand, Black Ops, briefly showcased a team of commandos who travel the world avenging acts of terror against Americans. It is being supplanted by another high-adventure line with a bit of a science fiction twist, in the works for 1997 and to be released under the Deathlands house name, James Axler. And, perhaps as a bit of balance, Gold Eagle recently got the license to publish The Destroyer series, created by Warren Murphy, which sends up the whole genre. Together, these male-oriented books represent less than five percent of Harlequin's overall volume and have been on a sales plateau for the last half-dozen years.

Harlequin has always been overly protective of its Gold Eagle heroes, especially Mack Bolan. Its executives even contemplated, although never acted upon, a plagiarism suit against David Morrell, the Canadian creator of the Rambo character, and the makers of the film versions starring Sylvester Stallone. They also considered suing the producers of the TV series *The A-Team* (with Mr. T and George Peppard) for allegedly ripping off Gold Eagle's Able Team. These outlandishly macho heroes have presented problems for female Harlequin staff. In the mid-eighties a stand-alone action novel called

Mad Dog precipitated a crisis among editors. One male editor describes it as "easily the most sadistic, misogynistic novel to come through Harlequin – and a special favorite of Mark Howell's." All of the female copy editors and proof-readers refused to work on it.

Mohammed was involved in the post-Pendleton process that extended The Executioner's reach to encompass international terrorists as well as the Mafia. He had met Don Pendleton and found him "a very nice, gentle man . . . so erudite and well read. Pendleton had said very early on that Bolan's enemies are not stupid people. They know exactly what they are doing. It's just not good enough to say, well, 'Middle Eastern terrorists.'" The books tend to cap-italize on current events: the 1996 *Hunting Cry*, dealing with a European white slavery ring, begins in war-battered Bosnia. Readers have responded enthusi-astically to the content and tone of the continuing series, wanting to get in touch with Pendleton and thank him, in some cases, for starting them read-ing. "We're talking about literacy here," Mohammed says.

He also runs the Worldwide Mystery program of first-time paperback edi-tions of hardcover fiction, 36 cozy mysteries a year starring amateur detectives, medium-boiled private eyes, and police procedurals. For several years, he had worked under Howell and an editorial director named Randall Toye, the author of an authoritative work on Agatha Christie for the company's Jonathan-James book-packaging division and a freelance Harlequin editor in the late 1970s. After Howell was fired and Toye moved up to become director of the entire editorial operation, Feroze Mohammed took over as Gold Eagle's senior editor and editorial coordinator. At any one time, he has 12 to 14 writ-ers working on the various Gold Eagle lines, most of them Americans, includ-ing a lawyer, a police officer, and currently a creative writing instructor at the University of Oklahoma. A veteran Bolan author, Michael Newton is a Pendleton protégé, a former schoolteacher who has written an encyclopedia on 20th-century killers and *Armed and Dangerous: A Writer's Guide to Weapons*. Feroze Mohammed met with three of the Executioner authors in Oklahoma City not long ago. "We do try to draw things from today's head-lines," he says, "but by the time you get the book out, it's forgotten. We wanted to see what's current, what's the mood of the U.S. . . . We didn't want to sug-gest that we pounce on the militia groups, but was there some sort of truth, legitimacy, to the existence of such groups and such behavior . . . ? We came away with what we call, in-house, the splintering of America." Which means? "Just what it says: American society is not this cohesive thing. You have people with different agendas."

Amid her term as vice president, editorial, romance, Star Helmer found her fiefdom splintering as colleague Richard Lawson tried to act out his different agenda. Dick Lawson, vice president, North American publishing services, had been one of Josh Gaspero's gang from Western Publishing and eventually married Gaspero's ex-wife, an airline stewardess. With his cleft chin and dimples, Lawson was Harlequin's Cary Grant – in appearance. He was a decade older, much smaller in stature, and much less flamboyant in nature than Helmer, though no less steel-willed. Their battlefield was the burgeoning role of computers in a company that seemed made for them. Lawson was determined to revolutionize the production of Harlequin books the way Larry Heisey had transformed their sales and marketing. He purchased a flotilla of slightly used P C s from I B M , just down the road in Don Mills, and in a bid to romance Star's staff with the pleasures of on-screen editing, he had officials of an Atlanta-based software company fly up to Toronto to present a word-processing program called Samna 3. In practice it was an unwieldy, unproven program that slowed the work of editing. "Basically it was a pain in the butt," Brian Henry says. "You'd have a manuscript on four different disks. It was a lousy system." In fact, some of the fatter novels took up seven disks. The editors complained to their boss, and she took their fight up to the highest levels of the company. The battle between Helmer and Lawson was an old one: the responsibility for copyediting had bounced back and forth between the editorial and production departments, and this was just another skirmish.

"I was basically told this is a fait accompli: we are going to edit on computers and it's going to start, like, now," Star Helmer recalls. The one feature she wanted was the use of modems to streamline communications between her office and authors across the continent. But she was told that the modems were too slow and that long-distance charges would be too high. Nor did all the editors have their own computers; the P C s were put on rolling carts to be shared among the staff. Lawson reasoned that the editors were not all working on manuscripts all at the same time. "But then again," Helmer argued, "they might be." Lawson had failed to take into account the fact that editors sometimes worked at night and on weekends, and editing on a P C meant they could only work at the office. Helmer estimated that with such slowdowns and the flaws in the software, productivity might have been cut in half.

Harlequin hired a computer expert and a psychologist to mediate between Helmer and Lawson. Helmer says, "One of the recommendations was that Richard and I needed 'marriage counseling.' *Excuse me.*" Finally her head boss, Brian Hickey, convened a meeting in the lunchroom and brought in the software expert, who upset the editors by assuming in his remarks that they all had P C s at home. An editor finally asked how much the computers were saving in costs. A hesitant Lawson admitted: "Plus or minus $150,000."

To which Helmer commented: "We might be losing money on this? And you haven't even taken into account the fact that the editors aren't working at home anymore because they can't take the P C s on the subway."

Hickey pulled the plug on the computers for the moment – while today's editors have access to better hardware and software, they still don't edit on-screen – and Helmer threw a little champagne party to release tension. An editor at the celebration says Helmer went into the hallway at one point, jumped up and down, and chanted, "Nyah, nyah, nyah" in the direction of Lawson's office. "Maybe in retrospect it was the wrong thing to do," she says of the party. "Obviously Hickey and Lawson didn't like it."

As time went on, Helmer became increasingly bored with her work, a state of ennui noticed by some of her staff. Her immediate superior was Horst Bausch, who had run Cora Verlag, the editorial side of Harlequin's joint venture in Germany with the Springer group. Bausch had been moved to London to replace Alan Boon; he had also assumed Fred Kerner's upper-echelon role in overseeing the romance field in North America. In 1986 he went to Toronto as editor in chief and a vice president, supposedly moving the editorial decision-making power with him. "I have no idea what he did," editor Brian Henry says, expressing a common feeling in the editorial department at the time. What *did* Bausch do? "That's an interesting question," Helmer says. "If you find out, let me know. He did lunch." Needlessly unkind words, but Kerner also wondered about his effectiveness. "He's a nice guy," Kerner says, but adds: "Why a European with no experience in the North American market, which is the biggest market for Harlequin? Totally incapable of talking to authors even." Bausch's English, while good, wasn't attuned to the subtleties of the language that an editorial chief should appreciate. Even Brian Hickey would raise the issue later, posing him the rhetorical question: "Why would a North American company go with a German editor in chief?" As for Bausch, he says, "I had always a very good relationship with Brian, but it wasn't a close relationship. Brian wouldn't be that forthcoming with his thoughts. . . . The strange thing is, as a person you might feel more warmth in him than in David [Galloway], but you couldn't get as close to him."

Helmer told Bausch in the summer of 1987 that she wanted a special project to keep her occupied. She says he promised to get back to her on it but never did. A year later, she was among three high-level executives fired in what was becoming an almost routine Harlequin housecleaning. (As an editor describes the purges, "it was like a cold wind blowing through.") She was replaced by Karen Solem, vice president of the Silhouette editorial operation, who stayed in New York but remained with the company only briefly. "Initially," Horst Bausch admits, "we had some difficulties because she used to be her own boss, and suddenly she had to report to me." Solem has since worked for HarperCollins as a respected editor of single-title romances and for Writers House in New York, where she is now a literary agent.

The same year that Star Helmer left, 1988, the dark-haired Frances Whitehead became editorial director of Mills & Boon. While doing her master's thesis on popular fiction at Sheffield University, the ex-librarian from Lancashire had met Alan Boon. In 1976 she became his general assistant, which meant manuscript reader. "Even if Alan made the decisions," says his successor, Horst Bausch, "she really carried the can when it came to editing, and he trusted her judgment – as did I." As Boon wound down his duties and Bausch went to Toronto, Whitehead moved up the editorial ladder and eventually commanded a staff of two dozen in M & B's office, appropriately relocated on Paradise Road in south London's Richmond. "Alan Boon is an absolutely wonderful man," Whitehead once told the British trade journal *The Bookseller,* "really the old-fashioned type of eccentric publisher, marvelous with authors and really good at bringing a young editor on." In 1986 Boon's reputation (and his brother John's) had not been held in quite that high regard by some of the writers Alan always said he adored.

There was plenty of smoke and a fair amount of fire that [Mills
& Boon and Harlequin] tried to extinguish.
— Mark Le Fanu, Britain's Society of Authors

12

Scandals and Secrets

THE BOONS AT BAY

The headline in Britain's *The Mail on Sunday* read: CRUEL SHADOW OVER
PARADISE: TALE OF REVENGE IN THE HIGH-FLYING WORLD OF
ROMANCE. The article in February 1986, written in a parody of romantic
prose, began:

> She should not have had a care in the world, yet as she sped through the
> balmy Bahamas afternoon in her gold Mercedes, the wind teasing her hair,
> Anne Hampson's mind was in a whirl.
>
> The memories spun before her. How foolish she had felt that day, a
> dowdy schoolteacher taking the manuscript of her romantic novel to the
> Post Office – and how amazed when Mills & Boon said: "Yes."
>
> Then there were the champagne years, the 134 novels published world-
> wide, and the excitement when a glamorous New York publisher signed her
> up from Mills & Boon.
>
> She should have been happy, driving back to her mansion in paradise.
> But she was not. For the first time in her career, Anne Hampson realised
> with a sick feeling that she had been deceived.
>
> The tale of why the prolific Mrs Hampson has not produced a novel
> since August 1984 is as lurid as many of her stories. It even has a teak-jawed,

racehorse-owning central character, Alan Boon, the man who runs Mills & Boon with his brother John.

Mrs Hampson claims that she and as many as 100 other authors have been cheated out of up to £1 million in royalties. She says she is owed £200,000, in unpaid advances, too.

And last week the authoress of classics like *Eternal Summer* and *Windward Crest* asked the Fraud Squad to investigate. . . .

Alan Boon had long had a reputation for courting his authors, lavishing praise on, and listening to, the women during boozy luncheons at his regular table at the Ritz. He was soon to celebrate his 50th anniversary in the book business, amid a roomful of Mills & Boon and Harlequin colleagues in London, where he would be introduced as "a legend in his own time." Modestly he would respond, "More correctly, a legend in my own lunchtime." But in that *annus horribilis* of 1986, his standing with some of his authors would become increasingly wobbly as news of Anne Hampson's serious allegations spread.

And they did spread in England, with the flames of approaching scandal being fanned by a disaffected ex-employee and a British writers' organization. Norman Shields had worked in M & B's accounts department since 1976. Laid off a decade later, he was more than disgruntled and decided to act on his anger by revealing a secret he had been keeping for some time. In late 1985, Shields approached Mark Le Fanu, general secretary of the Society of Authors. An independent trade union, the Society offers individual advice on legal and financial matters to its 5,500 members and campaigns on their behalf with governments and other groups. For their membership fee of £60 a year, the authors can seek counsel on all forms of contracts and ask the union to intercede when necessary with individual publishers. The Society's chairwoman was the celebrated crime novelist P. D. James, and its president was the distinguished short story writer and essayist V. S. Pritchett, who had a C.B.E. after his name, like John Boon, but also an F.R.S.L., as a Fellow of the Royal Society of Letters.

Essentially Shields alleged that some of Mills & Boon's authors had been deprived of substantial royalty payments from their sales in the United States during the 1970s. At first Le Fanu (pronounced *Leff*-an-you) had his reservations about the charge given that it came from a fired employee. "You want to take it with a pinch of salt," the general secretary told me, "but he was certainly pretty convincing." Shields presented him with "masses of calculations" to support his allegations, and "lots of our members were obviously involved." The figures, combined with anecdotal reports from some society members, were enough to convince Le Fanu to write to the publisher.

If he originally had some doubts about the source of the accusation, he had others about Mills & Boon's vaunted reputation for treating its authors splendidly. "We complain about their contract, which we don't think is quite fair," he said when I first talked to him in 1995. "They ask for a waiver of moral rights [which demands an author's approval for changes to her book] and give themselves a very long time in which to publish [after accepting an author's manuscript]. They're something of a law unto themselves."

By now M & B had been alerted and was quietly assuring any fretful authors or their agents that it was conducting an internal review. Le Fanu's first letter to M & B managing director Robert Williams in December 1985 stated the Society's case:

> As you probably know, we have been contacted by a number of our members who write for Mills & Boon concerning the apparent underpayment of authors' U S royalties and we have subsequently been in touch with Mr. Norman Shields, who was formerly employed by your company.
>
> Mr. Shields tells us that when he joined Mills & Boon in early 1976 he inherited the practice of paying authors 50 percent of all royalty income from North America. He says that he realised that this practice was wrong (authors being due 75% and 50% shares from the usa and Canada respectively) and so started to change the system of accounting to authors by separating out American and Canadian receipts. However, he maintains that he was instructed to revert to the practice of including all North American receipts as one entry on royalty statements (thus obscuring the us element) and to continue to pay 50% thereon.
>
> A good many of our leading authors are members of this Society and we obviously therefore must treat the information that we have received extremely seriously. Quite apart from the general implications of Mr. Shields' revelations, the sums of money involved seem to be substantial. I understand that your auditors are conducting an enquiry and that there is no doubt that a number of authors are owed considerable sums.

Le Fanu concluded by asking Williams to report on the progress of M & B's own investigation. The managing director replied a week later in a letter marked "Private and Confidential," saying he had passed along the request to Bob Massie in Harlequin's Toronto office. Massie was then the executive vice president responsible for all overseas operations, which included M & B. Williams confirmed that "there is indeed an inquiry underway, being led by prominent international and U K attorneys who are reviewing the author contracts and payment practices during the period in question." However, he added, "At this time, our international auditing firm does not believe that monies are owing, but we are endeavouring to obtain a complete legal assessment." Late in January 1986, prodded by Le Fanu, Williams said the internal review had been delayed because the publisher's legal counsel was heavily committed in court.

Mills & Boon realized that this was not a tempest in an English teapot to be contained without further controversy. It had become a full-blown issue. The populist *Mail* was one matter, but details of the claims had also appeared in that old-boys' bastion of conservative thought, the *Sunday Telegraph*. In early February, the newspaper, under the headline SOFTLY SHE BREATHED: 'I WANT MY ROYALTIES,' reported on the allegation of impropriety and noted in a "We understand old chap" tone of voice:

> The suggestion has caused considerable pain to senior members of the firm, which has always prided itself on its treatment of authors, some of whom have become millionaires.
>
> Last week the firm's chairman, Mr. John Boon, said: "We have had the whole matter investigated by our accountants, Arthur Young, and also by our lawyers. We have also taken advice from counsel.
>
> "We are near the end of the whole process. Whatever the judgment, we will be abiding by the advice of our experts, which will be impartial."
>
> Mr. Boon said that a "fair amount of money" could be involved. He added: "We have been in publishing quite a long time. We have looked after our authors."

At which point Anne Hampson surfaced in the press. The author who now drove a Mercedes and kept a Bahamas mansion had dropped out of school in Lancashire at 14, run her own café and fish-and-chips shop, and worked in a sewing factory before going back to school and getting her teacher's certificate.

She was teaching when she took the cruise to Greece that inspired her to spend five months writing her first romance novel. Mills & Boon published it, and within four years Hampson had sold enough books to convince herself that she could be a full-time writer. By 1986 her childless marriage of 17 years had long since ended. If necessary she could console herself with the fame and wealth she had found in creating her mildly provocative novels, including the first Harlequin Presents, *Gates of Steel*. She had her Bahamian residence and, like her sister author, Sheila Holland (Charlotte Lamb), an address on the tax-haven Isle of Man – she lived at Windward Crest, the very name of one of her bestselling books.

Of course Hampson was no longer a Mills & Boon author. She had gone over to the competition, Simon & Schuster, during its dustup with Harlequin – Silhouette's first romance, remember, was her *Payment in Full* – and when Harlequin acquired its rival, she was left out in the cold. In fact, she told the press that eight of her manuscripts had been returned as suddenly unsuitable. "Alan Boon is a rake," she insisted, "just like out of one of my novels, a dashing, most attractive rogue." Hampson herself had gained a reputation as something of a scold. The Society of Authors' Mark Le Fanu told me that "she was a slightly unhappy lady and malcontented with everybody. She just faded out from membership. She wasn't easy. She had a top American agent known for his sharklike jaws, but somehow it didn't work out for her." That agent would be Mort Janklow, chairman of the high-powered New York literary agency Janklow & Nesbit Associates and a friend to many of the most powerful in publishing, including Simon & Schuster's Dick Snyder.

As Le Fanu continued to press Mills & Boon, and the Fraud Squad of Scotland Yard looked into the affair in London, David Galloway and Harlequin were scrambling in Toronto to keep the potentially damaging fall-out to a minimum. The company knew two things for certain. One was that authors have a right to a full accounting of their royalties. Actually, as New York literary agent Richard Curtis points out, they can audit their publishers' books. He tells authors that they have that right in the United States whether their contracts stipulate it or not. A publisher "can make it damn hard. . . . But he must, ultimately, let your accountant go over the books." So it was imperative that Mills & Boon head off any attempt at such an outside audit. The other certainty was that the company was in deep trouble because, in spite of all the protestations to the contrary, the brothers Boon had screwed up, badly.

As a senior executive of the time admits, "Brother Alan was the only one who handled the authors' accounts. We were let down by the auditors and by him. He didn't pay a lot of attention to what he should have." Harlequin, in acquiring M & B, had discovered the anomaly in the British company's contracts between the American and Canadian payments. I have learned that at least one North American colleague had told Alan Boon to clear it up and, in checking with him a few years later, was told, "It's coming along fine." It was not, and a discussion with brother John failed to resolve the issue. This executive has said of Alan Boon: "He was too timorous to do anything. . . . He just wasn't paying [the additional royalties owed to the authors]. It stayed in the company. Instead of doing it, he did in effect *not* do it. The auditors never caught on all those years."

Meanwhile, Scotland Yard decided not to pursue the matter, presumably satisfied that Mills & Boon would do the right thing. Mark Le Fanu, however, was upbraiding M&B's Robert Williams for declining to tell the Society of Authors the outcome of the internal investigation:

> The list of names and figures produced by Mr. Shields runs to nearly 100 authors, a good many of whom are members of this Society. I am sure you will understand that we cannot let the matter rest until we are sure that it has been resolved satisfactorily. I really cannot see why you are so reluctant to reveal the outcome of the enquiry conducted by your professional advisers, as disclosure of that information and your subsequent action would help to establish confidence that errors are being remedied. As it is, your secretiveness simply breeds suspicion.

"It actually worked pretty well," Le Fanu told me. "We meant what we said: we would have taken legal action. But as it turned out, we didn't have to spend a penny because they knew the game was up."

On March 25, 1986, under Alan Boon's signature, Mills & Boon sent the numerous authors involved a letter marked "Without prejudice and in confidence." It said that although the publishing contract in question was not clear, and that advisers had assured M & B it was justified in interpreting the provisions the way it had, and that the lapse in time would probably not make it liable, in spite of all that, "we do not intend to rely on the strict legal position."

Mills & Boon would repay them the additional royalties plus interest.

It was a good sum. One executive estimates it at "probably hundreds of thousands of pounds, about one and a half percent of 10 years of royalties." Le Fanu says that one author alone – was it Anne Hampson? – received at least £100,000.

For all the publicity in Britain, M & B's parent company did manage to prevent the controversy from spilling over on the other side of the Atlantic. Aside from those writers (and their agents) who received what they could have believed were windfall profits, North Americans in the book business appear to have had no idea of the rumpus. In the U.S. trade press of the time, I could find nary a report, not even a mention, of the situation.

Had Mills & Boon learned its lesson? Was it prepared to treat its writers fairly from then on? Harlequin's British division had another chance to prove itself to them six years later when one of its authors, Pauline Harris, was accused of plagiarism. In 1992 David Lodge, honorary professor of modern English literature at the University of Birmingham, wrote a newspaper article drawing links between his 1988 novel, *Nice Work,* and her bestseller of three years later, *The Iron Master.* Harris, a former schoolteacher who had written 23 romances as Rebecca King and Rachel Ford, denied that she had ever read his book. As it turned out, both authors later admitted to being influenced by Elizabeth Gaskett's *North and South.* But in the wake of Lodge's charge, Mills & Boon dropped Harris from its list of authors. She sued her accuser for libel and won substantial damages for the "considerable distress and consequent depression" she had suffered. "Mills & Boon behaved very badly towards me," she said. "They are obsessed with lawsuits, and within 10 days of Lodge's article, I was out." After her libel action was settled, Mills & Boon declined comment, except to say: "We reached a settlement with her in 1993."

In the decade since the royalties storm shook Mills & Boon, Harlequin itself has had its own controversies to negotiate with writers: among them contract terms, the use of authors' pseudonyms, editing practices, and the general feeling that as a virtual monopoly in the category-romance field, the company can make and enforce its own rules. "A monopoly – even a near monopoly – puts too much power into the hands of the greedy," a romance author named Linda Hilton wrote last year in PANdora's Box, the Romance Writers of America newsletter distributed only to the organization's published writers. She was making the case that the industry needs a major competitor to the Canadian company, perhaps its old rival, Simon & Schuster:

> Those who write for Harlequin/Silhouette have seen their royalties drop as subscription book clubs flourish and corporate profits soar. Gains in foreign royalties are offset by nefarious contract terms that make authors bear the burden of the publisher's errors in judgment. Authors complain of heavy-handed editing until their unique creative effort becomes just another carton of homogenized milk. . . .
>
> I don't write for Harlequin/Silhouette, but if I did and another well-established publisher offered me a contract that didn't require me to sign over my rights in perpetuity, accept insulting royalty rates and twisted logic that justifies paying authors less for book club sales while the publishers report higher profits, and all the other nonsense I've seen in this new Harlequin/Silhouette contract, you bet your booties I'd sign. If there's no publisher's loyalty to authors, why should there be author loyalty to a publisher who doesn't play fair?
>
> I think the time is ripe for a new silhouette to step out of the shadows. Simon & Schuster – or Dell – or Berkley – or NAL : where are you when romance writers need you?

Having a forum for such wonderfully polemical writing is just one of the strengths of the RWA, perhaps the most potent writers' lobby in North America. Agent Richard Curtis says, "I recognized a few years ago that Romance Writers of America had the potential to be a very, very powerful political force, and I have for years said that there must be collective action by authors' and agents' organizations if you are going to achieve anything. Because, you know, even the most powerful agents can only negotiate so much for their authors, but to get certain other concessions, you really need clout. The Mystery Writers of America, while they certainly give the best party in the world, have not in my opinion used their collective potential to any political good. They are essentially a writers' organization, but not a lobbying group the way RWA has become."

When editor Vivian Stephens conceived the idea for the organization, she intended that it would create a support network of sister writers who felt kinship with one another in the writing of romantic fiction. It began in 1980 with a meeting of working professionals at a savings branch in Houston's North Oaks Mall. The first president was Rita Clay Estrada, a Silhouette author who went on to write for Harlequin. Six hundred writers had joined RWA by the time of its first conference the following year, and its executives were soon dealing with publishers and agents as a collective force. Along the way, there has been internal strife, much of it about the role that hopeful writers, with votes equal to published ones, should play in shaping the alliance. Glenda Sanders, who wrote for Vivian Stephens's Candlelight Ecstasy line and later for Harlequin, told me, "For many years, there was plenty of room for everyone, and the group was more supportive. Now there are 1,500 published writers and 5,500 [or more] trying to storm the doors. . . . There's a feeling that we're doing too good a job in training our replacements." An early attempt at setting up a separate organization for professionals was the Society of Romance Novelists. More recently some of RWA's published writers have switched their allegiance to, or shared it with, Novelists, Inc., a coalition of writers of popular fiction who must have published at least two novels. Among its members are heavyweights such as Judith McNaught and Jayne Ann Krentz. In an effort to stem the flow from RWA, a Published Authors' Special Interest chapter held its first conference in 1996 to address the specific concerns of professional writers, as opposed to the hopefuls and fans who pad the larger group's rolls ("The effort has raised a few eyebrows, a few tempers, and even a few defenses," says the chapter's contact person, Linda Hilton). In Canada Jo Beverley of Ottawa – one of about 40 writers across the country currently publishing in the genre – has been a spark plug of the recently formed Canadian Romance Authors' Network.

Despite the divisions, Romance Writers of America has changed its members' working lives through spirited lobbying. One effective tactic has been the annual Publishers' Summit; in 1995 five RWA representatives met with executives of 27 publishing houses in New York, including all the major romance publishers. The writers were pushing most strongly on two financial fronts with Harlequin: to increase its royalties on both book club and foreign sales. The company gave in on the English-language foreign payments, doubling the rate to four percent of cover price for books sold in England, Australia, and Canada. Of course, that leaves hanging the larger issue of all the royalties from publishing in foreign languages in the rest of the world. Nor would Harlequin budge on raising the royalty percentage for book club sales. Libby Hall was at that meeting and would be at the next one in 1996, when the RWA would resurrect the long-simmering issue. She is the organization's vice president, a former computer engineer on the U.S. space shuttle program who has since written 37 Harlequins and Silhouettes under her own name and as Laurie Paige ("I decided they needed romance heroines who were something besides secretaries and nannies, so I started writing them with math geniuses"). She says that most members feel Harlequin's book club royalty rate is unfair. "It still stands at half the normal royalty rate [six percent], minus 15 percent, which actually comes down to 2.55 percent on the price of the book. What bothers our writers is that we look at their annual report and see that they made over $70 million from their book club sales, which is by far their biggest money maker. They don't pay 45 to 50 percent to IDs [independent distributors] or booksellers. And they've really been pushing the book club sales, from everything we can see." As David Galloway has said quite publicly, the real magic of Harlequin is its book club, and Larry Heisey agrees: "That's a wonderful business – it still is. It's probably the largest segment of profitability to the company – by faithful subscribers who buy anywhere up to 25 books a month." The same is true in the British operation, which, urged on by the North Americans, improved its direct-mail business to the point where, John Boon says, "in the end, it contributes 50 to 60 percent of the profit."

The authors received other concessions from Harlequin, however. They no longer had to sign a contract that gave the company rights to a book "in perpetuity." And new writers could finally have ownership of their pen names, taking them along if they left Harlequin for another house. On the other hand, authors who had already been writing for the company would have to seek written permission from Harlequin to use their pseudonyms elsewhere (although, truth to tell, a majority of its authors were by now writing under their real names). This was an issue that had caused the publisher some embarrassment. *The Nation,* for example, had run an article three years earlier under the headline ROMANCE SLAVES OF HARLEQUIN. It quoted New York literary agent Anita Diamant as saying that she couldn't get a contract from Harlequin for her 20 romance authors unless they agreed to write under a pseudonym. The left-wing journal called the requirement "a Harlequin ploy aimed at keeping its stable of writers strictly tethered to the corporate hitching post" and reported:

> Harlequin has threatened to convert its contracts to "work for hire" if its authors keep making a fuss over pseudonyms. As matters now stand, authors own the copyrights on their books and receive royalties of 6 percent on sales. But under work-for-hire agreements, writers would be paid a flat fee for their manuscripts, would not own the copyright and would get no royalties, however well their books sold.

Current publisher Candy Lee gave me the corporate rationale on the issue: "There is a body of work that has a particular flavor and feel to it. Both the author and the publisher jointly had an investment in that body of work. . . . The idea here was that we couldn't use the pseudonym for anything else, and the author couldn't either." She was obviously not comfortable with the policy. But as Richard Curtis, literary agent and sometime adviser to RWA, explains, "Harlequin is somewhat Kremlinesque." Lee is a friend of his and "a very articulate spokeswoman for the powers that be – she has tried very much to be the authors' friend, but she's not the last word." On this issue and financial matters, he says, "With other publishers, there's a quid pro quo, but with Harlequin it's really take it or leave it, and the percentage to which the authors are entitled is seldom negotiated. They have essentially held the line on everything, because to give in to one is to set a precedent that could open the dike and flood them with negotiated changes."

When RWA had shown some early signs of hesitancy on the pseudonym controversy, Novelists, Inc. and The Authors Guild began pressuring Harlequin – along with two of its bestselling novelists, who preferred anonymity in hiring lawyers to protect their pen names. By the time of the Publishers' Summit in New York in 1995, the company had backed down from its long-defended stance. Of course, it was continuing to demand that veteran writers seek approval in writing each time they wanted to use their noms de plume with another publishing house. "This has not been fought in court," Libby Hall says, "but there's no way they can control your career like that. So that once they give the permission, it's given – you don't have to come back again on every book you publish. They know that in 100 percent of cases, the courts have always come down on the side of the writer in the use of the pseudonym and the control of their work."

The Romance Writers are now pursuing another contentious point on a new frontier: on-line publishing, with its potential for readers simply to call up entire books on their computers and download them. Publishers are looking to the Internet as a potential source of income – where they could avoid the usual production costs and discounts to distributors and booksellers. Writers are looking at their contracts and discovering that Harlequin, among others, lumps electronic publishing royalties under the same clause as those for book club sales: effectively offering a mere 2.55 percent of cover price. They intend to ask for the 50 percent rate that a few small entrepreneurial firms are already offering authors.

Meanwhile, RWA continues its nurturing role with a bevy of services to its American and Canadian members. It supports more than 150 local chapters; sponsors writing contests; runs a hot line to report up-to-date industry news; arbitrates grievances between writers and publishers or agents; critiques manuscripts for a fee; offers medical and indemnity insurance; holds an annual national conference; and publishes two bimonthlies, the magazine *RWR, Romance Writers' Report*, for all members, and the newsletter *PANdora's Box*, for its Published Authors' Network. The more public magazine addresses less controversial, more positive matters on subjects such as self-editing, the selection and handling of agents, and the tricky nature of sex scenes. (Writer Robin Schone presented an example of erotica from her own work: "'Oh, God, yes, yes, that's it, let me hear you, moan for me, baby; moan, I want to hear you,' he groaned, nibbling, sucking, head wildly rooting from one breast to another." And Schone added her editor's comment: "'Baby' is twentieth-century slang and does not belong in a book that takes place in 1883.") A popular theme in the magazine of late has been the Internet, particularly E-mail. Romance writers have been quick to embrace the new technology, certainly for self-promotion but also to set up forums on commercial servers such as America Online, GEnie, and Prodigy on which they chat, swap gossip, and E-mail one another manuscripts for criticism – in an electronic extension of the countless real-life critique groups that these most organized of genre writers have spawned across the continent.

The professionals-only newsletter is where the working writers vent their gripes more vocally, among themselves. There is a lot of monitoring of the media and its routine disparaging of romantic fiction. Recently the publication has begun a "Gag Me with a Spoon Award" for the most offensive piece of reporting. A typical winner was Susan Ager of the *Detroit Free Press* for writing: "Romance novels are bad for women. Evil. Worse than whipped cream. More crippling than high heels. They perpetuate false images of romance and love that no real man or relationship can live up to. They dull women's brains. They make women suckers for swagger." The newsletter also becomes a forum for personal critiques of various publishers, often contained in long letters to the editor. A couple of years ago, several were aimed at Harlequin's editing practices. One, who had asked that her name be withheld, reported the case of a friend, an award-winning writer, who once received a 17-page revision report in which her editor argued that the color of a suitcase be changed and a minor character renamed because no one in her city would bear that sort of sobriquet. The letter-writer herself, who said she had earned her book-writing stripes at Harlequin, complained: "The more books I wrote for them, it seemed, the more they reshaped the plot, characters, motivation, you name it. I've had names changed because the ones I'd chosen weren't WASP enough, had minor characters added or deleted, had plots turned in different directions."

While that letter went unsigned, many other writers insist their names be used. However, there was one piece of correspondence in the fall of 1994 from several published RWA members that the editor positioned on the front page as an open letter but decided on her own to print it without identifying its authors. One point in the letter concerned a convention that romance writers and readers had attended that year in Tennessee:

> We are also concerned about the freewheeling atmosphere that prevailed at the Nashville convention. Again, we're not the thought police and we all love a party, but public spats, personal attacks, and the impromptu lectures featuring foul language tend to diminish the celebration of romance we all strive for. Why give the press more ammunition for ridicule?

The letter – which would be debated on *PANdora's Box* pages – was a wide-ranging attack on the operations of that entrepreneurial powerhouse in the romance industry, the publisher of *Romantic Times* and the promoter of the annual Booklovers' Convention, the formidable Kathryn Falk.

Look, I have a lot of respect for a person who can keep a little business going. And if she has a genius, it's for self-promotion.
— Ballantine editor Carolyn Nichols on *Romantic Times* founder and CEO Kathryn Falk

13

Tempting Eve

THE READERS

It started as a shoving match between the two petite redheads and wound up with one of them going to hospital. The combatants encountered each other in April 1994 on the front steps of a convention hotel in Nashville. Kathryn Falk ordered Charlene Keel to get off the premises. A year earlier, Keel had helped to produce the first Mr. Romance Cover Model Pageant for Falk in San Diego during the annual *Romantic Times* Booklovers' Convention. But now she was covering the second pageant in the Tennessee capital as managing editor of *Playgirl*. And, if truth be known, she was also snooping around for material to include in *I'll Take Romance*, a fan publication she was planning to launch in competition with Falk's. The publisher of the 13-year-old romance magazine was well aware of that *Playgirl* person's intentions. As scores of witnesses watched, Falk grabbed her rival's purse, and in the ensuing scuffle, Keel fell or was pushed and, she claims, kicked in the head before Falk was pulled away. An ambulance took Keel to hospital to be treated for a slight concussion.

The unbecoming sight of the 53-year-old Falk and her 49-year-old competitor involved in a fracas would spur romance writers on the scene and others who heard of it to write a flurry of letters to *PANdora's Box*. "Last time I checked,"

Kathryn Falk – a power unto herself. ROMANTIC TIMES

one remarked, "romance writers weren't in favor of dealing with business rivals by committing assault." Another, who signed herself "I left my boxing gloves at the door," pointed out that Falk had later made an impromptu speech to fans awaiting a writers' book-signing and that these "readers were not amused by the foul language Falk used when referring to her rival." The front-page open letter in a subsequent issue went beyond the convention carryings-on to criticize the publisher for downgrading the image of the romance-novel industry. The authors who wrote the letter said they would love to see the cover-model pageant disappear, and they asked Falk to stop perpetuating the lie that celebrity models such as Fabio actually wrote novels that bore their names. They also resented having to pay her $100 a table to autograph books at her conventions and deplored the ads for "spanking stories" she ran in her magazine. Finally they demanded her promise that no author would be penalized for supporting another publication, even if it was a competitor. This fear of retaliation was real: as romance writer and *PANdora's Box* columnist Deborah Camp later wrote, "Successful authors I admire have admitted to me that, while they don't approve of some of Ms. Falk's business practices, they would never say anything publicly about them because they fear she would destroy their careers!"

"I defend my turf," says the woman who created romance-fan magazine publishing out of whole cloth in 1981 and has since become a real-life link with the world of romantic fiction for her 135,000 readers – many of them aspiring writers. As many as 900 sign up for Kathryn Falk's conventions to meet their author heroines, attend writing workshops, rub shoulders with the editors and occasional publishers on site, and perhaps rub up against cover models during photo opportunities. Harlequin sent two of its editors to participate in panels at the 1995 convention, and two female vice presidents appeared the year before to show the company's colors to *Romantic Times* readers.

Falk's readers are, for the most part, similar to the most faithful of Harlequin's. In their devotion to the genre, they parallel the subscribers to the book publisher's direct-mail Reader Service. Certainly book club members who may receive anywhere from four to a dozen titles a month – and some double that amount – display the same degree of fealty as the readers of a $42-a-year monthly magazine that consists mostly of publishers' and writers' ads and uncritical reviews of romance novels. The publishers I talked with would prefer to have, rather than a fan magazine, a real trade journal like *Boy Meets Girl* was when Vivien Lee Jennings began publishing the market letter in 1981, the same year *Romantic Times* began. Jennings, a bookseller in Fairway, Kansas, reported on the romance trade without falling into the trap of running invariably favorable book reviews. Over the four most frenetic years of romance's boom time, she distributed several thousand copies each week of the $125-a-year newsletter to booksellers, publishers, writers, and the media. Regretfully, she now says, "one of the things I did not succeed in was raising the level of respect for the business."

It is doubtful whether Kathryn Falk, with all her shenanigans, has entirely succeeded either. Her tongue can be impolitic: "One of the problems with editors is they all whine. Publishing is a poorly paid profession. The girls are right out of college, and they probably don't know anything. . . . They have little offices. They're trying to get married and get pregnant." At the time, she was advising a group of wannabe writers at her 1995 Fort Worth convention on how to handle an editor. "Mother her," she said. "They love to be mothered." Her feuds with colleagues in the business have become the stuff of legend. Carolyn Nichols was editing the Loveswept line in the 1980s when her publisher, Bantam, placed an ad in *Romantic Times* that included book endorsements from various romance authors and reviewers. When it appeared, some of the endorsers' names were missing. Nichols called Falk, only to be told, "My darling, you don't think I would actually put in the names of people I detest." For a long time after, Bantam refused to advertise in the magazine.

Falk is loyal to many writers, but not all. In my presence, she called Kathleen Woodiwiss, author of the trendsetting *The Flame and the Flower,* "Woodi*shit.*" At least one agent – Richard Curtis, who represents Janet Dailey and other mainstream romance writers – admits aloud: "I was born to hate that woman, and I think vice versa. She wrote a very insulting thing about Janet once, and we threatened to sue, and I said I would have nothing to do with her, and I would not encourage any of my clients to have anything to do with her until she retracted it. She never retracted it, took off after me by telling any author who would listen that I was a thief – so, you know, I have a lot of opinions about her, but probably none you could print without getting sued."

Falk's first allegiance is, as it should be, to her readers. Given *Romantic Times'* grip on such a dedicated audience, publishers – even Harlequin, which needs its support least of all – are not prepared openly to criticize the fanzine or its owner. The one publisher who had a public tiff with Falk felt compelled to make peace with her. Walter Zacharius of Zebra Books learned she was miffed when one of his editors said he would not give Falk some information she wanted. After she wrote to Zacharius that he was too busy counting his money to return calls, he phoned to say he was going to see her. She greeted him with the assurance that she wanted to "break bread" with him, Mafia style – and had a loaf ready in the shape of a penis. "Why didn't you call me?" he asked her. "I was afraid of you," she replied. Zacharius professes friendship with her ever since: "She's a gutsy lady."

She is that, and despite her often outrageous behavior, I confess to a grudging admiration for what she has accomplished in the past decade and a half, if not always for how she has done it. Falk's early years were part fairy tale, part horror story. Born in 1940, she has intriguing looks that spring from her parents' melange of backgrounds: father Irish-German-American Indian, mother Scottish-Alsatian. He was a physical education consultant to the school board in moneyed, conservative Grosse Point, Michigan, and with his wife ran a boys' camp in summer across the border near Windsor, Ontario. Kathryn was the eldest of five, pretty enough to be a cheerleader and a Miss Bond Bread. What she learned only later was that her mother was a manic-depressive and had once tried to kill herself. The daughter, desperate to flee the Grosse Point lifestyle, left college for acting and singing in New York, where she says she managed to land some chorus line roles on Broadway. Hand and face modeling led to public relations work for a medical company, which took her to Europe. She lived in London, and about 1971 in Vienna, she says, she began dating Maximillian Schell, the Austrian Oscar winner for *Judgement at Nuremberg*. She also paid $4,000 for a mountainside farmhouse outside the city, which she still maintains. A year later, Falk opened a dollhouse and miniatures store in New York, which flourished over five years, and published two books on those areas of expertise. She then produced four quarterlies on the subject until the publisher of the magazines collapsed. It was at that point her whole world began crumbling. By then her father and mother had separated, and one day she got a call that her father's summer camp had burned down. Her mother, hearing the news two days later, committed suicide. Her daughter found her hanging, dressed all in black, and had to cut her down. "It was very tough," she remembers. "The anniversary came along for a couple of years, it was like a movie, and I had to relive the whole day."

Falk was then romantically involved with Kenneth Rubin, whom she had met on a Mississippi steamboat. The owner of a jewelry business and a serious collector of antique coin-operated machines, Rubin had a carriage house in Brooklyn Heights brimming with his expensive playthings. Falk had contemplated another offer. While living in London, she had met the former Maharaja of Baroda, from west-central India, whom she describes as one of the country's richest men. Jackie, as Falk called him, was a dozen years older than her. Visiting New York, he had asked her to move in with him. She told Rubin, who invited her to live with him instead. "Okay," she said, "I'll give up an Indian prince for a Jewish prince."

Intrigued with historical romances, Falk had been interviewing veteran writers of the genre with the idea of doing a book. Pinnacle was interested but wanted only the most recent romance writers. Falk enlisted as her personal editor a former neighbor in Greenwich Village, Bonnie Golightly, the author on whom Truman Capote had modeled heroine Holly Golightly for *Breakfast at Tiffany's*. Falk's book of profiles appeared as *Love's Leading Ladies*. It was 1980, and she realized there was a niche in the expanding romance field for at least a newsletter chronicling the phenomenon. Backed by Rubin and cash flow from a mention in Janet Dailey's report to her readers, she put together a 24-page newsprint tabloid in a windowless walk-in closet in her boyfriend's house, sold some ads, printed 20,000 copies, and in June 1981 began distributing them mainly through bookstores across the United States.

Her timing was superb. For 18 months, Harlequin and Silhouette had been battling *mano a mano,* their high-stakes competition encouraging other publishers to enter the romance market. *Romantic Times* generated enough interest to prompt Long Island's Institute for Continuing Education to collaborate with Falk on the first romance booklovers' conference in 1982. That year Crown Publishing asked her to compile *How to Write a Romance and Get It Published,* a hardcover reprinted as a plump Signet paperback several times since. Eventually she bought a former Brooklyn tire shop and garbage dump and turned them into her antique- and doll-adorned offices and charming little tree-shaded garden. In 1983 she hired an assistant, Carol Stacy, a former rock singer who found producing the magazine much like patching together the quilts she loved to make. She had neither editorial expertise nor any ardor for romance novels. They are too slow-moving for her ("I like reading about serial killers"), and she reads them only to satisfy her curiosity about certain authors. The magazine grew as Falk conceived the profitable notion of charging writers as well as publishers to advertise their books (a full-page black-and-white ad is about $1,200). "We're mostly author-driven with advertising," says Stacy, now president and publisher. "Right now, out of the 10 [major romance] publishers, there are probably five that consistently advertise" – Harlequin among them.

While newsstand sales are sluggish, she says the magazine has a 95 percent renewal rate with its subscribers and a 75 percent sell-through in the nationwide Waldenbooks chain. One of the publication's strengths is its relationship with The 950 Bookstores That Care – that is, the booksellers across the United States that carry Falk's magazine. Not all bookstores do care: unlike the chains, many higher-brow independents even refuse to stock brand-name novels such as Harlequins, which can be bought so readily in supermarkets and drugstores. The ones that do sell them usually have a cadre of faithful readers: as

Linda Scott, a mass-market paperback buyer for Canada's Coles Bookstores chain and a former store manager, told *Quill & Quire,* "the customers practically know what time the truck pulls up." But more than most genre fiction, series romances are to be found in abundance in shops that sell used books; they have an active secondary market through these outlets and at garage sales. The two Book Bugs in Sikeston, Missouri, are typical small-town stores selling mostly secondhand romances, although one has a special Romance Room bedecked in wooden hearts, lace, and roses, a platform rocker, and cutouts of Fabio and the Topaz Man. Owners Joyce Hagy and her husband, Merlin, were at Falk's 1995 Booklovers' Convention to videotape events for replay in their stores and to connect with authors for personal appearances. "I'm impressed with Kathryn Falk," she says. "She's a very strong woman."

As Falk was turning *Romantic Times* into a more polished production on glossy paper, she was also reshaping herself. "She had more plastic surgery than a dog had hair on it," says Zebra publisher Walter Zacharius. Visiting him one day, she asked if he wanted to see some high-priced sculpture. He protested as she was about to bare her enhanced bosom; a little later, he heard one of his editors yelp when Falk paid her a visit. With this kind of chutzpah, Kathryn Falk has beaten off all serious competitors. Today only a few small romance publications survive. The long-running *Affaire de Coeur* of Oakland, California, is a monthly magazine notable for its glad-handing reviews. *The Literary Times* of Miltounboro, New Hampshire, is a 36-page quarterly that grew out of a writers' support group, The Literary Connection. Both it and the newsletter *Romantic Notions* of Salem, Oregon, have an Internet presence as well. Romance newsletters aimed at specific readers' interests include *The Regency Reader* of Federal Way, Washington (early 19th-century England), *The Gothic Journal* of Forest Lake, Minnesota (suspense, mystery, Gothic, supernatural, and women-in-jeopardy romances), and *Rawhide and Lace* of Gig Harbor, Washington (western women's fiction). As for Charlene Keel's *I'll Take Romance,* it took a nosedive in 1995 after two issues, although her former partner resurrected a successor called *Forever Romance.*

In 1995 the theatrical Kathryn Falk made herself a lady by buying an English title, to Barrow, which gave her the right "to market and fayre" along with a cottage on 2,677 acres of freehold land and wastelands near Newmarket, the racing town that Alan Boon frequents. "Basically," she says in hinting at how much she paid for it all, "the Marquis of Bristol needed to pay off his wine bill." But long before she became Lady Barrow, Kathryn Falk had become the Maharini of Romance. Through her passionate if self-promoting cultivation of her readers, she helped to raise the profile of romantic fiction throughout North America. Not all the members of the RWA responding to that open letter to Falk in their newsletter were critical of her. Among supporters was associate member Beatrice Sheftel, who wrote: "To me, Kathryn Falk is God-Mother to the Romance novel industry, encouraging and inspiring its growth through her various promotions. I think she should be praised instead of condemned. . . . Kathryn Falk is a business woman who has created an enterprise which has benefitted readers and writers."

The readers of romance fiction – like *Romantic Times* readers – are, first of all, nearly 100 percent women. (Larry Heisey, when advised that a 1970 survey had shown only one percent of Harlequin's readers were men, said, "I don't want to meet him.") The clichés are that these women are elderly, love-starved spinsters in low-paid positions and middle-aged wives and mothers pining for a little romance in their duty-bound lives. In reality they are Everywoman, reported one of the first social scientists to survey the romance readership seriously. Peter H. Mann, an English sociologist at the University of Sheffield, began analyzing the field in 1968 and within five years had come up with such myth-revising statistics that Mills & Boon published his updated results in posh pamphlet form as *A New Survey*. Looking back on his first study of romance readers, Mann notes what he calls a conspiracy of silence about romance novels and their readers: "Very little at all was known about them, and, such was the climate of opinion at that time, my survey aroused a great deal of interest, since not only had no one until then written about the readers of romances, practically no one in the world of books ever mentioned them in conversation."

Mann found that romance readers, in his country, anyway, represented a general cross section of the female population. Neither all young girls nor ancient spinsters, readers crossed every age group, nearly half of them between 25 and 44 compared with fewer than a third of women in that age range in

England as a whole. Only six percent were 65 or older, compared with 20 percent in the national population. Only a third were single; 45 percent were married women with children at home. Responding to the criticism that romantic novels cater to women with too much time on their hands, Mann pointed out that a third of the readers were full-time housewives, 30 percent were housewives with either full- or part-time jobs, and 22 percent were unmarried and employed. Most of the readers are factory girls? No, only 19 percent had manual jobs, while more than half had office or clerical positions, and 10 percent worked at a professional or higher technical level. Poorly educated? Nearly half of the readers had not left school or college until 16 or over, 12 percent at 18 or over. Among the sociologist's conclusions: "Romance reading for sheer relaxation after a hard day's study or mental work is clearly popular with numbers of women at college or in quite intellectually demanding jobs." Other surveys have shown the continuing popularity of romantic fiction in Britain. Romance is the largest single sector of the adult paperback fiction market there, and Mills & Boon has about a 54 percent share. One study estimated that 40 percent of the 24 million British women aged 15 and over had read a paperback romance novel, 4 million of them an M&B or Silhouette.

The same year that Mann was releasing his study, 1973, Harlequin was finding that the average North American romance reader was 35.5 years old, was married with two children, had a high school education, and lived in her own house. Now the average age is 42 (up from 39 a few years ago); not surprisingly the average age of the books' more mature heroines has simultaneously risen from about 26 to the mid-thirties and early forties. However, just over 50 percent of today's readers start to sample the genre between the ages of 15 and 17. Harlequin's own statistics claim that 48 percent of romance readers generally have attended or graduated from college, that 57 percent are employed, and that the average household income is $41,900 U.S. While the company reports that the average romance fan spends up to $30 a month on the books – with half its customers buying an average of 30 books a month – the major Barnes & Noble bookstore chain estimates that its typical romance reader spends $100 a month.

Along with its market research through focus-group testing and readership surveys, Harlequin has long tried to encourage closer communion with its audience. In Larry Heisey's era, the most remarkable example of such contact began with a letter in 1969 from a woman in Austin, Texas, named Helen-Jo Hewitt. She even volunteered her personal statistics: 42, five foot nine, and 195 pounds, at the time pursuing her doctorate in linguistics with a thesis on Melanesian languages and intending to teach English as a second language. Her letter began: "Are you interested in your readers? H A R L E Q U I N R O M A N C E S are a sort of hobby of mine and I have a curiosity concerning them which I doubt Simon & Schuster would bother to allay, so I write to you in hopes that a Canadian firm might be less depersonalized." She represented a group of Harlequin readers and collectors – housewife, secretary, short-order cook, and herself, a Ph.D. candidate. They were seeking missing titles for their collection as well as satisfaction of their curiosity; among their questions: what moral guidelines, if any, were given to writers of Harlequins? "While some are comfortably forthright," she noted, "many are almost simpering." But the meat of Hewitt's letter came at the end, where she mentioned that she kept a record of her evaluations of the 400 Harlequins she had read, grading them by author. "Marjorie Norrell, for instance, out of fourteen titles has only once (in 1057) risen above C. [Eleanor] Farnes, on the other hand, in her dozen, ranges all the way from F to A+++ (a grade shared by only two other titles)." Other symbols ranged from an asterisk for "super" to a "z" for "I'm darned if I'm going to read any more by this author!"

Although she had addressed her letter "Gentlemen," she heard back initially from Ruth Palmour, who said the company sought a high standard of "morality" in selecting the titles. And yes, Harlequin would be interested in seeing her evaluations. They arrived on 14 typewritten legal-sized pages, and over the next couple of years, Hewitt continued to send her grades of books as they appeared. Larry Heisey, as the new president, was fascinated. "Let's meet a real serious reader," he told his colleagues, and he invited Helen-Jo and her girlfriend the cook, twentyish Susan Glover, for an all-expenses-paid visit to Toronto. Both were large women swaddled in New Zealand muumuus (Hewitt said she had "the more-than-ample proportions of the late Queen Salote of Tonga"), and they had tea with Heisey in his dark-paneled, art-bedecked office and dinner in a rooftop restaurant. The friend, a high school dropout, especially impressed him with her knowledge of Harlequins. The company had published nearly 1,300 romance titles by then. "I could give her any number, and she could snap back with the title, author, and plot," Heisey recalls. "If we showed her cover artwork, she could do the same. It was fantastic."

Such obsessive collectors continued to surface. An American couple vacationed in Canada two years in a row during the 1970s to look for titles missing from their Harlequin collection, they returned to the United States with more than 600. Richard Griffin of Grove City, Ohio, 74, has been subscribing to the Harlequin book club for years so that he can read to his wife as she drives – and when teased about his own lifelong love of romances, he points out that he fathered seven children. Rosine Levy of Georgetown, Ontario, in her late middle age, won a prize in 1989 for owning more Harlequins than anyone else in the province and now has about 6,000, which she buys from the Reader Service and consumes at a rate of 20 a month. There are enough passionate romance readers to prompt a Louisiana company to develop a software program to computerize their "keepers"; Twilight Publishing's Personal Book Collection has room for 90,000 records.

Beginning in 1979, the year it was planning to drop Simon & Schuster as its distributor, Harlequin actively courted these fans through readers' parties across North America. Representing the company at the first one in San Diego were editor George Glay and a public relations manager who had been in place less than a year, Pam Galsworthy. A former executive secretary to the president of Carnation Foods, she was a vivacious redhead who married a Harlequin product manager, Jay Whiteside. The parties, another publishing first, were billed as thank-yous to loyal readers, chosen by lottery from responses to newspaper ads. The format was similar in every city: luncheon with pink linen and the good crystal, pianist playing romantic music, well-known romance author as speaker, question period, book-shaped cake for dessert, door prizes, and take-home bag of gifts (including a romance novel and sometimes a potted corporate history, *Thirty Years of Harlequin*). Fred Kerner soon took over for Glay at the lunches, which cost about $12,000 to mount; in his later role as editor emeritus, Kerner would get $1,500 a day to play host.

Pam Galsworthy died of cancer at 32, but she had already retired to care for a child after hiring Katherine Orr. Her replacement was the daughter of an

Establishment figure, John Orr, the managing partner of a prominent Toronto accounting firm. A voluble blond, a keen skier, she went to the private girls' school Branksome Hall and studied journalism at the University of Western Ontario. Her first reporting job was with Maclean Hunter's weekly tabloid *Marketing,* in which she wrote a people column, and then for six years she was production manager at *Homemaker's,* a successful national monthly magazine. Orr was briefly married to a teacher at the private boys' school Upper Canada College; she has been unmarried since, although she now lives with a companion. As Harlequin's consumer relations director – PR manager – she had her public baptism in 1980 at a readers' party in Saddle Brook, New Jersey. "I was a nervous wreck. I cried," she remembers. She was there with Kerner when some readers commented on the fact that Harlequin authors were deserting for Silhouette. "Authors are not slaves. They can go wherever they want," he replied, and invited any hopeful authors in the audience to submit their manuscripts.

A year later, Toronto played host to the first Canadian readers' party. In attendance at the Vanity Fair Ballroom of the King Edward Hotel, along with 350 fans, was Sandra Martin, an acerbic-tongued paperbacks columnist for the *Globe and Mail:*

> Where once they (or their mothers or grandmothers) foxtrotted at tea dances, now they sat at round tables eating rare roast beef, roast potatoes and broccoli and sipping water – there wasn't even the scent of anything stronger – while Fred Kerner flattered and teased them. . . . Kerner, a slippery devil who can play his crowd like an accordion, invites questions, offering as an incentive the floral centre-piece at each round table to the first woman to raise her hand and speak.

The bow-tied Kerner also did his party trick of tossing a bridal bouquet over his shoulder into a circle of happy women. The readers'-party promotions ran out of steam in 1992.

In the past decade and a half, Kathy Orr, now a vice president, has been an attractive corporate symbol, representing Harlequin to its readers. She handles the company's major sponsorship of Big Brothers/Big Sisters of America, to which it has donated a few hundred thousand dollars while creating innovative promotions such as placing ads in Harlequin novels to recruit volunteers for the organization and making all of one year's Superromances heroines Big Sisters helping young girls. Working with outside P R experts – currently Leslee Borger of New York's Dunwoody Communications – Orr develops publicity-generating programs such as the annual Valentine's Day *Romance Report*. One survey in the 1996 version, based on telephone interviews of 1,000 adults, reveals that 46 percent of obviously stressed-out American women agree that "a good night's sleep is better than sex," 34 percent say that "if they could have anything in the world, they would like more sleep," and 38 percent say that they "can never get enough sleep."

That report (which Orr signed as usual with a heart replacing the *O* in her name) also announced that Harlequin was now reaching out to its readers electronically by establishing a site on the World Wide Web (*http://www.romance.net*). Its classy home page opens with weekly romantic tidbits, such as travel agents' top 10 tropical escapes for couples and phonetic ways of asking someone to marry you in another language. Illustrated profiles feature The Book of the Moment and Author of the Month (in April it was Rachel Lee, whose biography mentions that she met her husband on the Internet). And there are details of all current Harlequin, Silhouette, and Mira books, the current romance survey, a daily horoscope, a Loveletters area for reader feedback by E-mail, and a form to print out for ordering the company's books by regular mail.

Harlequin was a latecomer to the Web; its writers were on-line first. The Internet is just one more resource for them. The more entrepreneurial romance authors have long been using a cornucopia of gimmicky promotions, most of which they create and pay for themselves. The most common is the old-fashioned bookmark, but even it can be offbeat. Harlequin author Glenda Sanders had one for *Not This Guy!*, her Temptations novel featuring a veterinarian hero, that listed his six requirements for a woman in his life, including: "4. Drives a relatively new car still under warranty and has an established rapport with a professional mechanic." Sanders has given readers fridge magnets, perfume sachets, and for *Doctor, Darling*, mock prescription pads ("Rx to avoid winter blahs"). Booksellers have received a yellow plastic sign with a

suction cup to stick on shop windows to announce: "Glenda Sanders scintillating love stories sold here." To promote her series of Temptations with *Secrets*
in their titles, she had a four-page newspaper designed with all the subtlety of
a newspaper tabloid. The headline on *Sanders Scoop* screamed LOVERS'
SECRETS REVEALED! beside a photo of her peering secretively out a window.
Inside were a self-profile, reviewers' comments, and a draw for a secret prize
to readers who sent in a questionnaire based on her latest book. Sanders and
many other romance authors also publish pamphlets with brief extracts – first
chapters or compelling scenes – of forthcoming books. Some promotions are
more imaginative than others: Nora Roberts's favorite was for her novel *Public
Secrets*, whose heroine is afraid of the dark: Bantam gave away little plug-in
night lights.

Romance writers are the most omnipresent of any authors in bookstores,
meeting readers and making nice to booksellers. At the *Romantic Times*
Booklovers' Convention in Fort Worth, a special workshop on the bookseller-
author relationship had a Zebra Books representative urging authors to involve
themselves in local writers' groups, which are sometimes tapped for bookstores'
author events, and to research the stores and their employees with on-site visits. "Then start schmoozing. Go in, get to know the people in the bookstore."
At that point, someone in her audience mentioned that they were mostly booksellers, not authors. "Oh-oh," she said. Bobbi Smith of St. Charles, Missouri,
took over to schmooze with them. The Leisure Books author, who had sold
books herself, defined the difference between the two breeds of people to be
found in a bookstore: "Clerks are the people who, when an author comes in,
say, 'Hi, how are you? Your books are in the back, nice to meet you.'
Booksellers go, 'Ohhh, an author!' They grab the books, have you sign them,
and sell them all by five o'clock that afternoon." Smith also satirized her reaction in a bookstore after she became an author. If her books were not there, she
thought the bookseller had failed to order them; if they were there, she
thought, *Oh, my God, nobody is buying my book*. Romance writers also actively
court librarians, having convinced the American *Library Journal* in 1995 to run
a thrice-yearly romance-review section over some of its readers' objections.

At the Booklovers' Convention, I met the Wyrd Sisters – three of them
writers for Harlequin and Silhouette who have banded together with two others to pool their resources and magnify their presence at public events like that

one. Defining the Old English *wyrd* as "that which is unusual or different," they felt the word described their individual and collective styles and subject matter. They had buttons made – I READ THE WYRD STUFF – and published a newsletter, *All Things Wyrd and Wonderful*, which profiled their careers and books and listed upcoming personal appearances. The front page quotes actor Kenneth Branagh: "Friendship is one of the most tangible things in a world which offers fewer and fewer supports." Industrial engineer Pam McCutcheon and former telephone-company engineer Laura Hayden, who writes for Harlequin Intrigue as Laura Kenner, met as unpublished writers at a critique group in Colorado Springs, Colorado. "We just bonded one day," Hayden says. She was writing time-travel romances (*A Margin in Time*); McCutcheon was composing tales of the future and a Harlequin American about a six-foot-four leprechaun (*A Little Something Extra*). Then Hayden met English teacher Yvonne Jocks, who was about to publish a Silhouette Shadows about magic under the pseudonym Evelyn Vaughn (*Beneath the Surface*). "We're psychic twin sisters," Jocks says. Hayden suggested the Wyrd Sisters name, inspired by the three witches in *Macbeth,* as a marketing ploy with booksellers, distributors, and readers.

Hayden and Jocks, who lives in Texas, met through a romance writers' forum on the Prodigy on-line service. It is one of several that have sprung up on the Internet, which, through electronic critique groups and E-mail communication, has become an effective new tool for the isolated writer. Romance authors in particular are driving the information highway with abandon, and a key motivation is to build readership through the use of promotional home pages. Individually and together, they have created countless sites for Web surfers to visit. An interesting one is the home page of Stella Cameron of Seattle (*http://www.seanet.com/vendors/bryan/stella.html*). The award-winning writer, whose novels have made the USA *Today* bestseller list, wrote Harlequin Superromances and American Romances for several years starting in 1985. A visitor to the site is presented with her name in Day-Glo orange lettering above her city's skyline. The full-color covers of her two latest books, for Warner and Zebra, are set against a champagne-bubble backdrop of pastel blue. The visitor can click on a cover to enlarge the image or call up a love scene from *Bride* or the prologue of *Sheer Pleasures* ("Men like Roman Wilde welcomed the night . . ."), or he or she can download a brief audio message in which Cameron reads the opening line of that book and ends with, "Roman Wilde – now I give him to you." Her biography includes a color photo of a barefoot Stella; her bibliography has a black-and-white one gracing her booklist, which reveals that she also wrote as Alicia Brandon and Jane Worth Abbott. Browsers can join her mailing list to keep informed of her career; send her an E-mail message; sign or simply read her guest book, which has scores of messages from appreciative fans and sister authors impressed with her Web site. They can also visit the *Ask Stella!* area to pose questions, as at least one rejected writer has: "How do I know if I'm any good?" To which Stella replied, "One rejection from an agent is a drop of water in an ocean as far as this business goes," and then went on to tell the inquirer to send her manuscript directly to publishers and to find a critique partner. There are even related links to explore from her home page, such as the Romance Novel Database and The Eclectic Writer, which can lead to the GEnie-Romance Writers Exchange Online Newsletter, which has categories for readers to communicate directly with authors. A Stella Cameron fan can happily spend an hour or more here, reconnoitering and reading.

All the Internet experience lacks for a reader is an in-the-flesh romance author. This may help to explain why 900 women came to the Fort Worth Booklovers' Convention. On the first day of the accompanying Book Fair, they and visitors from the local area stood in long lines for autographs and a few words from the superstar authors, the McNaughts and Henleys. They had more time to chat with the second-tier writers such as newcomer Anita Williams (pen name Maggie Ferguson), an Afro-American lawyer in Springfield, Illinois, who writes Harlequin Intrigues and Americans with both black and white heroines. She had interesting stories to tell about her budding career. At one point, the surprised editor of *Looks Are Deceiving*, her first book, remarked, "You know, your characters are black." As for writing nonblack characters, Williams said: "My best friends are white. I think I have a pretty good understanding of white people."

One of the fans I found prowling the floor of the two-day Book Fair was Ella Combs, her buggy half full with 30 books and a Fabio calendar. Freshly 46, short and plump-faced with smiling green eyes, she was a happily wed wife, mother of daughters aged 17 and 22, and bank teller from the ranching and oil town of Carthage, a five-hour drive. "It was almost like my back door," she said, a true Texan. She had been planning her visit for nearly a year, but her reservation the previous August was too late for a room in the official convention hotel this March. Combs thinks TV is a waste of time and never goes to movies; instead, she reads romance novels three to four hours a day, including her quiet time at work, and runs through two or three fat historicals in a week – "I can do a Harlequin in a day." She subscribes to *Romantic Times* to keep current with new releases and, to keep up with the monthly deluge of titles, even listens to audio romances on the tanning bed; over a year, she might spend a couple of thousand dollars on the books and tapes. "Harlequins are terrific stories and not bogged down in a lot of description of sex," she told me. "You can only rub so vigorously so many times." She prefers the heroes to be like her husband, Bruce, an electronics engineer who is "so caring, so protective, he doesn't want you to do anything – mow the yard or pick up anything heavy." He can just about read her thoughts and always remembers anniversaries and birthdays. In fact, he teased her about being at the Book Fair on her birthday and "being here with all these hunks." Not far from us, cover model John D'Salvo and Steve Sandalis, the Topaz Man, sat signing autographs.

The hunks were nowhere to be seen the next morning, Sunday, nor were any but a handful of the romance writers. The exhibitors were mightily displeased that the big-name authors were not scheduled to be at the Book Fair that day. Claiming to be victims of at least bad communications with Kathryn Falk, the entrepreneurs were so angry they called a meeting on the floor to discuss getting some of their money back. Falk and her president, Carol Stacy, were just as disappointed at the turnout for the Book Fair. "I told Kathryn if we don't get thousands and thousands of people through our Book Fair, we're never going to get it," Stacy said long afterward. "And we didn't."

But the readers had not come to sample the painless hair-removal service, have their auras photographed, or buy juicers and hot tubs. Not many were that interested in the onstage wedding ceremony of two exhibitors. Some had come because they, too, wanted to write romantic fiction and just might find the secret formula from real writers. "The secret," Glenda Sanders would tell them, "is you have to tell a damn good story, get it to an editor who appreciates it and to readers who discover it – and that can be an exhaustive process." But most came to the Book Fair and Booklovers' Convention because they wanted to meet the women who write the stories they love, the books that let them escape on their own terms, quickly, easily, into fantasies.

I met Joan Cullum at a welcoming dinner on the first night of the convention. The exuberant 30-year-old manicurist from Grande Prairie, Texas, with a heart-shaped face, was wearing a Valentine-red dress, and her polished nails were impeccable. "I have four kids, so I don't have a lot of time," she said, explaining her preference for short-read Harlequins. "I call them my dessert books. I belong to the Reader Service, where you get them in the mail. My husband calls them smut novels. I trade them in, or he would burn them. I've got an easy 100 in my house right now." What else was there to say? "I've been reading Harlequin books since I was 16 – my grandmother read them, and my daughter will probably read them."

It is dangerous to condemn stories as junk which satisfy the deep hunger of millions of people. . . . People like stories that embody fantasies which fuel their imaginations and in some measure give meaning to their lives; of these, the Cinderella fantasy is the most powerful.
– Robertson Davies

14

No Cure for Love

THE LURE OF ROMANCE

Yvonne Jocks – English teacher, Silhouette author (writing as Evelyn Vaughan), and one of the Wyrd Sisters writers' group – gave me a copy of her master's thesis during the Fort Worth Booklovers' Convention. Entitled "Adventure and Virtue: Alternating Emphasis in the Popular Romance Tradition," the paper offers the compelling argument that today's romance novels, whether considered dessert books or smut books, have a history that goes well beyond 18th-century England. The theory is worth exploring, especially given the conflicting criticisms of feminists for and against romantic fiction. As Jill Barnett, a Pocket Books romance author, has observed, "Love stories have a timeless quality about them. After all, romance isn't a modern phenomenon – something just dreamed up by the president of Harlequin." Or, as Margaret Atwood says, this kind of book has been around since the first books were written, and this kind of story has existed ever since people in the West started telling tales to one another. Jocks makes the point that there are enough surviving examples of the ancient, orally communicated fairy tale, with its romantic subject matter and happily-ever-after conclusion, to connect the genre to popular romance. And she believes that our erotic historical romances have their more tangible roots as far back as ancient Greece, while the sweet contemporary ones had their antecedents in the works of an aristocratic social and literary group in 17th-century France.

Many critics tend to date the birth of the romance novel we now know to 1740, when Samuel Richardson published *Pamela, or Virtue Rewarded,* about an innocent servant girl who wards off her rape-minded master, wins his respect, and winds up happily marrying him. In writing what is generally thought of as the first real English novel of any kind, the prosperous middle-aged printer showed surprising psychological insights into women. Others trace the lineage of the Mills & Boon romances of the 20th century to Jane Austen's *Sense and Sensibility* of 1811 (successfully translated onto the screen in 1995) and the Brontë sisters' *Wuthering Heights* and *Jane Eyre* of 1847. Frances Whitehead, as an M&B editor, thought that Mr. Darcy in Austen's comedy of manners *Pride and Prejudice* was the archetype for the strong and silent, tall and handsome hero of the popular modern romance. Certainly that comparison with the earlier, sweeter Mills & Boons is apt: in both a young heroine of modest means charms the well-to-do eligible hero with her spunk. Of course, what Austen also brought to the table was her satirical social criticism, so that even a curmudgeonly male reader such as British author Martin Amis can confess to reading *Pride and Prejudice* six times for the "undiminished catharsis" of its happy ending.

Yvonne Jocks, however, looks back more than 2,000 years to find the beginnings of at least one form of romance, the erotic historical. During Greece's Hellenic period, the wellspring of Western civilization, several writers whose work survives wrote stories of young couples surmounting major problems to win love. Many were written in an early book form, the equivalent of our paperback, rather than the more literary papyrus roll. Despite their popularity, these Greek novels were scorned, perhaps in part because they were among the few classical genres with a female audience. And in content they were remarkably similar to the erotic historicals that began flourishing in the 1970s. The ancient Greek authors wrote long and sentimental love stories flavored with travel and adventure – with beautiful, spirited, prideful heroines kidnapped by pirates or sold into harems and saved by handsome if character-flawed heroes. The books were often set in earlier times, always drenched in endless inner dialogue, and concluded with the requisite happy climax.

These Greek romances were popular in 17th-century France with the group known as the *precieux*, aristocrats who held weekly salons in Paris and wrote reverential stories of overwhelming, lifelong love. Some were written by women, the most notable being Madeleine de Scudéry, whose two pseudo-historical novels bore the name of her brother Georges on their title pages. French feminism was in bud, and many of the novels reflected that movement. Just as in our own sweet romances, their smart and plucky heroines psychoanalyzed their feelings and kept their virginity intact, their sensitive heroes mirrored feminine values about the worth of women, and the stories inevitably ended with at least the promise of marriage (although de Scudéry was pragmatic enough to note that "marriage and love are two things that do not often last together"). In England during the next century, the sweet contemporary romance was cemented into place, starting with Samuel Richardson's *Pamela*. Yvonne Jocks says, "This English branch of the subgenre continued in a fairly straight pattern until it crossed the Atlantic in the form of English Mills & Boon romances reprinted by Harlequin Enterprises."

These works were spat upon by a whole school of feminists throughout the 1970s and beyond, with what now seems slightly outdated criticism. Typical of the time was a 1980 attack by Columbia University English professor Ann Douglas. She called Harlequins soft porn shaped to suit female emotionality and wrote that "the timing of the Harlequins' prodigious success has coincided exactly with the appearance and spread of the women's movement, and much of its increasingly anti-feminist content reflects this symbiotic relationship." In harsher language than most critics', she said the hero and heroine of these books were emotional illiterates locked in a duel of sexual stupidity. If the statistics were true that middle-aged women read Harlequins, the professor was seriously concerned for them: "How can they tolerate or require so extraordinary a disjuncture between their lives and their fantasies?"

Scholars who came along later were somewhat more understanding, sometimes even revisionist about popular romances. Tania Modleski's *Loving with a Vengeance* (1982) suggests that they tell stories about how women have managed not only to live in oppressive circumstances but also to invest their situation with some dignity – which explains their timeless attraction to female readers. Ann Barr Snitow, co-editor of *Powers of Desire: The Politics of Sexuality* (1983), wrote:

While most serious women novelists treat romance with irony and cynicism, most women do not. Harlequins may well be closer to describing women's hopes for love than the work of the women novelists. Harlequins eschew irony; they take love straight. Harlequins eschew realism; they are serious about fantasy and escape. In spite of all the audience manipulations inherent in the Harlequin formula, the connection between writer and reader is totally seamless. Harlequins are respectful, tactful, friendly toward their audience. The letters that pour into publishers speak above all of the involvement, warmth, human values.

But then she added the stinger: "The world that can make Harlequin romances appear warm is indeed a cold, cold place."

The most influential of the critics was Janice A. Radway, now a literature professor at Duke University, whose *Reading the Romance: Women, Patriarchy, and Popular Literature* in 1984 was based on a field study of a group of female romance readers and how they reacted to the novels. She concluded that for these women, who believe in a system of heterosexuality and monogamy, romance reading "can be conceived as an activity of mild protest and longing for reform necessitated by those institutions' failure to satisfy the emotional needs of women." The women claimed that romance reading was a declaration of independence and a way of telling others, "This is my time, my space. Now leave me alone." In a new introduction seven years later, Radway recalls that the women saw their reading as buying them time and privacy while compensating for "the physical exhaustion and emotional depletion brought about by the fact that no one within the patriarchal family is charged with *their* care." While Radway acknowledges that the very act of romance reading might well disarm their impulses to change their lives in any meaningful way, she also says it might lead them to a new sense of strength and independence. In the end, she says, no one has done the studies to know which is true.

What Radway does know is "the fact that the romance *is* being changed and struggled over by the women who write them." If the criticism has evolved, so has the romantic fiction. As North American authors became more prominent during the Harlequin-Silhouette contretemps, they wrote a more liberated heroine and a more sensitive hero who could learn to express his feelings with a lover's help. In effect, the new heroine held the power more firmly in the relationship and would no longer tolerate the overt rapelike lovemaking that had become so prevalent in the hot historicals of the 1970s. The first issue of *Romantic Times,* in 1981, had a column by Barbara Michaels (pen name Elizabeth Peters) that bemoaned the fact that the worst of the so-called bodice-rippers of the era pandered to "the nastiest of sexual perversions – the age-old male fantasy that women love to be raped." After Jude Deveraux lost her contract with one publisher because she refused to include rape scenes, she moved to another and became a bestselling author.

What many of the revisionist feminists now point out – corroborating a belief of the authors – is that the best of the current romances can actually be empowering for women. In *The Romance Revolution: Erotic Novels for Women and the Quest for a New Sexual Identity,* Carol Thurston talks about the "new romance" whose happy ending "now is possible only through the heroine's emergence as an autonomous individual, no longer defined solely in terms of her relationship to a man." Stevi Jackson, a lecturer in sociology at England's Strathclyde University, argues that "in both fairy tales and romantic fiction love tames and transforms the beast: love has the power to bring him to his knees." Margaret Atwood, as a writer of novels that could never be called romances, has long held a similar view. A decade ago, the author of *The Handmaid's Tale,* a chilling allegory of a future antifeminist society, spoke about the romance novel in an interview with the Canadian feminist magazine *Herizons:*

> Now, Pride and Prejudice is about romance, but it's about discovering that the beast is actually a prince in disguise. And that he's helpless in your power. There are two sexy scenes in Pride and Prejudice. One is when he proposes to her in a rather snotty way and she rejects him for being a snot. And he's very offended. The other sexy scene is when they go walking in the shrubbery and he reveals his intentions. She realizes that she can make or break this man with one little word. It's total female power fantasy. People wonder what people see in Harlequins. Well, that's what they see. They see the possibility of this kind of control and self-aggrandizement.

And what do the romance writers themselves see in their genre today? Jayne Ann Krentz of Seattle – with a history degree from the University of California at Santa Cruz and a master's in library science from San Jose State – has been writing for Harlequin, Silhouette, and Dell for more than 15 years. "I was sick and tired of seeing romance novels critiqued by the media without any real understanding," she told *Publishers Weekly* in 1992 just before the release of the book she edited and wrote with 19 other romance writers. *Dangerous Men and Adventurous Women: Romance Writers on the Appeal of Romance* was published by the University of Pennsylvania Press. It is more of an offensive attack than a defense or apologia. In her introduction, she discusses the unifying threads of the essays: "First and foremost among these themes is the exasperated declaration that the romance novel is based on fantasies and that the readers are no more confused about this fact, nor any more likely to use their reading as a substitute for action in the real world, than readers of Ludlum, Parker, Francis, and McCaffrey."

Krentz mentions the theme of empowerment – the honorable, courageous, and determined woman always wins in a romance novel – and the fact that this is an inversion of the real-world patriarchal power structure. She also raises the interesting notion that romantic fiction is written in a coded, figurative language, a concept that she explores with Linda Barlow, who left her work as a lecturer in English at Boston University to become a full-time author of romances for Silhouette, among others. The co-authors write that the codes of romance celebrate feminine wisdom, power, and communication; the integration of male and female in the mental and physical worlds; the healing and renewing strength of love; and the woman's capacity to do mythic and epic battle – translated to the human plane with the union of lovers at book's end. They mention typical code phrases: "a lust for vengeance," "marriage of convenience," "teach the devil to love."

Romance novels also celebrate life, Krentz writes, often literally by ending with the birth of a baby. Their optimism allows them successfully to cross cultural and political boundaries, as Harlequin has in Japan and China. She quotes Harlequin author Margaret Chittenden about meeting 250 Japanese women a few years before who talked about the unhappy endings of their indigenous stories and how they enjoyed the Western romances – "Happy ever after, yes?" one woman said.

Krentz says readers may identify with either heroine or hero or both, as the writers often do, particularly in love scenes in which they feel the experience as seducer and seduced at the same time. Another sort of duality is the role of the male protagonist, whom the heroine must vanquish as villain without taking down as hero. "Such a task is far more complex than that faced by the protagonists of westerns and mysteries."

One of the contributors to *Dangerous Men and Adventurous Women* is Suzanne Simmons Guntrum, another Harlequin writer. In her essay, "Happily Ever After," she poses an obvious question: "So why read a novel when we already know how it is going to end? Because it is the process, not the conclusion, that we are reading for. Indeed, it is *safe* for us to enjoy the process because we are already guaranteed of the ending."

Guaranteed. I wonder, when I hear literary critics castigating romance novels, whether the genre is that much different in its predictability, its so-called formula, from the sort of book I like to mellow my mind with: the mystery novel. For the sake of comparison, specifically a Dick Francis mystery. The immensely popular English writer, an ex-jockey, always has a horse-racing setting, and horses always play some crucial part in the plot, but perhaps more telling is the fact that the hero – although he has a different name and a different occupation in each of the nearly three dozen books – is always essentially the same character. He is the stalwart, trustworthy, endlessly capable Englishman. Perhaps a bit less brooding and glamorous than the typical protagonist of romantic fiction, yet a stock hero all the same. I go to a Dick Francis, I suspect, for the same reason many women go to a Harlequin: for the comfort zone it surrounds me in, for the sure knowledge that I will receive a certain number of thrills, learn a certain amount of facts about an occupation (though Francis is fairly light on physical description and setting), and reach a cathartic climax the equivalent of the romance's happy ending. As Mary K. Chelton, a county library coordinator in Rockville, Maryland, pointed out in *Library Journal,* "Just as Sara Paretsky's fans know that she will solve the mystery by the end, so Nora Roberts's fans know that her protagonists will ultimately wind up with a fascinating, attentive lover. Mass audiences demand the reassurance that predictability provides; only the means of getting there varies." Although the Dick Francis plots are pleasantly puzzling, there is enough sheer dependability about what they will deliver that brings me back to his books time and again.

Speaking of time, however, this is where I might diverge from the stereotypical romance reader. I enjoy Francis and can gladly read his book a year, but to consume him or his type of mystery novel several times a month, or even week, is beyond me. Perhaps I don't need that much escape. Or my mind needs more mental provocation from a variety of literary stimulants. Whatever it is, a diet of one brand of book – whether mystery or romance – seems constipating. Janice Radway, in *Reading the Romance,* offers one explanation for women's rereading of romances: it is a ritual of hope. "Repetitive engagement in it would enable a reader to tell herself again and again that a love like the heroine's might indeed occur in a world such as hers. She thus teaches herself to believe that men *are able* to satisfy women's needs fully."

The other important point to be made is that I never feel bound to defend myself reading a Francis novel, the way many women do when reading a romance. Somehow the fact that the book is by a man – and presumably for an audience at least equally male as female – legitimizes it. John F. Kennedy could admit that he was a fan of James Bond, just as Richard Bonnycastle did, and nobody thought him a mental midget. Rather, they said that the poor president, what with all his stressful official duties of state, deserved something relaxing, mind-numbing, escapist. Do the wife and mother and career woman – often one and the same – deserve anything less if they seek it? "I've always been offended by the feminists who demean romance fiction," the outspoken Glenda Sanders told me. "These romantic fantasies are written for women by women, which means if a woman wants to escape, she doesn't have to be James Bond. I tend to write very traditional women, but none would let men treat them badly. And my heroines have always been responsible about birth control."

The romance reader may not have to *be* James Bond, but at least one interested observer feels that she may *want* a Bond in her arms. Dr. Julian Boon is the son of Alan Boon, editor emeritus of Mills & Boon. As lecturer in the psychology of personality at the University of Leicester, England, he gave a series of interviews in the early 1990s about how the stereotypes in his father's romantic fiction are scientifically correct. "What every woman wants," he said, perhaps simplifying for the press, "is a rugged James Bond type, an archetypical Mills & Boon alpha male, and what every man wants is a young, beautiful woman." In another interview, he said, "The plot[s] of Mills & Boon books are quintessential examples of the attraction theory as applied to women. Mills & Boon novels are hardly ever read by men, because they are motivated by the competitive instinct and need escapism which has an element of aggression and contest."

It may be a pity that men don't read romantic fiction. The most insightful of the novels can be catalogs of the social and sexual relationships that women dream about: commitment with communication, tenderness with strength. As sex manuals, they can be wonderfully instructive for a man who wants to know a woman's fantasies: explicit and lustful though they can be, they are far, far different from the objectified ruttishness of the man's. Dr. Gay Guzinski, chief of gynecology at the University of Maryland, says good romance novels can be sex information services: "They help women expand their sexual repertoire, in a good, clean, and harmless way." Some psychiatrists use romance novels to help treat couples suffering from "diminished desire," as several therapists mentioned during a 1992 meeting of the American Psychiatric Association. And eight years earlier, Atlanta psychologists Claire D. Coles and M. Johnna Shamp did a study of 48 housewives and working women who read romances to chart their sexual, personality, and demographic characteristics. They found that the romance readers averaged between 25 and 35 years old and read for escape. The most intriguing revelation was that romances acted as a socially acceptable type of sexual stimulation: their readers reported making love twice as often per week as nonreaders (an average of 3.04 times a week compared with 1.75 times). As chronicled in *Archives of Sexual Behavior,* the romance-reading housewives especially were "more satisfied with sex than were nonreaders." Coles, at the Emory University School of Medicine, explains, "Readers reported using fantasy to improve their experience during sexual intercourse, while nonreaders did so seldom or never."

When David Galloway was still Harlequin's president, he spoke to a largely male audience at a Harvard Business School alumni meeting in Toronto. Before beginning his formal presentation to fellow grads, he asked how many of them had read the *Globe and Mail* that day. All the hands went up. How many had read his parent company's paper, the *Toronto Star*? About half the hands rose. *Tough crowd,* he thought. How many, he asked finally, had read a Harlequin in the past three months? Only his hand was in the air. "Well, let me tell you," he said, "Harlequin readers *read* – and watch television less than the average [person]. And they have better sex lives." Amid laughter he added, "I guess you'll have to take my word for it." One man in the audience piped up: "How many books does it take?"

*I think the fall of the Wall gave Harlequin a new
dynamic, which will carry on for some time until
these markets are saturated.*
— Horst Bausch, Harlequin's former editor
in chief and vice president

15

The Awakened Heart

WOOING EASTERN EUROPE

Ralf Kläsener, director of international affairs for the Axel Springer publishing conglomerate in Germany, was visiting Toronto on business in early 1989. He was in town for a meeting with Harlequin in his role as the Springer shareholders' representative for Cora Verlag, the West German joint venture his company had long enjoyed with the romance publisher. Taking a taxi, he chatted up the Hungarian driver, a former language professor who had fled his country.

"Would unification of the two Germanys ever happen?" the cabbie asked his passenger.

"We all hope so," Kläsener told him, "but we never think there is a real chance in the next 20 years."

He had been studying in Berlin in the early 1960s when East German authorities closed the border between the two halves of the city and erected the Berlin Wall to halt the mass exodus of East Berliners to the West. Nearly three decades later, as Soviet citizens began gaining rights and other Eastern European nations forced out Communist governments, a shaky East Germany was celebrating its 40th anniversary. The Soviet Union's Mikhail Gorbachev came to visit and betrayed his hosts by encouraging their citizens to engage in perestroika-like protest against the regime. That month, October 1989, Kläsener was among colleagues meeting in Springer's building in Berlin, so close to the Wall that they looked down on Checkpoint Charlie. It was a momentous time to be there: the embattled German Democratic Republic was in crisis. Within a matter of weeks, amid widespread emigration through Czechoslovakia, President Erich Honecker resigned in disgrace to be replaced by his hard-nosed security chief Egon Krentz, who promised no real accommodation with pro-democratic forces.

In Toronto on the evening of November 9, Brian Hickey – just a year after becoming Harlequin's chief executive officer – was meeting over dinner with his troops from around the world. They were assembled for the twice-yearly gathering of overseas managing, marketing, and finance directors. David Galloway was present in his new capacity as president of Torstar Corporation. Sitting with a group of non-German European executives, Galloway directed the conversation to events in Germany. He posed a couple of questions – would the Wall ever fall? how did they feel about a reunified Germany? – and the group talked on the topic for half an hour. The consensus, summed up by a finance director from France, was that the Germanys would not rejoin in their lifetimes.

The next morning, Galloway picked up the *Toronto Star* to read that – as the G D R suddenly allowed citizens to exit without visas – thousands of East Berliners had thronged through openings in the Wall to the West. The hated barrier of cement and barbed wire had fallen overnight. "Everybody thought I was clairvoyant," he recalls. "I was just making conversation."

A year later, in 1990, Ralf Kläsener was back in Toronto and hailed a taxi. The cabbie looked at him and asked: "Do you remember what you said a year ago?" It was the same Hungarian driver, whose homeland had declared itself a democratic republic with multiparty elections. He was now heading back to Budapest to reclaim his old position as language professor.

By then, as Communist control of the Eastern Bloc nations crumbled along with the Wall, Harlequin Enterprises was solidly entrenched in both Hungary and the former East Germany. They were the first two countries it would colonize through joint ventures to distribute that most befitting symbol of capitalistic publishing: brand-name books.

In the wake of the Wall's demolition, Cora Verlag, the German partnership of Harlequin and Springer, sprang into action. The East German government had announced the new travel freedoms on a Thursday. By Friday tens of thousands of jubilant people an hour were flowing over the border into West Berlin, the guards simply glancing at their identity papers and waving them through the Wall. Some climbed it or chopped chunks off the barricade. The West German government immediately said it would give any East German 100 of its deutsche marks ($54 U.S.) in welcome money. On that first weekend, West Berlin businesses began distributing free milk, coffee, and other drinks to the visitors. Meanwhile, at Harlequin headquarters, the key management and distribution people were in deep discussion. They had access to potentially hundreds of thousands of unsold romance novels, in the German-style magazine format, which wholesalers could return to them intact. Why not give them away to all the East German women crossing the border?

"We discussed this together and thought, 'What a brilliant idea!'" Ralf Kläsener says. "So we took all the books back for a certain period of time and gave them to the people of Berlin. They had to pass through certain passages, so we had people placed at strategic points in the first two or three months." Cora employees took truckloads of books to the border, handing out bags holding three or more free samples – 150,000 copies in just the three weekends before Christmas. In all they distributed 720,000 books to appreciative women, some of whom wrote the company in thanks:

> I was in Hamburg on December 9 and couldn't imagine that a surprise would be awaiting me this eventful day. I would like to thank you and your staff who stood at the border crossings, regardless of the cold, in order to prepare pleasure for us. Although I am already 46 years old, I still let myself be carried off into the world of the romantic.
> Helga Skoeries
> Bruel, G D R

> Returning home, we experienced a pleasant surprise as we were given your lovely present. We were very happy over it and want to express our thanks. It was a very good gesture on the part of your publishing company. Perhaps the day will soon come when we will be able to buy your literature in the

form of romance books in our own country. For this, we wish you and your publishing company successful efforts.

Joachim and Gerda Hindemitt
Kindelbrueck/Thueringen, G D R

The Hindemitts would not have to wait long for that day to come. Harlequin's executive vice president of overseas operations, Heinz Wermelinger – still based in Toronto but soon to relocate to Baar, Switzerland – was spearheading his company's end of the East Bloc publishing putsch. He was well aware that it represented one of the few growth areas in a world that was rapidly becoming Harlequinized. "We are everywhere," he told a Canadian business journalist grandly. His move across the Atlantic in 1990 would be prompted by the fact that Western Europe's retail sales were reaching a plateau. East Germany had an alluring 30 percent of the reunified nation's total population. "Therefore," says Wermelinger's counterpart at Springer, Ralf Kläsener, "every German publisher from the first day considered this a beautiful new market." Within four months, Cora was selling romances to that audience. But Kläsener points out the problems the joint venture faced, along with other West German publishers, in entering this untested territory: "Distribution had been handled by the postal service, the only institution with a nationwide distribution service. There were only 2,000 selling points, in the biggest cities – and everybody tried to work on how to improve the distribution business. Hundreds of thousands of new selling points were created. At the end of it all, German publishers had collectively lost 100 million marks." Much of the distribution had been placed in private hands, some of which made off with money not theirs. And publishers – eager to capture market share – were accepting East German marks on an equal basis with West German ones, when the official ratio was closer to one to seven. "We have to confess that in the first three-quarters of the year, most German publishers shipped far too high [a volume]." When the new industry shook down, the former East Germany had only 20,000 distribution outlets, Kläsener says, which was about 10,000 fewer than it should have had to serve the population.

With all the frustrations, however, Cora's romance novels did sell reasonably if not spectacularly well. "This product was really unknown to the population there," Kläsener says. "From visitors to East Germany, we knew before unification that people were reading Cora books. Older people were allowed to come to West Germany to visit relations and used to bring the books back. This was the kind of literature that Communist Germany used to consider a sign of Western decadence." The fact that the books were not German worked in their favor: "We translate them, but we don't adapt them. They have foreign names and foreign settings, and this is one of the secrets of their success – even in West Germany. This is armchair travel for the readers. One of the reasons East Germans wanted to unify was that they were not allowed to travel." Although Kläsener describes Cora's sales to this new audience as "satisfying" over the first half of this decade, he told me they have not yet reached the equivalent of 30 percent of the country's eastern population.

Larry Heisey watched all this enterprise with pride. His boyhood dream of running a company that operated worldwide was having its fairy-tale – romance-novel – ending. In 1989, the year the Wall went down, Harlequin kicked sand in the faces of its 98-pound weakling competitors with a 40th-anniversary promotion that made *The Guinness Book of World Records.* The concept was the release of *A Reason for Being,* by globally popular British writer Penny Jordan, in 18 languages in 100 markets simultaneously. Among the countries were Turkey, where Harlequin had signed a licensing agreement in 1981, and Korea and Iceland, where it made a similar arrangement six years later. "This symbolizes the fact that Harlequin can manage the translation and distribution of a book around the world," said Brian Hickey in announcing the promotion. The idea actually came from Heisey. Corporate insiders say that when he first pitched it to Hickey, who did not share his sense of corporate history, the newly appointed C E O simply asked: "Why?" And Heisey replied, in effect: "That's what I did with my life."

He was to retire a year later, in 1990, at the age of 60. Harlequin had been good to him. A multimillionaire, he had a 42-foot Bertram yacht, a lavish summer home on Ontario's Georgian Bay, and a winter home in Florida. In Toronto he and Ann lived in Rosedale, a downtown neighborhood ringed by ravines and lined with maples and elms, a graceful old upper-middle-class enclave of lawyers and stockbrokers. Their 22-room, three-story Tudor-style mansion was built in 1911 by the developer of the area. In the dining room, a chandelier dripped from a ceiling inlaid with hexagons of light oak, and an antique chinoiserie filled one wall. The living room had a Basendorfer baby grand piano, and the billiard room had the original carved-rosewood table, both of which he still played. In the solarium, a bronze French harlequin figure reminded him of the source of the surrounding beauty. On the walls or plinths were a couple of Picasso drawings, a Henry Moore bronze maquette, a Van Gogh of a woman in a field, an Andy Warhol of ballerina Karen Kain, ceramic sculpture by the contemporary French Jewish artist Georges Jeanclos, and two Impressionist paintings by Pierre Bonnard, one of them Heisey's treasure.

He remained a romantic. A few years before, on the 20th anniversary of the day he and his wife had met, he took the silver-tressed, attractive Annie out for dinner alone – without signaling the occasion. At the end of the meal, he announced: "I have something to tell you." She was sure it was bad news: he had another woman perhaps, or they had lost all their money. He told her the significance of the date and then said, "I just want to tell you that you've given me the happiest third of my life."

After his retirement, the state of his health reared up as an unhappy reality. He had a quintuple bypass in the summer of 1994, a legacy of the heavy smoking and double-fisted martini consumption of his Harlequin years. But he recovered well and continued a busy life. In a reprise of his 5B X exercise-timer venture, he and a friend tried and failed to promote an invention that allowed a rental videocassette to be played only once. More successfully he invested in the Toronto production of *Cats*, produced by Garth Drabinsky, who went on to bring an acclaimed *Show Boat* revival to Broadway. Heisey has served on the board of Aetna Insurance of Canada, the Atlas Group of Funds of Toronto, and the Canadian division of the American office-supplies chain Staples. He has been a governor of The Banff Centre, the continuing-education school in the Alberta resort town, as well as of the National Ballet of Canada and York University, and he has chaired the ballet's and university's foundations. For these involvements and his services to Canadian publishing, he was named an Officer of the Order of Canada in 1995.

As chairman emeritus of the company he helped to build, Heisey maintained his office on the ninth floor of the Harlequin building. It was just down the hall from the boardroom with its decorator wall of ceramic pottery; a Royal Doulton of a nude couple in a passionate kiss, in honor of Anne

Mather's 100th novel; and a bronze bust of Alan Boon – "the father of the business," Heisey told visitors. His own office, capacious and dark-paneled, had Oriental rugs, heavy rust draperies, and a sculpture by Canadian Gerald Gladstone on a buffet. On the shelves were an old Mills & Boon penny-library hardcover and a copy of the first Harlequin, *The Manatee,* and on the wall a plaque marking the publication of the one billionth book on March 29, 1985. Beside his desk was a globe, where Larry Heisey could continue to track Harlequin's movement into areas of the world he might never have imagined occupying as a young boy dreaming of his global business.

Before entering East Germany, the Harlequin-Springer joint venture had already tested its wares in a formerly Communist country. The ruling party in Hungary had officially become Socialist when Cora Verlag initiated a licensing arrangement to distribute romance novels there in 1989. The Hungarian deal happened too late for a photo of a book in the Magyar language to be included on the 40th-anniversary poster that accompanied the promotion. The globe-girdling Penny Jordan novel did circulate in Yugoslavia, a country about to implode over the next couple of years, offering Harlequin no happy endings there. But in the more stable and equally westernized Hungary, the company replaced the licensing agreement with a joint venture with a local partner in 1990 to print 48 titles a year. In a country where it was difficult to rent space with more than one or two telephones for an entire building, the Hungarian team managed to settle in a new structure whose offices had their own phones. Horst Bausch, the Toronto-based editor in chief at the time, recalls other challenges faced by the seven university-educated staff who started up the operation: "Italy, France, and Germany were countries where romance fiction had a tradition. Whereas in Russia, since 1917 there was a total break, and in the other Eastern countries since 1945. There was nothing where you could compare content and the special language of romances. You really had to develop a sense of what's behind the words. It's a particularly tough job in Eastern Europe. Hungary was launched by the German company. They still have more people [in Hungary] who speak German than English, so they translate from the German translation. So there are more possibilities for error. They still feel that in the long run, it would be better to move directly from English." Bumpy translations did not dissuade appreciative readers, who wrote fan letters. "I simply cannot stop reading them," B. Agnes of Nyirbogdany reported. "If I get one, I do not bother about anything else, even at a bus stop or during a math lesson." And B. J.-ne Szigetszentimiklos said in her thank-you: "I bought my first Romana after seeing your advertisement on T V. . . . These books meet a long-felt need in Hungary."

Printed on relatively slow Hungarian presses in the same magazine format and with the same series names as in Germany, four books a month were distributed through the postal-service network set up by the national government. Harlequin, which had to deal with virtually monopolistic periodical wholesalers in North America, was now having to accept the vagaries of Communism's exclusive distribution channels. As Harlequin's Heinz Wermelinger explained it, "the post office tells us how many books each retail outlet should get. On the up side, we are guaranteed complete and highly efficient distribution, and we know their numbers are correct. We trust them." There were other benefits to the system, Hickey told Torstar shareholders in 1991: "The dissemination of propaganda required a literate population, efficient periodical distribution, . . . and a large-volume capacity for paper, ink, and printing presses. The infrastructure for our books exists, and it does work." And local partners were anxious to ally themselves with the Western company, he said. "Harlequin has a reputation for making profits, and they want to do business with us."

Within the first six months, the Hungarian start-up had broken even – selling 6.5 million books, nearly triple what it had hoped to do in a year. Returns were only six percent. Thirty-second T V spots supported new titles in a country where television advertising was still a novelty. The demand moderated to 7 million for all of 1991, but by the following year, it had increased to nearly two books sold for each of the nation's 5.5 million women – then the highest ratio of any of Harlequin's operations. They sold at first for the equivalent of 85 cents, a price based on both cheaper labor costs and local competition from magazine publishers. When paper prices climbed within a year, the Hungarian managers were hesitant to raise cover prices. Urged on by their partners at Cora, they did, anyway, by about 10 cents, and sales continued strong – enough to add a $2.10 triple-volume book each month and a new line of the old reliable doctor-nurse romances. The one series that failed to find a readership was a leftover from a tame, short-lived, young-adult series, *Crosswinds,* launched in North America in 1987; young Hungarian women also preferred sexier stories with bold covers of clinching couples. As rival publishers entered the market, Cora's volume decreased to about 7 million in 1994.

That year was also a more difficult one for Harlequin in Poland, where it had established a wholly owned subsidiary known as Arlekin in late 1991. The venture had started well – the first million copies of eight titles sold out in five days – and maintained the momentum for the next couple of years with increased print runs despite increased cover prices. Its early success was due in no small part to the marketing-savvy managing director, Nina Kowalewska. Born in Warsaw in 1958, she was educated for six of her teenage years in New York, where her father was commercial attaché to the Polish delegation. In 1974 she brought American optimism back to a pessimistic Poland. "When people ask an American how he's doing, he replies okay, even if he has cancer," she explained to a journalist from the Parisian newspaper *Liberation.* "A Polish person, even if he just bought a Jaguar, will always answer, 'Everything is bad.'"

For Kowalewska – a stylish woman with a face like a heart framed by bountiful dark curls – almost everything was good. Back home in Warsaw, the maverick young woman, a feminist by her country's standards, studied Japanese and married an artist, with whom she had a daughter three years later. In 1990 she was distributing *The Financial Times* of London throughout Poland when she met a representative from Harlequin, shopping around for management. Despite her New York stay, she had never heard of the company. But the challenge was irresistible, as was the salary: Nina Kowalewska was soon earning 50 million inflated zlotys a month – $5,000 – when the average wage was only 2.7 million (10,000 zlotys equaled about one Canadian dollar). Poland was just emerging from four decades of Communist rule as Solidarity leader Lech Walesa became president. After suffering through a period of great inflation, when prices soared by 600 percent, the country was undergoing the shock therapy of an overnight transition to a free market. That translated into an abundance of consumer goods and a shortage of spending money.

No major research was necessary to test the feasibility of selling Harlequins in a nation of 40 million people who had gone without popular romantic fiction since before World War II. Heavy readers, the Poles had been limited to state-controlled classical literature, which was inexpensive if serious. For the two exceptional years of 1989 and 1990, a gaggle of Polish commercial publishers started up to satisfy an audience hungry for once-banned Western bestsellers. With free enterprise firmly in place, book prices leaped, and retailers now insisted on products that would sell swiftly. Cheap, commercial Arlekins were one answer. The novels would appeal to women who had won the right to vote in 1918 and most of whom – wives and mothers alike – had to have jobs outside the home: the ultimately sensitive hero portrayed in American and British romance novels was a revelation for Arlekin's Polish readers. More than 30 percent of them had not picked up a book since leaving school; nearly 40 percent were younger than 19, only six percent older than 40. A major difference between the romances packaged for Hungary and strongly Catholic Poland was the sexual discretion of the covers. To test them, Kowalewska had created focus groups of four dozen women at a time who got perfume and munchies in trade for their opinions – which, overwhelmingly, were to downplay the passion in the cover illustrations.

In October 1991, with a small operating staff – including three editors under editorial manager Leszek Kaminski – Kowalewska launched eight 188-page books in the first two series, Romance and Desire (the series titles remained in English for their exotic appeal). The managing director read as many Harlequins and Silhouettes as she could, not as a fan but as a pastry chef sampling her wares. Fifteen Polish women volunteered to read them to help decide which should be translated by 77 freelancers, who were paid 25 million zlotys ($2,500) a book. The editors and eight proofreaders vetted their renderings for style, spelling, and grammar. The translators had the usual trouble other Europeans would encounter. At first some of them were well-known Polish poets and novelists, who used less clinical lovemaking euphemisms such as "she felt the happiness inside her." Other professional translators, who had handled the likes of Margaret Atwood, expressed frustration with the language of romance: "The details are very detailed. And the kiss: it's almost always the same," Ewa Godycka told the *Washington Post* not long ago in an article that so upset Harlequin's head office that it forbade Kowalewska and her staff to talk to Westerners without permission. "When I read it in English, it's okay. But when I read it in Polish, I can't digest it. It's ugly, really. When it comes to sexual language, we have a somewhat different tradition. We really do not have the vocabulary for it in literature. So we try to soften it. We want to be less open and literal . . . and we don't want the Church to comment. We want peace and quiet." Piotr Amsterdamski, an astronomer when not moonlighting as a translator of romances, wondered, "I wish I knew why they were so popular. My livelihood depends on it." And then he answered himself: "Many women here live in tough conditions. Their husbands are drunkards, their children don't learn well, the money is tight. This offers a respite."

Arlekin delivered the books to readers through the two government-run periodical and book distribution channels and eventually, when the state book distributor went bankrupt, through private operators and directly to a 660-store book chain. The surviving government periodical channel, Ruch, shipped 80 percent of all the company's books to 22,000 kiosks – the majority of them now privatized and starting to bypass Ruch to buy from independents who gave them a higher margin on sales. To widen its reach, Arlekin even approached the post office to test its outlets as a retailer of romance novels. Originally priced at 10,000 zlotys apiece, the books were selling for 50 percent more three months after the launch as print runs rose to 175,000 per title.

By then Harlequin had spent 3 billion zlotys on television alone. One of three commercials, played thrice daily on the two national channels, opened in black and white with a wistful-looking woman alone in a café. As a male voice-over said "Escape into the world of dreams," the screen burst into full color, and the setting became a fabulous yacht, complete with a handsome hero. It ended with the line: "Harlequin is a garden of love." Buttressing the commercials were radio spots, media events, and 300 million zlotys' worth of ads in women's magazines. In 1992 the advertising and promotion budget mounted to 25 billion zlotys. A fifth of that went to print; when a competitor borrowed the "garden of love" line, Arlekin rejoined with the magazine ad: "There are many romances but only one true love." As well as running regular commercials on government and private radio stations, it sponsored an Arlekin Club talk show featuring women's concerns. Television advertising increased to 50 spots a month, complementing the sponsorship of popular shows such as *Dynasty* and *The Bill Cosby Show*. Romantic cover illustrations began appearing as posters on bus shelters in downtown Warsaw. A hundred guests attended the first readers' party. The enterprising Kowalewska also sponsored cultural events and even an intellectual magazine called *Res Publica*.

The monolithic Palace of Culture in Warsaw sprouts a heart on Valentine's Day 1992, announcing Harlequin's arrival in Poland. HARLEQUIN ENTERPRISES

The company awarded scholarships to students and made donations to a children's hospital – and when a Polish court ordered a local publisher to pay Arlekin the equivalent of $125,000 for pirating its books, Arlekin gave most of the money to charities, presenting its adopted hospital with an ambulance.

That was just before Kowalewska's most ambitious, and outlandish, promotion. On Valentine's Day 1992 – an event never before celebrated in Poland – Warsaw awoke to an immense red heart bearing Arlekin's name atop the monolithic Palace of Culture that Stalin had bestowed as a gift on Poland. The biggest and oldest building in the central capital had suddenly become a Western billboard. It was just the beginning. A special Valentine-themed book was launched. Major radio stations, newspapers, and magazines interviewed Arlekin people. And that evening the company was on television – with a vengeance.

David Galloway remembers asking Kowalewska later about the TV promotion. "Gee, that's great, Nina, you prepared some advertising and put it on that evening?"

"No," she said. "I programmed it."

"What do you mean, you programmed it?"

What she meant was that she took over the entire channel, buying eight full hours of time, presenting 11 programs – dubbed American sitcoms such as *The Love Boat* and another mimicking *The Dating Game*. There were romantic film stars on talk shows, and she herself gave a state-of-romance speech. To many Poles, February 14 has been Arlekin Day ever since. Kowalewska followed up this coup in 1993 with another imaginative promotion. Harlequin sponsored a Woman of the Year Award and presented it to the wife of the nation's dynamic president; interviewed on television, Danuta Walesa said she not only knew Arlekins, she also read them.

After two years of exciting growth in Poland, the company began to hit a bumpy stretch. Its growing competition included one private Polish firm publishing eight series romances a month, including Bantam Loveswepts, and another releasing bestsellers such as Robert Ludlum and a line of Barbara Cartlands. Although Arlekin had sold 40 million books by October 1994, sales were not accelerating. The Polish economy was wracked with problems. Nina Kowalewska was sorry that the company hadn't started in 1989 and enjoyed those two boom years before the marketplace began to get so crowded.

She had her own problems as well. Now a single mother of a 10-year-old, she was in the middle of a divorce in which she would have to sell her house and share the proceeds with her ex-husband. "My life is not really a Harlequin kind of life," she admitted to an interviewer at the time. Within a year, she had decided to leave the company to work on her own. She would represent *The Financial Times* again and produce films and documentaries for television, perhaps even some for her former employer. In compensation she would have the knowledge that the company she had helped to start in Poland brought comfort to many women. As many as 2,500 of them a month wrote letters to Arlekin. "We are more than a publishing company," Kowalewska told *Liberation*. "We are considered experts in women, we are consulted on everything – fashion, food, children's education, the couple. I represent the Harlequin woman."

The same phenomenon was at work in the Czech Republic, where Harlequin opened a wholly owned subsidiary in 1992. Here the company again hired a local woman as managing director, Dagmar Digrinová, owner of an ad agency called digdag and publisher of a teen magazine, *Watch Out Girls*. Her experience emboldened her to conceive her own commercials for television and cinema screenings to introduce Harlequin to the newly created nation of five million. The three T V spots had different hues to reflect the cover colors of the various series: white for the tame Romances, purple for the Temptations, and red for the Desires. In each a woman in a reverie left a humdrum man to wander a long corridor to seek a faithful hero. "Wake up to a world of desire," the voice-over said. "With someone who will never leave you." Digrinová combined the ads with promotions as clever as her Polish counterpart's: using direct mail to position Harlequin as a women's club and throwing costume balls to attract media attention and parties to celebrate a Valentine's Day that had only surfaced in the republic in 1989. Perhaps the most unusual promo was a calendar designed for a female reader to track her menstrual cycle as well as the release dates of new romances. The calendars were distributed at newsstands, where most of the novels were sold for about $1 apiece. Digrinová also recruited 55 volunteers to promote the company in their hometowns in return for free novels. All of this activity spawned an ongoing spate of letters: nearly 20,000 women wrote to her in the two months after the launch – and, as in Poland, they were asking for advice, mostly about men. So much mail continued to flow in that Dagmar Digrinová retained a

On the Vltava River in Prague – one of the thousands of Czech women who woke up to a world of desire. HARLEQUIN ENTERPRISES

psychologist to help her staff answer the heartfelt inquiries. And from these missives, the managing director developed a mailing list of about 50,000 names. The Czech operation was soon generating the equivalent of about $10 million U.S. a year. At the same time, however, a new Harlequin subsidiary in Bulgaria was faltering.

In 1992 the publisher also edged into the former Soviet Union, whose Russian-speaking market was 140 million strong. With a state-owned publishing house, now forced to be profitable, Harlequin began with an encouraging test run at the 10th of that total who live in Moscow and St. Petersburg. The seven titles released over two seasons sold out quickly at about 25 cents each. "From a business standpoint," Harlequin vice president Hugh O'Neil said after his visit to Russia the year before, "the potential is phenomenal. It's like discovering America. It's a vast untapped omnivorous consumer. . . . The literacy rate is almost 100 percent." Russia was emerging with abandon from the long, dark night of social repression to embrace a new freedom in portraying sexuality – a topic that Russian anthropologist Igor S. Kon says had until recently been "indecent and unmentionable, a subject only for the degenerate underground." While the populace was primed for Western romance novels, the marketplace was not yet working. Paper was in short supply because

80 percent of it had already been allocated. Distribution was a horrendous problem, which is why Harlequin began collaborating with other publishers – Germany's Bertelsmann and Denmark's Egmont – in an attempt to streamline a new system for delivering books and periodicals. In 1993 Harlequin was telling Torstar's stockholders: "Russia's deteriorating infrastructure, creating difficulties in distribution and printing, have prevented start up of full operations." A year later, it told them that while Russia offered the most significant growth potential of all the former Iron Curtain countries, its "infrastructure and fledgling financial system are major obstacles to expansion of the business." The financial factor then was the instability of the ruble, a nonconvertible currency, which meant that profits couldn't be taken out of the country. Meanwhile, rivals for the female readers' attention were appearing, including old faithful Barbara Cartland.

But by early 1996, when I talked with Brian Hickey, Harlequin's situation in Russia had improved. After visits there, the C E O told me he was "excited as hell. I mean, Russia's been wonderful for us. We have a copublishing agreement with Raduga [Rainbow] Publishing. It had to be economically self-sufficient, so we were an immense opportunity for them. And they have a wonderful lady, Nina Litvinets, who runs the company, who fully recognized this potential and has grown in her understanding of it and is quite aggressive about it. So we work very closely with Nina, and things work out very well there."

Visiting Harlequin's head office in 1991, Nina Litvinets forecast some of the challenges that lay ahead. Among them were Raduga's relationship with the government: "The only way the state assists us is by overseeing finances to make sure there are no untaxed profits. . . ." In Russia at the time, the publisher, not the printer, had to buy the paper on the so-called free market, and "as a rule, the first two shipments are all right, but then you have to send telexes." The printer earned what she called an absurd 20 to 25 percent of the profits under an antiquated system she compared to "some typically Russian bicycle that doesn't exist anymore." Competition – an opening up of the market – has since taken care of many of those concerns. Distribution does remain a problem, although a system of private independent dealers now buys books and periodicals and moves them through the country. And currency regulations have relaxed somewhat: "We repatriate substantial funds out of the Russian marketplace," Hickey says. "Yes, we make money."

In summing up Harlequin's overall Eastern European operations, Torstar chairman David Galloway admits, "It's not all roses there. We started really well, but the economies there are tough. Poland – we took off. We made a lot of money the first two years. Bulgaria, we never made any money. Czech, we're doing okay. So when you add these up, it's not all roses."

In the end, the new dynamic – along with the high profits – that the liberated East Bloc nations were supposed to bring to Harlequin haven't materialized as dramatically as many within the company had hoped. The most recent Torstar annual report, in discussing how ascending paper prices around the world limited Harlequin's profitability in 1995, points out: "This is particularly true in Eastern Europe, where there has also been tremendous pressure on profit margins due to intense competition from the women's magazine market." While other book publishers in these countries have not yet become consequential competitors, magazine publishers have. Because Harlequin novels are largely published in magazine format there and distributed like magazines, as they were in West Germany from the beginning, the conventional women's periodicals can become serious direct challengers.

"This competition," the report went on to say, "has not only hindered Harlequin's ability to increase prices in the face of severe cost increases, but has also taken money out of the leisure reading market. Despite all of these market pressures, Harlequin has managed to maintain stability in its Eastern European operations and there were signs of improving trends in Poland and Hungary in the latter part of 1995." Meanwhile, the company had closed down operations in Bulgaria while promising to sustain a business presence there and operating through what it hoped would be a more profitable licensing arrangement with locals. To assuage shareholders, the report had to look to a more hopeful tomorrow in overseas operations: "The most significant opportunity for future growth lies in geographic expansion with the development of new markets in Russia and the republics of the former U.S.S.R., China, Central and South America, India and Southeast Asia."

A reader of the report didn't have to be a Kremlinologist to decipher the direction that the romance publisher was heading – and the implicit dismay at the fact that it was lagging behind the competition: "Harlequin's best opportunity for expansion in existing markets is through the release of single titles as opposed to series romances. More than two of every five books sold in North America have romance themes and many are single titles, an area Harlequin has yet to exploit in a consistent manner." The company's competitors were the experts in single-title romances. One of them was the so-called Mr. Romance, Walter Zacharius, the owner of Zebra Books' parent company, which Harlequin had tried – and failed – to buy.

An early Russian Harlequin with its English equivalent. HARLEQUIN ENTERPRISES

They're so powerful that they think they can do so many things, and they know that they can't, down deep, but they use their muscle. And in some respects, if I had that muscle, I might use it also.
— Walter Zacharius on his competitor, Harlequin

16

Seduced and Betrayed

HARLEQUIN BRANCHES OUT

Kathryn Falk labeled Walter Zacharius Mr. Romance, but Clint Eastwood would probably not play him in the movie. A leaner version of Walter Matthau might, perhaps; Zacharius has the same rumpled look and big-nosed, rumpled face. With his boyhood in polyglot Brooklyn as the son of a Jewish immigrant architect, his electrical engineering education at New York's populist City College, and his carving of a publishing career through pulp paperbacks, men's magazines, even a gospel music publication – with this kind of résumé, he stands in some contrast to the well-born, M.B.A.'d Torontonians David Galloway and Brian Hickey and their General Foods marketing backgrounds. Zacharius once described to the *New York Times* the difference between his firm – now the last privately owned paperback firm of any size in the United States – and its more powerful, publicly held competitors: "The people who run [Zebra] are free to operate as they see fit and can react quickly to changing conditions. The conglomerates that own all the other houses require their M.B.A.-type executives to spend most of their time preparing projections and plans for years to come."

In 1992 the Torstar conglomerate's Harlequin division made a bid for

Zacharius's New York business and even signed a letter of intent to buy it. It would not secure an impressive flow of cash with the acquisition of its relative pip-squeak of a competitor, which had sales of $40 million on 400 titles the year before (or $12 million less than Harlequin had earned in *profits*). What it would gain was a line of ingeniously produced and marketed romance novels in a category in which it was weak, a growing book club, and a company that had some insight into single-title publishing. Over two decades, with nearly half a century of frontline experience and a gut instinct for good marketing, Walter Zacharius had built one of the most innovative paperback houses in the country. In recent years, his Kensington Publishing Corporation – including Kensington hardcovers and Pinnacle and Zebra Books paperbacks – had competed in the romance market with imagination in place of deep pockets. As a fellow publisher, Bill Black of Dorchester Publishing, told me: "Dr. Z: he is a legend. He built a business out of nothing, for God's sake. Obviously Zebra is a real player in the poker game. . . . They're a very creative force, endlessly inventive, and I think Walter more than any other individual *is* probably Mr. Romance."

But as he reached his seventh decade, Zacharius was faced with the fact that fleet-footed creativity and invention no longer loomed as large in an industry in which the conglomerates reigned. He and his partner, president and publisher Roberta Grossman, could not attract and keep more bestselling romance authors beyond the handful they already had (among them Janelle Taylor and Constance O'Day-Flannery). Although they gave Katherine Stone an advance of $225,000 for a book, she left for Random House and $860,000. "You don't have the financial backing to go out and buy these kind of people getting these huge megadeals," says Zacharius's son, Steven, who joined the firm as general manager in 1992. "Or you don't have the movie ties that a Warner might have or Simon & Schuster with Paramount [its sister company]. We were losing that end of the business. So I think my father felt, why not get out at the peak?"

It had been a long, curious climb up for a publisher now linked with romantic fiction. After soldiering overseas in World War II, Zacharius went to engineering school at night for nine years while getting his first publishing job running figures in the distribution department of McFadden Magazines. With his calculator-like head for numbers, he became a circulation manager with

Mercury Publications, which published science fiction and mystery magazines as well as the iconoclastic *American Mercury* magazine. In fact, the company had created a line of American Mercury Books in 1937 that predated the marketing techniques of Zacharius's eventual competitor, Harlequin, in three important ways. Mercury was the first to distribute mass-market paperbacks through magazine outlets, where they stayed on the racks for only a month; it numbered each book to help readers keep track of the similar-looking products (and make them collectible); and in deciding by 1940 to focus on mysteries, it became the first true category book publisher in the United States, as Mills & Boon had with romances the previous decade in Britain.

Walter Zacharius soon moved on to Ace News, owned by magazine publisher A. A. Wynn. When Wynn started a paperback line, Zacharius conceived the idea of Ace Double-Decker Books, named for the sandwiches he liked, which combined two novels bound back to back, each with its own cover. Aaron Wynn renamed them Ace Double Novels and released the first of them in 1952. They were a popular feature on the racks for almost a decade until the company realized that wholesalers were returning *both* covers of unsold books for refunds. The wholesalers were a tough bunch – "the guys in New York City had shotguns in their cars; you never crossed them," Zacharius says – but his Brooklyn upbringing and direct manner disarmed them. Some were among his silent partners when he cofounded Magnum Royal Publications in 1955 – "I figured it was a good idea to get them as my protection for distribution, and I tell you, I had the biggest, the best, and the toughest."

He had a more vocal partner, Irwin Stein. They published automotive, sports, and men's periodicals, including *Gallery*, which had been owned by superlawyer F. Lee Bailey; a European publication called *Playmen*, which Hugh Hefner, understandably, forced him to close; and the not terribly swanky *Swank*. In 1962 they launched Lancer Books. The company that had begun with $80,000 had annual book sales of up to $9 million within five years; among their titles was Mario Puzo's first book, *The Fortunate Pilgrim*, which they got for a $1,500 advance and which made them a lot of money after another house released *The Godfather*. Along with decent lines of science fiction and mysteries, the partners were responsible for dross such as the Conan the Barbarian and The Man from O.R.G.Y. series. The most contentious release was the sexually bizarre *Candy*, by Terry Southern and Mason

Hoffenberg, originally published by Olympia Press in Paris; Lancer put it out as a 500,000-copy paperback after realizing it could be considered in the public domain. When Putnam published an authorized version in competition, the firms sued each other, but to no avail. A more respectable venture was the introduction of Easy Eye books with larger type on nonglare greenish paper. Ultimately, however, the partners fell out over finances – "he knows to stay away from me," says a still bitter Zacharius. In 1973 the dispute forced him, he says, to shut down what he claims was a successful business.

Two years later, the woman who had been his unlikely editor at *Swank*, 26-year-old Roberta Grossman, convinced him to return to book publishing. He took over what remained of Barney Rossett's aggressive and litigious Grove Press, known mostly for erotic works by Henry Miller and D. H. Lawrence, which it had fought in the courts to publish. Zacharius acquired the beleaguered Grove's Zebra Books imprint for its indebtedness of $400,000 and paid it off within four years. He made Grossman president and publisher with a piece of the business; there was then only one other woman with that role in the industry. Educated at New York University and on the staff of the scandal magazine *Confidential,* bubbly but blunt (in size and tongue), Grossman was a shrewd and loyal partner.

The first title under their imprint pursued the sexual theme with the autobiography of a male porno actor. Later books were more decorous, as Grossman published nonfiction, westerns, thrillers, and the Gothics that eventually led to a line of romance novels. Some of them were contemporary and overly genteel, but by the beginning of the 1980s, Zebra had identified a market niche that Harlequin avoided: historicals. It paid $750 to $1,500 advances for slush pile manuscripts by unknowns and marketed the pants off them by marketing the pants *in* them. Its passion-laden covers became the industry standard for sheer novelty. The partners tried photographic covers for a series with mature and independent heroines, which flopped. They pioneered in adding die-cuts, foil, and embossing to the design, which succeeded. Zebra was the first to use an eye-catching hologram on the cover as a logo to identify a whole line. It spent about $1 million to research, develop, and market-test the innovation in the field; sales increased by 50 percent. A decade later, in 1995, it extended the concept to create an entire cover with three-dimensional artwork. The company was a pathfinder in publishing multicultural romances in the Arabesque line featuring women of color and in marketing them through distributors of perfumes and cosmetics to the black community. Arabesque was part of Pinnacle Books, which Harlequin had tried to acquire in 1978 and which Zacharius later bought out of bankruptcy. He was ever adaptive: at one point, Zebra raised its cover prices, and when wholesalers started to complain, he announced that paperbacks were too expensive and that other publishers should follow his lead by dropping their prices, too. Not long after, he began slowly raising his again. Zebra's parent company, Kensington, has published nonfiction such as an unauthorized Oprah Winfrey biography and the first O. J. Simpson book, produced by a writer and a researcher who got engaged after two and a half weeks of being holed up together in the publishing office. Oh, yes, and the music-loving Zacharius started *The Nashville Gospel,* a gospel music magazine he then folded after the media discovered that the former publisher of *Swank* owned a publication with religious overtones.

To distribute Zebra's books, at first he did what Dick Bonnycastle Sr. had done all those decades ago: Zacharius hired lower-cost salespeople retired from other publishing houses and put this Over-the-Hill Gang to work. In the late 1980s, Zebra and Harlequin shared Pocket Books as a distributor, and it was during those years that he got to know the Canadian company's executives. Zebra's parties for the distribution sales force were so rambunctious – song-and-dance skits, evenings on yachts, gifts for everyone – that Harlequin insisted on having its conferences beforehand so the salespeople would be fresh of face and mind. Eventually Harlequin demanded to have a separate Pocket Books sale force. Zebra itself later moved to Penguin as distributor and more recently set up a frontline sales network of its own people.

Zacharius wondered at some of Harlequin's practices, especially the fact that his competitor would routinely box and ship the same number of copies of each title no matter how marketable a name an author had. He questioned one of its warehouse representatives, who explained it was cheaper than putting six of one title and two of another in a carton.

"Do you know how many sales you're losing? You have big books here that could be selling out, but you don't know that."

He quotes the warehouseman as saying that Harlequin's method saved the company a cent or two.

"Yeah," Zacharius said, "but you're losing $2."

By 1992 he was prepared to admit that the industry had changed immeasurably and that it was time to shed his company. "He thought that the business is so dominated by these giants, and it's very hard to compete," son Steven told me. "We have to be smarter. We have to react quicker. We have to be more creative with packaging. And every one of these companies is pretty much foreign-owned now so that it's hard to compete with them. And he saw that the business he had created with Roberta, which was essentially a midlist-author business, was changing very rapidly to a huge bestseller list." Walter Zacharius approached a deal-brokerage firm to find a buyer.

The giant, foreign-owned Harlequin was an obvious one. Over the years, it had quietly and, as it turned out, unsuccessfully bid on large publishing concerns such as Doubleday and Addison Wesley. For the last two years in particular it had been looking for a suitable acquisition, and two years before that, it had begun casually discussing the possibility of buying Zebra. Now, with an open invitation, David Galloway and Brian Hickey sent in their team to research the company and make an offer. Both Zacharius father and son recall how Harlequin had more people doing due diligence than Zebra employed in its entire accounting department. The company was producing about 37 books a month with a staff of only 60, including three in the art department and four in production. After signing an agreement in principle, Harlequin had 10 people in place for two months looking at the accounts.

At the same time, Walter Zacharius's partner of nearly two decades was dying of rapidly spreading lung cancer at 45. "My father's head wasn't on straight at the time. He was very upset, obviously. Roberta was almost like his daughter," says the son, who began to sit in on the meetings with the prospective buyer. As the bargaining began, Roberta Grossman died. But by then there was an offer on the table, and Harlequin was disagreeing with some of the figures on items such as inventory and potential returns.

In Walter Zacharius's memory, things soured after his partner's death. "Once she died, I said, 'Let's stop for 30 days. I want to catch my breath and see what I want to do with my family.'" He claims Galloway refused to delay the negotiations. "Then we started knocking the price around. And I said, 'Knock wood, I don't need any money. Drop it.' We went on for six months. Then I called him and said, 'It's all over, David. The end of it.' He said, 'No, let's keep talking.'

And he's really a nice guy, but they're tough business people."

Not unexpectedly David Galloway has a different recollection: "If he'd asked us for a 30-day hold, we would have done it. My memory of it was that the figures in the end were the problem. It had nothing to do with the tragedy that his partner had passed away." One of Galloway's truisms at the time was that 75 percent of acquisitions made in the last half of the 1980s did not work because the original price paid had been too high. As for Zebra: "In our due diligence, we believed the inventory wasn't as good as Walter thought. We thought returns were going to be significantly higher than Walter thought they were going to be. . . . To me the interesting part is that Walter thinks I'm the bad guy in this deal. Which is sort of funny." As Torstar's C E O in charge of Harlequin, Galloway was involved with Brian Hickey in the negotiations over price – which was now significantly lower than the figure mentioned in the letter of intent. "What happened was Brian and his team said we shouldn't pay any more than X. And I looked at the original price, and I looked at X, and I thought we could go to X plus and we'd have a good deal. And I remembered Silhouette: you know, there'd be more there than meets the eye, right? And so I thought we could pay more. . . . But Brian and his team have to deliver, right? We buy it and say, 'Okay, Brian, you've got to run this thing, and you've got to get the return to justify this price' – it better be *his* price. In other words, if I overpay for this thing and then hammer them for not delivering, it's a little awkward. . . . Walter always calls Brian and says, 'Christ, if it wasn't for that goddamn Galloway, we would have a deal.' He might not have accepted *my* price, but it was certainly higher than what we offered."

Zacharius walked from the deal. However, a couple of years later, he approached the Harlequin heavyweights again, this time to discuss an idea he had for collaborating on each other's book clubs – presumably for them to manage his, which represents about eight percent of his business. "But they didn't think there was enough in it for them." When I saw him in the summer of 1995, he seemed to have gained some renewed vigor. He had begun a new imprint the year before featuring single titles by well-known names such as Alexandra Thorne and Joan Elliott Pickart. The Denise Little Presents line was named for its editor, a former buyer for the B. Dalton book chain who is legendary in her knowledge of romances. Zacharius now also had his son working with him as president and chief operating officer. During our conversations, both of them expressed a lingering suspicion to me that Harlequin had learned enough in its rooting around Zebra's operations to equip itself to enter at last the single-title market with a new imprint called Mira.

"They came out with Mira after doing all the due diligence here," the son told me.

"That's what pissed me off," the father said. "I told them exactly one of the things I would do with [Harlequin], and they came out with what I told them."

For all its supremacy in the series romance field, Harlequin had never managed to make sense of the single-title business, in which the best bestsellers could earn publishers, along with their authors, small fortunes. A Danielle Steel novel might have a paperback print run of 3.5 million compared to a Harlequin series romance's 200,000. Throughout the early 1990s, pressure was increasing for Harlequin to move into this market, sometimes called "one-offs." As Walter Zacharius pointed out in a controversial 1995 article in the Romance Writers of America's magazine, *RWR*, "romance as a genre is changing. Like fiction, it's moving away from a level list, and toward a hierarchy that emphasizes bestsellers and is less viable the farther down the list it goes. . . . [W]holesaler participation has dropped dramatically and is now limited to bestselling romance authors except in the largest wholesale outlets." And he posed a question on behalf of readers: "When you can buy a new hardbound brand-name author for $12 at the local superstore or Price Club, why pay $6 to take a chance on a book by an unknown paperback author?"

David Galloway told me that of any mistake he made during his era at Harlequin, the biggest was deciding to stay away from the one-off market (although the company had experimented with it in the late 1980s through its Worldwide Library). One consideration is that a publisher has less control over the author of a bestselling single title because sales are driven by the writer's name, not the imprint, as in a series romance. That might have been an unspoken factor when Galloway and Hickey studied the market and concluded, "This is big advances and lower margins. It's into the movie game, the bestseller game." Their reasoning was that while two books might sell well – often based on whether they get picked up as films – three others will be average and five will be flops, and in the end the return on sales might be a mere seven percent or so instead of 17. "And, gee, if this *works,* it will take away from our own [strengths], and we're getting into a business we don't understand – so stay out of it," Galloway says, summing up their thinking. They made that decision several years ago, and he estimates that the 40-plus percentage of paperbacks on the market labeled as romance probably split between single titles and Harlequin-style series. Today, to use his figures, it might be more like 25 percent one-offs and only 15 to 18 percent series. "So I mean we made a mistake. We should have been there. It's our genre. . . . If there's a better idea out there and it's going to take away from our business, it's better that we take it away than someone else."

Harlequin had tried the single-title market earlier. Its executives knew from sad experience that they were losing out on the blockbuster books. Before LaVyrle Spencer had become a big name, her agent asked Harlequin to return the rights to one of her books, which had been the first title in the company's Temptation series. She resold it to Berkley Jove, who repackaged the series romance as a mass-market, one-off paperback, and it made the *New York Times* bestseller list. About 1988 Harlequin set up a task force on single titles that included, among others, editor in chief Horst Bausch, Silhouette editorial director Isabel Swift, and Candy Lee, who was then in New York working for the company in a book-packaging division. "We did it under such pressure," Bausch says, "that they sent me the proposal to Yellowstone Park, where I was on vacation. In this task force, my contribution was that we should either develop our own single-title company, which would have to operate under a totally different mind-set, or we should acquire somebody, which would make life easier." In fact, Harlequin simply resurrected the old Worldwide name from earlier in the decade and hired an editor in New York. "But other than that," Bausch admits, "it was 'romance' thinking, and we had problems getting the proper distribution. We tried it with Worldwide, but we simply didn't go the full length."

Having failed to buy Zebra Books, Harlequin set about again to create a division that would focus entirely on mass-market, mainstream, author-driven women's fiction – as opposed to "romances." Brian Hickey had struck a series of global task forces: expansion into other businesses, which he oversaw; the core business, which Candy Lee headed as a new vice president; diversification in the Harlequin world (such as nonfiction and audio books); and single titles. Out of the last came a division named Mira – Latin for "wonderful," as well as one of the brightest stars in the southern sky. The parent company's name was nowhere to be seen on the covers of its books ("Don't put a Harlequin imprint on it," Fred Kerner had long ago warned in a report on single titles he left behind after retiring, "because that will be the kiss of death.")

Mira Books came on the market in the fall of 1994 with a first-year promotional budget of up to $5 million. Senior editor and editorial coordinator Dianne Moggy had signed up 20 authors six months earlier, among them bestselling Penny Jordan, Jayne Ann Krentz, and Heather Graham Pozzessere. The truth was that only one lead title a month was an original; three others were tarted-up reprints (like the old LaVyrle Spencer Temptation that Berkley Jove had recycled so well). Mira shipped from 140,000 to 450,000 of each paperback original and 180,000 to 600,000 of the reprints, priced at $4.99 to $5.99. The two hardcovers in the first year were the Canadian Charlotte Vale Allen's *Somebody's Baby*, about a heroine who had been stolen as an infant from a New York City supermarket; and actress Janet Leigh's *House of Destiny*, about two self-made Hollywood moguls. In 1996 two more hardcover and two larger-format trade paperbacks have been scheduled. And there are plans to have three original titles a month the following year. The bonus for authors is that Mira is also selling in Europe.

By the end of the division's first full year, its titles had appeared on *USA Today*'s weekly list of top 150 titles more than 50 times. Mira demonstrated its seriousness to the book trade by bidding against Avon and Pocket Books to sign Debbie Macomber, author of more than 90 romances, to a seven-figure contract for three books and one anthology. Some competitors thought it was an overbid, based on bravado. And at least one observer, who was retired from Harlequin in 1993, wonders about the long-term success of the Mira program: "To establish a real single-title division, it might be too late," says Horst Bausch. "The big guys are simply too big." Even David Galloway remains skeptical about the potential size of its success. "We should have been there," he told me. "So Mira is trying to correct that but, you know, we're late. I think Mira's doing very well, but imagine had we started it 10 years ago. We'd look a lot better. So I have to take responsibility for blowing that one."

Toronto-based Mira Books fell under the fiefdom of Candy Lee, who has had nearly two decades of experience with Harlequin. She is the buck-stops-here boss of the editorial divisions in Toronto, New York, and London. When she became vice president of retail marketing and editorial in 1992, it was the first time Harlequin had linked the two roles so overtly in a single title – although it seemed an overdue move for a company so marketing-driven. One result is a new initiative: the Vision Team of an editor, an art director, and a marketer for each line of books to make decisions such as what their series will look like and which promotions will market it. None of this concerns the actual editorial content, which remains the responsibility of the combined staff of more than 75 editorial people, plus numerous freelancers. As well as working with a string of 1,500 active writers, the company's editorial offices collectively receive 20,000 unsolicited manuscripts annually. They acquire only 900 or more titles a year, the majority of them for 13 romance series. Lee herself has never really been a frontline editor of fiction. "The amount of care our editors give to a manuscript – I wouldn't be able to do that," she confessed to me.

What she brings to her position, in addition to a lifelong love of the romance genre, is a sense of retailing, of marketing, of the business end of books. Born in St. Croix in the U.S. Virgin Islands, where her parents had moved from the United States, Candy Lee (her full maiden name) began reading romances at the age of 10; "I probably read a romance a day," she recalls. The grown-up continues to read them for pleasure: "I suspect I do have some kind of addiction, and I'd love to isolate that addiction and make sure that everyone else has the same chromosome." No single woman pining away, Lee – with long auburn hair, freckles, and brown eyes – is married to wine writer Joe Ward, whose work appears in *Condé Nast Traveler*. They have no children, but her office is adorned with a Babar poster, dolls, and toy trucks. She was educated in the Caribbean and then at Harvard, where she studied Middle Eastern literature and language with a minor in Irish Gaelic literature. That latter interest took her in 1972 to Ireland, where she landed a job with the country's largest publisher, Mercier Press, which was also expanding as a book retailer. All of 22, she went into bookshop management and stayed for more than five years, learning how books get into the hands of customers. England beckoned in 1978 when Bruce Marshall began his book-packaging company in London as a Harlequin subsidiary. Lee became a manager of Marshall

Editions, handling much of the day-to-day administration, including contract negotiations, and in the meantime learning about the manufacture of books and the appetites of the major publishers around the world who bought the packager's handsomely illustrated volumes.

In the mid-1980s, she attracted the attention of David Galloway, then Harlequin's president and C E O, who was trying to clean up a mess from the collapse of another book-packaging venture, New York-based Torstar Books. Among its projects were the affinity series *The Human Body* and *Stitch by Stitch*. The packager, although technically within the Harlequin orbit, had really been the baby of Torstar Corporation's president at the time, Paul Zimmerman, who had come from the Canadian Reader's Digest world, which had its own line of nonfiction books for direct-mail distribution. Larry Heisey remembers his concern about the project: "I was very dubious of Paul's ability to pull this off and was not beyond expressing my point of view at board meetings – not that I knew anything about the business. I was just very fearful it wasn't going to work. And at one meeting, I said, 'You know, I've been a Doubting Thomas about this project, but I must say that I'm impressed that it seems to be coming together, and it looks like it just might be what Paul thinks it is, and I'll be pleased if that's the truth.' And sort of three weeks later – maybe not that soon – the wheels fell off everything. We didn't know what we were doing. We lost a few million on that."

Candy Lee went to New York in 1986 to wind up Torstar Books, in which Galloway had taken such a personal interest. He delegated her to sell off the existing inventory, a task that required liaison with Harlequin's direct-marketing people in Toronto and offered her a chance to learn that side of the business. Meanwhile, she worked on new Marshall projects, including books for the American Automobile Association such as *Explore America*. In 1990 she moved to Toronto as director and then vice president of new business development, and within two years, she had responsibility for both retail marketing and editorial. "They knew how profoundly I felt the two areas should be together," she says. "I really believe that people should make books that sell. And people should sell books that they make." In a relationship that some at Harlequin are leery about, she still has close ties to Galloway in his position as Torstar Corporation's president and C E O.

The melding of marketing and editorial has led to Harlequin's reappearance, after several years of noticeable absence, as a television advertiser. Editorial collaborated with the direct-marketing division to produce T V commercials in 1995 sharing the same creative content prepared by Grey Advertising of New York. For Lee it was a test to see if the response to television could be measured at the retail level. The commercial for Silhouette featuring three female readers ended with a prompt to visit a retail store for a free gift such as a necklace. The test runs were successful enough that the company has been running the commercial nationwide in 1996; it plans to do another for the Harlequin line, and the direct-mail people intend to use it for their marketing. Another project, aimed strictly at the retail market, was a first in the publishing world: Pages & Privileges, similar in concept to the airlines' loyalty-inspiring frequent-flier programs. Buyers of Harlequins and Silhouettes could send in proofs of purchase to become a member of a program giving them hotel and airline discounts, free gifts of perfume, and an *Insider Tips* newsletter with sneak previews of books. Each additional purchase, the frequent-reader promotion promised, "brings you a step closer to even more FREE gifts." In her discussion of Pages & Privileges, Candy Lee seemed to express some slight doubt about how effective it had been to date.

Editorially during her tenure, Harlequin has been aggressive in creating new lines and new ways to deliver its product. One fresh focus has been an emphasis on the male hero: in 1993 the company began an occasional series called More Than Men about genies, mermen, and such; the following year, it launched another line entitled Men Made in America, featuring "red-blooded, true-blue hunks from every state in the Union"; and the next year, it started a subseries of Harlequin Intrigues known as Dangerous Men. The same year, 1995, it introduced The Best of the Best, an audiocassette program of popular romance novels read by actresses. Priced at $11.99 for two cassettes per book, at least $4 lower than the Time Warner and Audio Entertainment competition, the package was retailed in supermarkets, drugstores, and mass-market discount chains. In 1996 Harlequin has moved into nonfiction, with an abandon not seen for decades, with the first three of an original paperback line of Harlequin Ultimate Guides: how to *Make the Most of Your Love Life, Live Happily Ever,* and *Talk to a Naked Man* (including advice such as this sweet nothing to whisper in his ear: "Don't say anything, just nibble"). A more pragmatic guide is *I Can Fix That,* for women who want to do it themselves. A new line scheduled for later in 1996 formally acknowledges that romance can have its funny moments: Love and Laughter, launched with a writers' contest that offered three winners a critique of their manuscripts but no promise to publish. Harlequin is not averse to boarding bandwagons led by other publishers. One – the trend of casting babies as characters in romance novels – was leaped on with Marie Ferrarella's five-book series, Baby of the Month Club, about a quintet of women who meet at their obstetrician's office. Another is inspirational romances, which Candy Lee considers spiritual rather than formally religious books. Other houses will publish about 100 of them in 1996; she hopes to have some on the racks in 1997.

The inspirationals may be a counterbalance to a few books Harlequin has released in the past couple of years that can only be called soft porn. They were toes in the water in reaction to yet another trend. Britain's Virgin Publishing has an imprint called Black Lace, which sold a million books of erotic fiction for women by women in its first year, 1993. The subject matter ranges from bondage to sex with other women; the tone is generally explicit but less crude than if written by men. Similar lines include Headline's Liaison series for couples and Little, Brown's classier Ex Libris. *Romantic Times* has a rating system for degrees of heat that barely covers this trend: sweet, sensual, very sensual, spicy, and sexy – with a Virginia Henley and Johanna Lindsey spicy and a Bertrice Small and Rosemary Rogers sexy, with rougher erotic scenes.

Of course, Harlequin writers such as Charlotte Lamb had already introduced scenes with lovers handcuffed to a bed. But more flagrant recent books have been quietly brought onto the market to see what feedback they prompt. *Love Game* carried a cover warning when it appeared in 1995: "Outrageously sensual . . . a real sizzler!" Lee says, "We got about a thousand letters saying how wonderful it was and one or none saying they were surprised by it." As well as a bit of bondage and sadomasochism, it had the heroine uttering words such as "blow job" and "fuck." Public relations vice president Kathy Orr, like Brian Hickey, is not entirely comfortable with the trend: "The best books are still the ones with the sexual tension. The reader doesn't want it all done for them. I get very squirmy having to defend the sexier books. Both Brian and I didn't want to have to be spokespeople on *Love Game*." A Harlequin Temptation appeared the same year by the same Wisconsin author, Olivia Rupprecht writing as Mallory Rush. *Kiss of the Beast* was the story of a female scientist trying to create her fantasy man through virtual reality; he turns out to be a wolf-man from another universe. A scene from the book shows just how far Harlequins have come since Mary Bonnycastle's day:

> From his sumptuous cloak emerged a rigid sleekness that he slid between her legs. Like a moist tongue in texture, but it was unmistakably a penis testing her entry with a smooth, easy rhythm.
>
> "The mating dance of nature, Eva," he roughly crooned. "Come dance with me and meet my strength."
>
> She let him turn her over, guide her palms to the floor, arms braced. He roamed her belly, lifted her hips with a cinching hold. Stepping with her knees, spreading them apart, she enticed him with the swish of her buttocks to his groin. . . .
>
> It was an eloquent ravishing. She could feel the brush of mink slapping against her buttocks as he humped her. But inside, they were locked as surely as one entity of flesh.

Another trend that Harlequin is following is the increasing number of romances with African-American characters. The stimulus was the breakthrough success of Terry McMillan's novel *Waiting to Exhale*, which became a recent popular film. While not really romantic fiction, the story of four black women seeking love made the *New York Times* bestseller chart and prompted other publishers to wake up to the possibilities of novels for black readers. Among them were Zebra, with its Arabesque series, and belatedly Harlequin. Sandra Kitt of New York had written her first Harlequin with black characters in 1984, but after *Adam and Eva*, "I couldn't get them to accept the other black novels. They said they didn't know anything about the market," she told the *Boston Globe*. In fact, Harlequin got scads of letters complaining about the book, including one from a Philadelphia woman who said, "Those people should have their own series." A few years ago, the company asked Kitt for a novella about an interracial romance. "I found it ironic that all those years I couldn't get them to publish another story where the main characters were black, but, all of a sudden, they decided they were interested in interracial couples." In 1996 – on the heels of several New York publishers identifying a Spanish-language fiction market in the United States – Harlequin also began publishing the sensual Deseo and the milder Bianca romance series aimed at the nearly 10 million American Hispanic women aged 15 and over (authors got a measly two percent royalty for these books).

Two innovations in the first half-dozen years came not from Candy Lee but from Brian Hickey, her boss, who says he has the never-used power to veto but not to order publication of any book. One of his visions, as she describes them, was that "women are going to get busier and busier in their lives and that we should think about doing books that would give as much satisfaction as we currently have but in an even shorter time. We took the idea and developed it into something else that's been very successful, a bimonthly magazine for shorter stories." *Harlequin World's Best Romances,* with four stories in each issue as well as promos for full-length books, is sold to direct-mail subscribers, and Lee admits that it brings no significant revenue to the company.

Hickey's other vision was what the trade calls a continuity series, several books about the same cast of characters or the same locale. Harlequin's first centered on a small American town, Tyler. "Oh, yeah," he says, "I'll take credit totally for that one." Research had shown that while readers wanted to finish a book in a couple of hours, they also wanted more "story." Hickey, sick abed from time to time, would watch the occasional soap opera and observe the continuity of its plot – its ongoing story. Why couldn't Harlequin duplicate this continuity in print? Each book would have to be freestanding, able to be read on its own, but it could be part of a series set in the same locale or sharing a cast of characters. *Why can't we have a continuous environment,* he wondered, *so that when you walk into the diner, you'll recognize that lady who's running it, you already know what the apple pie tastes like, and you know who sits on the third stool down from the left at eight o'clock every morning?* He began cajoling his staff about the idea in the early 1980s. "The editorial people just laughed at me – what do I know about editorial? It took a long time before it finally came to fruition about '89. . . . The funniest part of all is that to define this for them, I kept talking about small-town Wisconsin. And you know, it's set in Tyler, Wisconsin. It's done quite nicely in reissue. But more important is the concept and the spin-offs." A Silhouette series, aimed at the young-adult market, has used a similar concept: set in Chicago, The Loop books have a running cast of characters in their late teens, or what Kathy Orr calls "Generation Y, dealing with adolescent problems like finances and unwanted pregnancies."

♣

Harlequin's own cast of characters has been changing since Candy Lee became vice president. After 17 years as art director, Charles Kadin retired in January 1993. His last years with the company were both satisfying and frustrating. He had helped to bring his department up to the minute technically with computer-aided design and electronic assembly of artwork. But after Larry Heisey's era, he never had a close relationship with David Galloway, ever since the new chief operating officer wrote an article for the internal newsletter about all the wonderful things that would be happening – without mentioning the art department. And insiders say that when Kadin was leaving, Brian Hickey never even bothered to say goodbye. Kadin had trained his successor, Shelley Cinnamon, an art buyer for him since the mid-1980s.

In 1994 two more of the company's older guard got shown the door, in London. Robert Williams, the managing director at Mills & Boon, had written those wriggling letters to the Society of Authors in 1986, warding off any suggestion that M & B had done anything untoward in its royalty payments to authors. His successor was Tony Flynn, a Canadian whose background as a chartered accountant was in retail finance with Royal Trust. Frances Whitehead was the editorial director who had been Alan Boon's devoted assistant since 1976. She and Williams had tried to keep up with the times in the £70 million British paperback romance market, of which M & B had a 54 percent share. She even launched a series of monthly romances set in each of the 12 capitals of the European Community member nations. In 1993 marketing director Heather Walton hired London design consultants Coley Porter Bell to redesign the covers: update the old red rose, add a half-heart frame around the visuals on some series, and introduce cover photos in place of illustrations to four of the six lines. None of it was enough, and the forced departures of Whitehead and Williams made the *Times,* whose arts correspondent quoted an insider as saying they were an attempt to resolve the growing tensions between the British and Canadian approaches to business: "There was resistance to North American ideas, new lines, new vehicles. There was a sense of wanting everything to remain the way it was." One of Whitehead's few comments was: "All I can say is nearly every author rang up and cried." Former executive editor Luigi Bonomi waxed eloquent: "The old culture was very beautiful, and a lot of people would still like to live, fantasize, and write in that world. But the harsh reality is that we are governed by the bottom line these days. With these people going, it really is the end of the old world of Mills & Boon."

Whitehead's replacement was Karin Stoecker, from Harlequin in Toronto, whom Fred Kerner had hired as a talented copy editor in the late 1970s. "If anyone can turn that British operation around," he says, "it will be Karin." Stoecker, a big-eyed blond with a plump, pretty face, brought fresh North American ideas to Britain, some of them easier to implement than others. She belatedly helped to introduce Mira Books there with established authors, but even then she had problems. "There are all sorts of internal complications that one faces because even though you are launching a new imprint, you are so indelibly associated with Mills & Boon and category romance. Our biggest difficulty is with the trade and bookseller media. They categorize us before we can get a book on the shelf. Your average reader doesn't know who the publisher of a book is except for Mills & Boon, which encompasses a type of book we don't even publish. Our challenge is to get past that and onto the shelf and see what happens with the readers."

If David Galloway has a leftover vision for Harlequin, it might be to see its enormous bank of romance novels translated regularly and effectively onto the television screen and then distributed as an ongoing video library. God knows, enough hopeful filmmakers had approached the company over the years to attempt such a translation. Galloway was already Torstar's president and lone chief executive officer when I met him in 1995. Until a year earlier, he had been sharing the C E O title with old friend David Jolley, whose responsibility had been the *Toronto Star*. Then chairman John Evans kissed Jolley off with a $2.5 million severance, and Galloway was now in charge of everything, the *Star* and Harlequin included. In that role, he takes more than passing interest in the potential to create a viable film and video division.

Several Harlequins have been adapted for the screen, beginning with the spotty performance of *Leopard in the Snow* as a feature film in the late 1970s. The U.S. Showtime pay channel did six others a decade later with misty titles such as *Clouds Waltzing* and *Tears in the Rain* and featuring no-names such as the Kathleens Beller and Quinlan. The deal with Yorkshire Television of London and the Atlantic Entertainment Group of Los Angeles, which was to have been for 18 films, never went any further because of the so-so ratings of the first half dozen. The video versions went on sale for $39.95. The first in the series, *Love with a Perfect Stranger,* had Marilu Henner of the *Taxi* sitcom and Canadian character actor Daniel Massey, and even the *Toronto Star's* own video critic was unkind: "The sets and scenery chew up the actors and it's just as well. Robin (*Lifestyles of the Rich and Famous*) Leach would have a field day with all the champagne and caviar consumed in baroque surroundings with violins playing and chests heaving."

The financing for those films was typical of the structuring Harlequin insists on: reportedly the filmmakers put up all the cash for a 50 percent piece and the publisher allowed the use of its books and its name in return for the other half. In 1994 Alliance Communications Corporation of Toronto cut a deal with Harlequin on those terms to produce four TV movies for CBS. Alliance, about to celebrate its 10th anniversary, is best known for its television productions, among them the prime-time CBS comedy adventure about a Mountie in Chicago, *Due South,* and the ABC computer-generated animation series *ReBoot.* Its theatrical films include *Johnny Mnemonic,* a $23 million science fiction feature starring Keanu Reeves, which did mediocre business. What Robert Lantos's Alliance brought to the table was a track record of getting pictures on the screen and the cofinancing smarts to put them there.

The troubled CBS was still tender from its jilting by the National Football League in favor of the Fox network. The idea behind the Harlequin movies was to snag a female audience by counter-programming them against the Sunday afternoon NFL games. CBS paid Alliance a fee equivalent to only about half the films' $3-million-apiece production costs because the network anticipated the relatively low ratings it, in fact, got. Alliance's financing partners were Canada's CTV network and the German media conglomerate Bertelsmann A. G. The first four films, bearing Harlequin titles such as *Broken Lullaby* and *Another Woman,* had young TV types in the leads backed by old hands – a Tippi Hedren here, an Ian Richardson there. Alliance has no pretensions about this sort of movie. Noreen Halpern, director of development for movies and mini series, says, "It's a Sunday afternoon, and women are helping their kids or balancing their checkbooks, and they can walk out of the room and get a drink of water." And David Galloway says, "These are made-for-TV movies. You're not going to pay eight bucks to go and line up for them."

Alliance did get the first four films on C B S and commissioned another two that were shown in the fall of 1995. Getting that last pair scheduled and shown was an exercise in frustration for both Alliance and Harlequin. At the time, C B S was looking to be bought, which Westinghouse finally did late in the year. "C B S is in disarray," Noreen Halpern had told me the previous summer. "People are only doing what makes them look good." When I saw her in July 1995, shooting was two weeks away, and no film crews had yet been hired.

Meanwhile, David Galloway was equally upset about what he would like to happen as opposed to what really does. "The reason we chose Alliance is that they're the first people who looked at this as business," he told me. As head of Harlequin, he had fielded calls almost once a week from people who wanted to do a film or T V series based on its romance novels. He would tell them: "There are only two things I want you to know. One is our right to look at the film and see whether we want to put our name on it. Two, it's your money and not ours." And the latter discouraged all the callers. Alliance, however, saw it as a business in which it might make movies paid for by international television revenues, while Harlequin would keep the video rights. "And if we had one a month," Galloway says, "then we could take videos out of video stores and do what we did with books – sell them in K Marts and Woolworths [at about $9.95]. . . . We'd then start a movie club like the book club." The problem has been the T V networks: "We go to C B S – and I've met with them – and we say, 'Look, we'll pull out all the stops if you tell us four months in advance what time this movie's going to be on, what day and what time. We'll put it on the front of the books. So if we can bring Harlequin readers to watch that, we could, I think, bump up the viewership of that program significantly for that time slot. And I think it's worth a test to find out.' All we hear back is 'David, look, you don't understand. We can't do that, that far in advance.' . . . They did four movies last year, but they didn't tell us in advance. So we couldn't bring our people to it. We didn't advertise. . . . I don't know if we can do it, but it would sure be worth finding out. Someday this is going to happen. I just believe it."

Like Galloway, Brian Hickey also appeared to be a believer in the beginning. When the deal with Alliance was announced, he was quoted as saying: "We look forward to a long and rewarding love affair." Yet even if the affair foundered, Hickey had a couple of other, more attractive sweethearts waiting in the wings to take him into the next century.

*My personal goal for the 1990s is to bring romance to millions
of Chinese women.*
        – Brian Hickey, 1993

17

Sleeping Tigers
TAKING CHINA

Brian Hickey, in some ways, is the very model of a modern major corporate
general. When I saw him at Harlequin headquarters early in 1996, he met me
in the ninth-story reception area, had my briefcase whisked away, and suggested we go downstairs to the modest cafeteria (featuring daily Chinese spe-
cials) where he could have a couple of cigarettes, guilt-free, away from the
smokeless executive floor. He wore a red tie with blue polka dots, black braces
over a black shirt, and black denim pants, and bounded around rather than
walked. Until then we had corresponded by mail and through intermediaries.
Officially he had me told, rather than telling me, that his company would not
be cooperating with my book. To pique his interest, I sent him a letter mentioning a couple of stories for which I required clarification, context, or outright denial. One was Walter Zacharius's suggestion that Harlequin, negotiating to buy Zebra Books, had been less than sensitive to the death of his partner. The other was about a former employee's alleged outfoxing of Harlequin
in forcing it to buy his faltering company just to get the right to use some of
the best lists of direct-mail subscribers.

The latter story involved John Biagini, who had been with the Harlequin

Reader Service and then ran the Hosiery Corporation of America, a mail-order distributor of panty hose and the like. Biagini had created Meteor Books to market the Kismet line of contemporary romances to its hosiery customers as a direct-mail competitor to his former employer. Apparently he and Harlequin had been renting the same lists, until Harlequin complained, so Biagini locked them up under an exclusive arrangement with the list provider. Then in 1993, when he unaccountably decided to close his publishing house after three years, Harlequin reportedly bought Meteor just to get back those lists that it had been using. It was the talk of the industry. One New York publisher told me: "Harlequin has a deal with Bantam over some lawsuit that neither company can make an exclusive deal on a list. But Biagini was able to. So now get rid of Biagini and the lists are freed up. Harlequin took over Kismet/Meteor and closed it up." Another publisher said of Biagini: "He really screwed them. It was a brilliant maneuver."

Brian Hickey's only reply to these stories was in a dismissive letter to me: "Concerning the two issues which you chose to share with me, I would caution you that your sources may just have an axe to grind when it comes to Harlequin. I would not give either issue any credence by responding to them." He never did. Nor did he want to see me for a long time, although I had been interviewing many of the key executives who have played a role at Harlequin – including his predecessors Larry Heisey and David Galloway, now his immediate superior at Torstar, both of whom said they would put a word in for me. Yet Hickey continued to refuse to cooperate officially. The reasons, as those who knew him well reported them to me, ranged from his not wanting to tie up his managers for long interviews to the inference that "he's frightened – that may be an unfair word, but he found your letter threatening." Finally, following back-and-forth negotiating through go-betweens, the president and CEO of Harlequin did agree to see me, almost eight months after my first formal approach.

If Brian Hickey has a dream, it might be to leave Harlequin a legacy – although he would vehemently deny it. We had barely sat down in the Harlequin cafeteria, surrounded by other smoking employees, when he protested as I raised the subject of legacies. "I don't feel any inspiration to at some point in time retire from Harlequin having made contributions that are enduring," he said, surprising me. "It's not to say I don't hope that happens . . . but it's not for the reason of a legacy. It's quite interesting. It's just something that – " He broke off, then concluded, "I have no interest in that." Moreover, he laughs at people who say they have a long-term career plan. Hickey went on to give me an upbeat dissertation on what does propel him: how he likes to come to work and see employees with smiles on their faces and watch them grow as people. "I don't mean to ignore the shareholders with that – of course, they win their reward then, too," he hastened to add diplomatically.

As we took the elevator upstairs, I wondered at his protestation. As long ago as 1990, discussing corporate expansion, he had said, "The Soviet Union is also of obvious interest, and my own personal dream is China." When we met, Harlequin had been in China for exactly a year, teamed up with two indigenous partners to do a test run of Western romance novels in that land of 1.2 billion consumers. The potential was obviously enormous, and Hickey, an old Asia hand, would speak of the China adventure with excitement in his voice. We settled into his corner office with its valley view and a sofa inhabited by half a dozen teddy bears (shades of Star Helmer?). There he spoke of another dream: to turn learning materials – or what is now called children's supplementary educational publishing – into a flourishing third arm after book publishing and the $115-million-a-year Miles Kimball catalog marketing division.

Both preoccupations, education and China, were among the few solid prospects for growth of the company and the conglomerate that owns it. In the fall of 1995, Dominion Bond Rating Service had downgraded Torstar's long-term rating because of an 80 percent increase in newsprint prices and a decrease in consumer confidence that was shrinking retail advertising. Meanwhile, the newspaper publisher was about to launch a sink-or-swim corporate strategy primarily to attract national advertisers. The *Toronto Star*'s slight profit of $2.3 million on increased revenue of $334 million in 1995 did not afford shareholders a satisfactory return, the annual report admitted. In the same year, Harlequin profits had risen to $77 million on increased revenue of $485 million. The book publisher was continuing its role of propping up the parent corporation. As Torstar president and CEO David Galloway had reminded me, "The *Toronto Star* is the flagship, and Harlequin is bigger and makes more money, lest we forget, and protected the *Star* in the early nineties during the recession. You can imagine. We spent $400 million building a new plant, and our earnings went from $75 million to zero. Without Harlequin, the *Toronto Star* – Torstar – would have been in serious trouble. So it was kind of nice it was there."

It was still nice, and Brian Hickey had been well rewarded for his company's performance. In 1993, for example, he earned more than either Galloway or his fellow CEO of the time, David Jolley. While Hickey had a salary of $279,825 and a bonus of $135,715 for a total of $415,540, his colleagues each earned $405,563 in salary but, given their newspaper's poor results, declined their bonuses of $29,201 based on Harlequin's results. Of course, that discrepancy lasted only one year: in 1994, when Galloway was suddenly Torstar's lone CEO, he took a combined salary and bonus of $726,347 to Hickey's still rewarding $453,743.

Harlequin had maintained its record profits year after year in the early 1990s, but Hickey knew that it would be increasingly harder to top himself through conventional publishing in conventional marketplaces. The company's home base, North America, was no longer the profit center it had been throughout its nearly half century of corporate history. Its 400,000-square-foot distribution center in Buffalo, New York, still shipped about 175 million books a year and up to 2.5 million direct-mail pieces a month. But that was roughly 25 million copies fewer than just a few years ago, and much of the erosion was in the United States and Canada, where romantic fiction was a mature market.

New York literary agent Richard Curtis is well positioned to view the rapid changes in the industry. "There are certainly signs all over the place of a possible recessionary trend in romance," he told me. "Because, first of all, we have lost about 10 or 12 percent of our wholesale rack space in the last few years owing to the incursions of superstores and chains. Paper prices have gone up by 25 and 35 percent [or more], making it more desirable to publish books that look mainstream so you can charge higher prices for something that feels big. So if somebody charges $4.95 for a flimsy-looking Harlequin-sized book, people are not going to pay that money. They want their money's worth. No one has licked the problem of returns. Harlequin has a higher sell-through rate than any other publisher, but returns are going up, and you just can't make a profit printing two books and taking one back for credit. So we have just seen a march over the last 20 years toward a smaller and smaller top of the pyramid. And I think that this is beginning to show up in romance. There's already a sorting out: the line below which you are out is higher and higher in terms of sales, so 15,000's okay this year, and next year it's 25, and the year after 50 – so you're a bum if you're selling under 50,000."

Harlequin itself had decreased its print runs to the point where, Candy Lee says, its average paperback release is now as low as 100,000 copies. Then, in mid-1995, two new developments were rocking the North American periodical distribution industry, both with potentially harmful repercussions on the romance publisher that had long considered itself powerful in its relationships with retailers and distributors. One development sprang from pressures by national wholesale magazine and book jobbers. These were the distributors who had been serving retail book chains such as Waldenbooks and B. Dalton and then began intruding into the nonbookstore territory, the virtual distribution monopolies traditionally held by the regional wholesalers. Several of these large regionals made the mistake of essentially warning major American publishing houses that they might no longer distribute the titles of publishers who refused to stop selling to these jobbers. Industry sources believe that the national jobbers then went to Washington's antitrust enforcers. "And," as one American regional wholesaler told me, "that triggered an investigation by the U.S. Justice Department into the whole wholesale monopolistic business, starting two years ago." Department investigators issued Civil Investigative Demands to survey the wholesalers' records – from correspondence to computer files – for the past five years. Meanwhile, they also interviewed publishers such as the Rupert Murdoch group and Time-Warner. "So the industry was very, very nervous," the wholesaler says, "because they knew damn well there had been these kind of unwritten protective market rules and that the government would view it as a monopoly."

The second development occurred in the summer of 1995 when the Safeway supermarket chain, by coincidence, decided to consolidate its magazine wholesalers for the sake of efficiency and cost savings. The idea, originating in the grocer's Bellevue, Washington-based division, was to have one or two regional wholesalers bid for the business in a large area that went beyond the wholesalers' traditional territories. In the past, a wholesaler, secure in his monopoly, would have responded to Safeway: "Look, I don't have the equipment, the ability. I don't really have the *desire* to bid on your whole division. Therefore, I'm only going to bid on servicing your stores in this area – and by the way, this is your price." However, because of the current Justice Department investigation of the distribution industry and because individual wholesalers had been getting bigger by acquiring competitors, Safeway was able to pressure some wholesalers to bid on all the business in the division. That meant about 200 stores from roughly Tacoma to Spokane. "So," as a wholesaler explained to me, "where there were traditionally 10 wholesalers servicing Safeway, it chose one or two, and about eight guys lost their Safeway business. And from then on, every major retailer in North America has done the same thing. For example, Wal-Mart consolidated their wholesalers from 300 to three in all the U.S. to distribute their products. So I'm going to lose my magazines in all the Wal-Marts that I have, which is significant business for me. As a wholesaler, you either get bigger or you get smaller. . . . We've never seen change this fast – whether in the bottling or food-broker or drug-store industries, who have consolidated significantly as well, but it's taken them 10 years to do it. This has happened in six months. Where there used to be 300 wholesalers in the U.S. in 1995, next year there might be as few as 50."

The unsettling result for a publisher such as Harlequin? "With that consolidation," this major wholesaler says, "companies like ours have a lot more clout than we've ever had. We used to have our own little deal, and that's why we allowed the national distributors like Curtis to beat up on us. Well, those days are gone. So now it's going to cost publishers to get their product to market. There's no doubt about it. And it's certainly costing the wholesalers a whole lot more money in terms of discounts to retailers." And that is also costing a publisher such as Harlequin, which might now have to pay a supermarket chain $50 or $100 simply to place a display fixture for its books in each of its thousand or so stores. "And they know the display's not going to last and they're going to have to pay for it again. But the point is that Harlequin now realizes they've got to use promotional moneys to keep the product on display at retail. And the question is: do you pay the retailer, or do you pay the wholesaler? The wholesaler is going to feel the same way, because Harlequin and Simon & Schuster [the parent of Harlequin's distributor, Pocket Books] on their own do not have the clout anymore. They're making lots of money because we've taken on a lot of their costs. Now they're going to make less if they're going to keep their market share."

Harlequin's North American market was getting smaller and costing more to maintain. Its Western European markets had reached a plateau and its Eastern European ones were failing to fulfill all their promise so far. Spin-offs of the romance business such as films and videos were spinning their wheels. With all this, Brian Hickey was looking to two areas of growth that he insisted were not consciously designed to be his legacies: supplementary educational publishing, and China.

There was some irony in the new focus on learning materials, because it was Hickey who, in one of his first jobs for Harlequin, had shut down its Scholar's Choice retail stores peddling that era's equivalent products. What happened to reinterest him in the field was again – like his ideas for a continuity romance series and shorter fiction packages – based on his personal experience. Nearly a decade ago, his son Josh was in elementary school in Toronto and needed some at-home help with his schooling. "So I wanted to get some materials to work with. And I was so frustrated. I started calling guys – I knew [the publisher] Houghton Mifflin in Canada – and they didn't really have what I was talking about, and so I kept saying to myself I can't be the only one. It seemed to me when somebody has that interest, boy, you have a real nice margin, because they're willing to pay if you can get something. So I identified what I thought was a real growth opportunity. We try to have an employee meeting once a year where we talk about the health of the company. I couldn't get anybody else here interested. It was the most fascinating thing. You just couldn't get them to bite on it. That's why it took so long. Maybe they didn't have the same sense of the opportunity that I had. Maybe they didn't have a kid. . . . I think it's a market that's still on the verge of explosive growth."

His first step into the market happened in 1993 when Harlequin paid $4 million to acquire 16 percent of Discis Knowledge Research, a privately held Toronto company that published interactive multimedia books on CD-ROM discs, which can store millions of bits of information to be called up on home and school computers. Hickey joined the Discis board, where he was positioned to watch the industry develop and, as it happened, have Harlequin buy, through Torstar, a company a year for the next three years. In 1994 the corporation spent a more assertive $81 million for the dominant supplier in the teachers'-aid field, Frank Schaffer Publications of Torrance, California, which had been creating nonelectronic materials for kindergarten through grade 8, old-fashioned things such as workbooks, bulletin boards, and teacher resource books. In 1995 Torstar paid less than $5 million U.S. for Warren Publishing House of Everett, Washington, a key producer of early-childhood teaching resources, with 100-plus products in its Totline brand sold through teachers' stores, book clubs, and a catalog. And in 1996 the company laid out more than $10 million U.S. for Tom Snyder Productions of Watertown, Massachusetts, an independent educational software developer that designed *Snooper Troops,* one of North America's first home games for the early Apple II computers. The Snyder company may soon have the highest profile of the group, because 20 percent of its $7.5 million U.S. in annual revenue comes from television production. Its *Dr. Katz, Professional Therapist* animated show on the Comedy Central cable T V channel attracted the attention of DreamWorks S K G – owned by media giants Steven Spielberg, David Geffen, and Jeffrey Katzenberg – which has commissioned Tom Snyder to do an animated pilot, *Giving Harry the Business,* as a possible prime-time show on A B C.

Women are prominent in the running of these operations. Jean Warren's Warren Publishing has since been integrated with Frank Schaffer Publications, whose female president, Lee Quackenbush, has launched its first software and religious education publications. They are part of Harlequin's new Children's Supplementary Educational Publishing Division, under vice president and general manager Donna Hayes, who had run the North American direct-marketing division for five years. She has already spent about $1.6 million and had invested a similar amount in 1996 on test mailings to market the group's products direct to the home, as the Reader Service does for novels. She also intends to start up a supplementary-education business in the United Kingdom as a prototype for further international expansion. "We understand the marketing of a retail product direct," Hickey says. "And, boy, I believe if there ever was a category that fit with direct continuity-type selling, it's this one. And our second skill is international. We've got infrastructures over there." His excitement is understandable: "It's very clear I can take ownership for this one. I did come up with the idea, and it was totally driven by me as a consumer and the frustration I was feeling. Your heart's in it, then, I'll tell you."

Brian Hickey's heart and head have been in China off and on since 1982 when Harlequin first indicated publicly that it was interested in the world's most populous nation, still growing by 21 million people a year. In fact, at his prompting, the publisher actually said at the time that it hoped to be there by the following year. That was not to be. He had begun learning patience in China, and understanding how to deal with its complexities, as far back as 1975. He headed a Johnson's Wax negotiating team to sell institutional cleaning products as the nation began embracing tourism. In Canton, now Kwongchow, he and a Chinese negotiator, each with a translator, sat on stuffed armchairs side by side like heads of state. Facing them were three of Hickey's people and 37 Chinese. "I had been warned that if you negotiate, there's going to be someone over in the peanut gallery that's really in charge. You've got to start trying to figure out who that is to read reactions. We'd negotiate for four hours, and then they'd disappear for a day and a half, then they'd come back – and we went on and on. We were a week and a half into the process, and I had clearance on four issues where I could make a decision on the spot. One of them was we were willing to accept payment in an [East] Bloc currency because this is a private company and we would have reinvested that money to train locals to work with the products that we sold them. So when I threw that concept on the table about 10 days in – you hold these back, right? – all of a sudden in the peanut gallery this little old fellow popped up in a gray Mao suit – just *boing!* – and that's when we knew who was in charge. They disappeared for three days. Then they came back and had a number of questions. What were we going to do with the money? They were very suspicious, and in the end they paid us in Hong Kong dollars. They were so intense about their currency not getting out of their country. . . . The bigger thing that mattered in China was that I really love being there. I think the people are fascinating. I have immense respect for their history and the history they've yet to write. When you like being somewhere, they can smell it on you."

At Harlequin Hickey had to be patient until autumn 1987 when he went to China with fellow publishers as the upcoming president of the Canadian Book Publishers' Council. On that trip, he made a solid contact with a representative of a state-run publishing house, Foreign Languages Press. Harlequin proposed an "arrangement" – formal joint ventures with foreign companies being illegal in China – to "coproduce" romance novels in a format that fostered English as a second language, with English on one side of the page and Chinese on the other. Negotiations progressed to the point where Hickey hoped to announce the deal at the Beijing Book Fair in September 1989. But in June, students demanding democracy and protesting government corruption were gathered in Beijing's Tiananmen Square. Chairman Deng Xiaoping sent in young Mongolian soldiers, who opened fire on the demonstrators, killing hundreds and perhaps thousands. Most international commercial transactions, Harlequin's included, went on hold. In the wake of the Tiananmen Square massacre, Hickey transferred responsibility for the China venture to the Australian office, under regional director Guy Hallowes, who continued discussions with the Chinese. India was also being considered, but Harlequin had no intention of competing with the 10-cent romance novels already being published in the many Indian languages. Nor had it convinced itself yet that the English-speaking audience there would ever offer more than 10 percent of China's potential with its single Mandarin literary language.

In the interim, Harlequin thought that Taiwan, the small island republic, might somehow be a springboard to the Communist mainland. It was, but in a backhanded way. Publishing small print runs of books in Mandarin there was one thing, delivering them to readers another. Distribution problems eventually proved insurmountable, and Harlequin abandoned the project in 1995. But as they were setting up Taiwan, Hallowes and his colleagues had need of some local research. Hickey suggested an associate from his Johnson's Wax days in Asia, Dr. Vincent Lo. He not only helped them to find a managing director, he also did some groundbreaking work for the company in China, introducing Hickey to power brokers in government and publishing circles.

In the first half of this decade, China took mighty strides in opening up its society to economic reform and, through it, to Western influences. Pushing the free market, it wooed foreign capital to dampen the economic unrest that led to the 1991 breakup of the U.S.S.R. After Tiananmen the government closed two-score book publishers and many independent printers. But Chairman Deng's desire to reshape the economy, while keeping the old political system intact, overcame such dictatorial impulses ("To get rich is glorious," he has said). Soon the West waltzed in with some of its most flamboyant symbols, such as the Hard Rock Café that opened in Beijing with posters of Elvis and the Beatles beside a portrait of Chairman Mao Zedong. The privatization of publishing had already begun during the previous decade and accelerated again in the renewed thaw as publishers, once supported by the state, suddenly had to be self-sufficient. Gone was the absolute power of the monopolistic and censorial State General Press and Publication Administration, which had reported to both the government and the Communist Party's propaganda department. China now publishes more new titles each year than any other nation (90,000 at last count).

The liberalization that had been in place by 1989 resulted in something called the second channel of publishing. The Chinese used a kind of color-coding to delineate the differences. The first or red channel comprised the newly profit-motivated state publishing houses and distributors such as Xinhua Book Distribution Company, with its thousands of bookstores. The second channel had a white arm, which included the operations of the nongovernment distributors, the entrepreneurial book kings who often also acted as publishers offering better advances than the state houses did. The black arm was the underground network of here-today-gone-tomorrow distributors, publishers, and printers who would handle anything, even pornography, to make a yuan. Chinese investigative journalist Jia Lusheng said that "the laws of commerce have become the determining factor in publishing, and the books that get published are those that make money." In fact, Lusheng himself later became a book king. By 1993 one of China's most distinguished houses, Joint Literature Press, was publishing a series of paperback romances by a Hong Kong novelist and launching it at a media event in a four-star Beijing hotel at which the publisher offered journalists gift bags that included a hundred-yuan bribe. In her recent book *China Pop,* Chinese-born Jianying Zha says many Chinese editors describe the second channel as a Mafia dominated by immoral, greedy swindlers, but others insist it has brought a professionalism and business sense to publishing: "Forced to compete with or to use the second channel, the state-run publishing houses have learned to keep close tabs not only on the Party's and the elite's preferences but also on those of the average readers."

Harlequin was dealing with the state houses, bringing delegations to Canada, offering the traditional courtesy gifts, and getting them into the corporate headquarters, where they could see the row upon row of 16,000 titles translated into two dozen languages. "We got very high scores and respect for the commercial viability of our global enterprise," Hickey says. Dr. Lo had been replaced as a consultant by Stephen Fitzgerald, the former Australian ambassador to China during the Cultural Revolution of the 1970s; Harlequin worked out of his Beijing office and employed one of his people full-time. By now the publishing contact Brian Hickey had first made in 1987 was in charge of Foreign Languages Press. And although it had taken seven years, a deal was finally struck: a test run with two of the newly entrepreneurial government publishers. Foreign Languages Press (FLP) would coproduce books under the Silhouette name in the provinces of Beijing, Hubei, and Jiangsu. The Chinese National Publishing Industry Trading Corporation (CNPITC) would do Harlequins in Shandong and Sichuan provinces. In all this would mean a market of 34 million women in central China. The titles included *Fire and Spice* by Carla Cassidy and *Two-Time Man* by Roberta Leigh, which are sweeter rather than spicier romances. Harlequin supplied the Western-created cover art and paid for the translations in the simplified nationwide Mandarin script; they were edited on site to accommodate local sensibilities and produced there with the help of a consultant from the Australian office. The books were released in January 1995 with a cover price equivalent to 75 cents U.S. (50 cents higher than the launch price in Russia). There were 550,000 copies of 20 titles in Mandarin and 200,000 copies of 10 titles in an English edition. None was designed to teach English as a second language. A typical cover, for Diana Hamilton's *Savage Obsession,* had the familiar Harlequin logo and name at the top, the title and author's name below – all in both languages. Two-thirds of the cover was filled by an illustration of a dark-haired couple (who look vaguely Asian) sitting on the side of a bed, the man in a housecoat leaning intimately into the nightgowned woman, who is patting her obviously pregnant tummy.

So far the response from Chinese women has been encouraging. It wasn't as if Western pop literature were an unknown quantity in the country; bestsellers have long been coveted on the contraband market. In *The Chinese,* the 1980 book by John Fraser of the *Globe and Mail,* he quotes a Chinese official who said he had simply ignored a widespread campaign to discredit a traditional Chinese novel in the early 1970s because he was more interested in reading a popular underground copy of *Love Story.* And while he was memorizing 16 quotations from Chairman Mao's *Little Red Book,* he also managed to read *Wuthering Heights.* Taking no chances, Harlequin helped the process along with its patented marketing and promotion. In the fall of 1995, it began sponsoring a time slot on Beijing's music radio station and made sure its titles were featured on a T V book-review program hosted by a popular twentyish female personality, Sunshine, who also ran a dating show. Meanwhile, the company worked with a dozen bookshops in the city to mount displays of both brands, even though F L P and C N P I T C books wouldn't normally appear together in the same store. "Boy," Hickey says, "all of a sudden, sales just rocketed." The books have since sold into the second channel of wholesalers, with Harlequin's encouragement: "That's where the immense success for us started to kick off." In 1997 the company is sending San Francisco author Tracy Sinclair, with more than 50 romances to her name, to promote its made-for-T V movies in China and equally prolific JoAnn Ross of Phoenix to promote romantic fiction.

Harlequin has been ingratiating itself with the government by responding to a request for ideas to improve the still rickety distribution system, which ranges from sophisticated urban bookstores to huts in the countryside. The company recommended a test in which well-trained people would go into the stores and organize, merchandise, and write orders responsive to local market needs. Hickey was careful to tell me that Harlequin is not yet in a joint venture. "We have sort of coproduction arrangements. We share the rewards fifty-fifty. They operate very similar to a joint venture." When I asked what the difference was, he replied, "I don't know. Really. I have to be very careful what I say here, but I don't know what the difference would be. Officially they are not joint ventures."

When asked when Harlequin would get beyond test marketing in China, Hickey told me, "It's a hard call," noting that the government policy on joint venturing had to change or evolve. "That's why, when dealing in a market like this, you have to have a lot of patience and be prepared to move quickly when the opportunity comes." And if the opportunity comes? "If we succeed," he said, translating the happily-ever-after dream into bottom-line reality, "China will be a quarter of our volume within six, seven years."

A quarter of our volume: added to the current total, that would represent more than 50 million books a year, most of them romances, perhaps some male action-adventure novels, all of them conceived in the West and superimposed on an Asian nation. Success in this, the most populous country in the world, would certainly be a suitable legacy for Brian Hickey, whether he consciously wants one or not. It would also be an astonishing sequel to a story that began in London, England, at the turn of the century and whose plot developed so casually, unsophisticatedly, in a small printing plant in the middle of Canada. Richard Bonnycastle, an adventurer at heart, might have liked this ending. His son, Dick Bonnycastle Jr., and Larry Heisey, who turned the company into a professional publishing house – a giant performing on the global stage – certainly would approve. As would the Mills & Boon brothers, John and Alan, and Torstar's David Galloway.

Yet the Harlequinizing of China raises a troubling question that I have purposely left to the last. The marketing of products and pop literature to non-Western cultures from the English-speaking world, primarily North America, did not begin or end with soft drinks, nor will it with romance novels. But if Coke represents America's most prominent single export, perhaps Harlequin is Canada's – although few readers around the globe even know the publisher is Canadian. The sweet love stories that Saudi Arabians and other Arabs could once buy were written mainly by Commonwealth authors for Mills & Boon. They were seductive enough that a large minority of Arabian men read them – to what effect, Allah only knows. Brian Hickey once mentioned to editor in chief Horst Bausch how strange it was that the Japanese prefer their tales of love to end unhappily, and Bausch idly suggested that perhaps Harlequins in Japan should have unhappy endings – which they never have had. The same type of stories about star-crossed lovers are cherished in China. As Margaret Atwood said in an interview a decade ago, after talking to an informed Chinese teacher, "People in the West don't realize that, but the Chinese have this kind of myth that you fall in love and it's a total giving of the soul to a woman that you can't have." My fear is that, like Hollywood movies, Harlequins potentially have the power to replace a people's plots and dreams and myths springing from their own culture with those manufactured in the West.

Even nonanglophone Westerners may resent these romance novels translated from English: France's conservative women's magazine, *Madame Figaro*,

Brian Hickey, king of the romance pile. North America, Europe, Japan, Russia, China. What's next — outer space? HARLEQUIN ENTERPRISES

observed in 1995, "After dozens of years of an unchallenged supremacy in Europe, French authors . . . have had their titles stolen by American authors. Nora Roberts, Judith Krantz, Rosemary Rogers assume the career of romance writer with no complexes, proudly pocketing their comfortable royalties and imposing their uninhibited stories in our homes. The only weak point is that the dream isn't the same in Paris as in New York. . . ." True, many North Americans and Europeans read translations of stories from other cultures and learn from them or are entertained by them – without losing their own sense of self and place. But for consumers who live in a have-not nation and have only meager disposable incomes or limited access to books, the inexpensive, widely distributed Harlequins might substitute for their own literature of any kind. Unfortunately the Chinese today seem not to be telling their own important stories; not enough serious literature is being written. Wang Meng, an author and literary critic who was China's culture minister in the 1980s, says, "In order to make money, writers have to serve the popular taste. . . . Since 1985 writers have become freer, but they don't know how to use the freedom to relate to people's pain." Instead, they are writing pulp novels about martial arts, mystery, and romance. So it seems that Western romantic fiction is becoming part of what Jianying Zha in *China Pop* calls the nation's current need for "Culture Lite."

And yet, as exports go, Harlequins may be less destructive than other products from the West. In the early months of 1996, when China was conducting war games around Taiwan, flexing its military muscle to influence the breakaway island's elections, stories surfaced in the media that Canadian companies were exporting military goods to the People's Liberation Army on the mainland. Among the equipment were target training systems and anti-mine detectors. The news, based on previously classified documents, raised concerns in Canada about the morality of helping to arm a nation that was demonstrating bellicose tendencies toward its neighbors while maintaining its poor human rights record with its own people.

Not long before that, I was in Toronto talking with Judy Burgess. The former editor of Harlequin Romances, now a freelance writer, had not been keeping up-to-date with the progress of the company her father had founded. And when I mentioned that Harlequin had recently gone into China, she was visibly surprised. Expressing a heretical thought for a Bonnycastle offspring, she remarked: "Of all the things we could be sending the Chinese. . . ."

I didn't say anything at the time, but afterward, when China began intimidating Taiwan, I considered what she had said and wondered if she was wrong in her judgment. If it comes down to the classic choice between guns and butter – in this case, military equipment and sugar and spice – I know where I stand. Call it Western arrogance or cultural chauvinism (as many will), but of all the things North Americans could be sending a country where personal freedoms are curtailed, where the standard of living is low, and where travel to the rest of the world is not an easy possibility, perhaps sending the Chinese our romantic stories set in faraway, exotic lands and always delivering on the promise of a happy ending is not such a bad thing, after all.

Index